Women Composers and Songwriters

A Concise Biographical Dictionary

Gene Claghorn

The Scarecrow Press, Inc.
Lanham, Md., & London

SCARECROW PRESS, INC.

Published in the United States of America
by Scarecrow Press, Inc.
4720 Boston Way
Lanham, Maryland 20706

4 Pleydell Gardens, Folkestone
Kent CT20 2DN, England

British Cataloguing-in-Publication Information Available

Library of Congress Cataloging-in-Publication Data

Claghorn, Charles Eugene, 1911–
Women composers and songwriters : a concise biographical dictionary / Gene Claghorn.
p. cm.
Includes bibliographical references.
1. Women composers—Biography—Dictionaries.   I. Title.
ML105.C593   1996   780'.92'2–dc20   95-51308   [B]   CIP

ISBN 0-8108-3130-9 (cloth : alk. paper)

⊛ ™ The paper used in this publication meets the minimum requirements of American National Standard for Information Sciences—Permanence of Paper for Printed Library Materials, ANSI Z39.48–1984.
Manufactured in the United States of America.

FARCA

Contents

Introduction   v

Preface   vii

The Dictionary   1

Sources   246

About the Author   247

Introduction

This book is two books. On one hand it is a book of facts gathered and presented in Gene Claghorn's caring, reliable organizational style, which we came to appreciate fully as we used his book *Women Composers and Hymnists*. On the other hand it is a sociological document, an account of the ways our lives have interacted with the women whose biographies are recorded here. For, as distinctive in time and location as each of these women is, they have one thing in common: They've been selected because they've touched our lives in some way.

Women who have composed choral or instrumental works, musicals, and/or operettas have brought pleasure, comfort, and inspirational thoughts to our minds. Those who have written hymns and songs also bring pleasure—or sometimes anger at the downtrodden paths of society. To the reader, it will become apparent that the authors and composers noted here were dedicated also to education, to the arts, to journalism, or to social work. It is evident that they have exerted collectively a profound influence on our society.

Some of these women have been passionately patriotic; others have cried out against injustice in their land. Some were born wealthy; others eked out their existences working as milliners, seamstresses, secretaries, or office clerks. Some lived in isolated and withdrawn seclusion; others were married and had children to raise.

Even before the current interest in women's studies had grown strong, Gene Claghorn published *Women Composers and Hymnists*. We know now that he was a man ahead of his time. And we know he has had to be tireless and uncompromising in his zeal. For there are many whose names do not appear with their work; in the nineteenth century a woman's text or tune appeared often under her husband's name, and there were times in earlier generations when an editor deliberately omitted or avoided using a woman's name lest it weaken the popularity of his publication. Fortunately, with all the scholarly research recently undertaken and all the reports now available, we appreciate even more the distinctive contributions of these women to every aspect of our common lives.

Mary Louise VanDyke, Librarian/Coordinator
Dictionary of American Hymnology
Oberlin College Library, Oberlin, Ohio

Preface

My book on *WOMEN COMPOSERS AND HYMNISTS* contained concise biographies of women who wrote hymns and who composed church music. It was decided this new book would cover secular music as well as sacred music. As a result the concise biographies of women composers of symphonies, instrumental and choral works, chamber music, the blues, jazz, heavy metal, rock 'n' roll, hard rock, soul, country and western songs are included as well as a number of younger or newer hymnists and composers of church music.

Thus a larger and more comprehensive volume will have a wider reference appeal for the musically inclined readers.

Biographies of a number of women who were or are members of the American Society of Composers, Authors, and Publishers (ASCAP) are included in this book. This author sent ASCAP several pages listing the names of women composers and songwriters to be included in the book, asking the organization to indicate the date of death where applicable. In response, ASCAP sent the author their ASCAP List of Members, consisting of 181 pages and published in 1994. The membership book lists those "Deceased". The author wishes to thank ASCAP for this information to be included in the book.

Also thanks to Lorraine Black and Gwen Birck, reference librarians at the Cocoa Beach Library, for obtaining books on inter-library loans and to Mary Louise VanDyke of Oberlin, Ohio, for her work.

Gene Claghorn, Cocoa Beach, Florida

The Dictionary

-A-

ADAMS, CARRIE B. WILSON (1859–1940)
Remember now Thy Creator
Composer, organist, and choir director, she was the daughter of David Wilson, a singing teacher, and was born at Oxford, Ohio, on July 28, 1859. She studied music with her father, and at age seven she was in a choir at a convention in Millville, Ohio, under the direction of Dr. Horatio R. Palmer. In 1880 she married bassist Allyn G. Adams and they settled in Terre Haute, Indiana, where he went into business. She served as director, chorister, and organist for the choirs of the First Congregational Church and the Central Christian Church. Her first anthem was published in 1876. She composed four anthem books, two sacred cantatas—*Redeemer the King* and *Easter Praise*—and anthems for the Choir Music Journal. She wrote for *The Choir Herald,* published by E. S. Lorenz.

ADAMS, OLETA
Evolution
Singer/songwriter from Kansas City, Missouri. Her first album with a rich blend of jazz, rhythm and blues, and gospel made platinum—*Circle of One. (See also* Kitty Margolis.) The title song of the album *Evolution* (1994) was written by pop songwriter Brock Walsh and a Brazilian, but Oleta wrote half of the remaining songs.

ADAMS, SARAH FLOWER (1805–1848)
Nearer, My God to Thee, Nearer to Thee!
Part in Peace; Christ's Life was Peace.
Daughter of Benjamin Flower (editor of *The Cambridge Intelligencer*), she was born at Great Harlow, Essex, England, on February 22, 1805. Her father was imprisoned at Newgate for six months for criticizing the political conduct of the Bishop of Llandaff. While there, he was visited by an admirer, Eliza Gould, a schoolteacher from Devonshire, whom he married upon his release from prison. In 1834 Sarah married William B. Adams, an engineer and inventor. She contributed poems and hymns to

1

the *Monthly Repository* (1834–35), edited by the Rev. William J. Fox, a Unitarian pastor. Sarah desired to be an actress, and appeared as Lady Macbeth at the Richmond Theatre in London (1837) in a successful performance. She found the work so strenuous, however, that she gave up the stage to continue her writing.

Rev. Fox published *Hymns and Anthems* (1840–41) to which Sarah contributed 13 hymns; her sister Elizabeth wrote 63 out of 150 tunes in the collection. Elizabeth died of tuberculosis in 1846, and Sarah of the same disease in London on August 14, 1848. Her first hymn (above) appears in *The American Service Hymnal* (1968); *Baptist* (1973); *Broadman* (1977); *Christian Worship* (1953); *Christian Science* (1937); *Episcopal* (1940); *Lutheran* (1941); *Methodist* (1966); *Presbyterian* (1955); *Songs of Praise* (1931); and the *Pilgrim Hymnal* (1958).

ADAMS, YOLANDA (1962–)
Through the Storm
Gospel singer/songwriter, she was born in Houston, Texas. Her album *Just as I Am* was on the top ten gospel hits in 1986. *Through the Storm* came out in 1992. She sang at the Republican National Convention in Houston in 1992.

ADKINS, DONNA WHOBREY (1940–)
"Glorify Thy Name"
Composer, born June 18th in Louisville, Kentucky, the daughter of Peare and Foster Whobrey, traveling gospel singers. At age two she sang publicly and at age twelve joined the family quartet. She was educated at Asbury College, Wilmore, Kentucky, and the University of Louisville (1961). She married administrative pastor James Adkins of the Covenant Church in Pittsburgh, Pennsylvania, and they have two children.

Her hymn appeared in *The Hymnal for Worship and Celebration* (Baptist 1986).

AGNESI, MARIA TERESA d' (1720–1795)
L'insubria consolata
Pianist/composer, she was born on October 17th in Milan, Italy, the sister of mathematician Maria Gastano d'Agnesi. She married Pierro Antonio Periottini. Her works include the pastoral cantata *Il ristoro d'Arcadia* (1747); the opera *Ciro in Armenia* (1753), of which she also wrote the libretto; *L'insubria consolata* (1766), which she wrote to celebrate the engagement of Princess Maria Ricciarda Beatrice of Modina to the Archduke Ferdinand. She also composed the music for the opera *Sofonisbe* and *Il re pastore*. D'Agnesi died in Milan on January 19, 1795.

AHEARN, LILLIAN M. (1886–Dec'd.)
Unbuckle your tongue
Composer/lyricist, she was born on September 17, 1886 in Virginia. She wrote songs, *Your Heart's Door, Unbuckle your Tongue,* etc.

AHLWEN, ELSIE R. (b. 1905)
Tune—"Pearly Gates"
Ahlwen was born at Örebro, Sweden, and came to the United States as a young woman. After studying at the Moody Bible Institute in Chicago, she became an evangelist and worked with Swedish-speaking people in Chicago. Later she toured the United States singing and preaching. She married Daniel A. Sundeen and continued her ministry, finally retiring to live in Manchester, New Hampshire. While Ahlwen wrote this tune, it is based on an old Swedish melody, and it may be said it was adapted by her. It was used with the hymn *Love divine, so great and wondrous* in *Hymns for the Living Church* (1974).
Her hymn tune also appeared in *The Hymnal for Worship and Celebration* (Baptist 1986).

AKERS, DORIS MAE (1922–)
Tune—MANNA—"There's a sweet, sweet spirit in this place"
Composer, pianist, gospel singer, born in Kirksville, Missouri. She wrote her first gospel song when she was only ten years old. Despite the lack of formal musical training, she organized the Simmons-Akers Singers in California and was director of the Skypilot Choir in Los Angeles, California, in the 1950s. Later she resided in Columbus, Ohio and was a member of the Full Gospel Church. She sang with Jim Bakker's PTL Club on programs from Charlotte, North Carolina. Her gospel songs include "Lead me, guide me" (1953), "You can't beat giving" (1957), "Sweet, sweet spirit" (1972), "Lord don't move the mountain" (1972). Her songs were sung by the Stamps Quartet in the film *Elvis on Tour* (1972). Her hymn "Sweet, sweet spirit" appeared in the Baptist 1986, Methodist 1989, and Presbyterian hymnals 1990.

AKIYOSHI, TOSHIKO (1929–)
Albums—*Kogun, Finesse, Wishing Place*
Jazz composer, pianist, and leader, she was born on December 12th in Dairen, Manchuria, China. While living in Japan she was discovered by Oscar Peterson, who convinced her to come to the States. She studied at the Berklee School of Music in Boston (1956–59), married saxist Charlie Mariano, and was a bop pianist in a group with Charlie Mingus. After divorcing Mariano she married flutist/tenor saxist Lew Tabackin and formed a band in Los Angeles. Their album *Kogun* was successful in Japan. She conducted the Toshiko Akiyoshi Jazz Orchestra at Carnegie

Hall in 1992. Her albums are *Akiyoshi plus Tabackin Big Band, Finesse, Wishing Place*. She was voted number one in the Big Band Category (down beat) and was the first woman in jazz history so honored.

ALEOTTI, RAFFAELA (b. 1570–d. after 1638)
"Cantiones sacrae"
Composer, daughter of Giovanni Battista Aleotti (1546–1636), the architect who designed the Teatro Farnese at Parma, she was born at Ferrara, Italy. A pupil of Ercole Pasquini and Allessandro Milleville, she published her compositions in book form at Venice in 1593. Other compositions were published that same year by Vittoria Aleotti, who could have been the sister of Raffaela, or this may have been her pen name. Later Raffaela entered the Convent of San Vito at Ferrara where she served as prioress. She died at Ferrara some time after 1638.

ALLEN, DEBORAH (1935–)
Baby I Lied
Singer/songwriter, she was born on September 30, 1935, in Memphis, Tennessee. She wrote *Baby I Lied* (1983), *Can I See You Tonight*, and *I'm Only in it for Love*.

ALLDREDGE, IDA ROMNEY (1892–1943)
They, the Builders of the Nation
Hymnist born in Colonia Juarez, Mexico, of American parents in a Latter-Day Saint Settlement. In 1912 she moved to Douglas, Arizona. Her husband, Lew Alldredge, worked as a merchant in Douglas and then in Mesa, Arizona. Her hymn above appeared in the Mormon hymnal (1985).

ALLEN, PENELOPE MOODY (1939–)
Let the Holy Spirit Guide
Hymnist born in Castro Valley, California. When she was eight years old her father died and the family moved to San Jose, California. She was educated at San Jose State College (B.A. summa cum laude) and Brigham Young University (M.A.). In 1963 she married Gary L. Allen, and they have four children. They live in Bountiful, Utah. She has written short stories, poems, and historical novels. Besides the hymn above, she also wrote "With Songs of Praise". Both hymns appeared in the Mormon hymnal (1985).

ALLISON, MARGARET (1920–)
Touch me, Lord Jesus
Composer, pianist, and gospel singer, she was born at McCormick, South Carolina. After the family moved to Philadelphia when she was a child, Allison played the piano and sang in the local church choir. She

played the piano for the Spiritual Echoes (1942–44). With two friends, Lucille Shird and Ella Mae Norris and her sister Josephine McDowell, they formed the Angelic Gospel Singers. Her gospel song "Touch me, Lord Jesus" was written in 1950, and "My Sweet Home" in 1960 became popular. Allison and her sister Bernice Cole performed in a trio in the 1980s/90s.

ALLTON, MINETTE (1916–)
Sweet dreams
Composer/lyricist, she was born on April 13th in Oakland, California, and was educated at the University of California. With Nat "King" Cole, Isham, and others, she wrote a number of songs—"I Get Sentimental Over Nothing", "Pink Shampoo", "Melinda", "Swan Song", "Come to the Party", "Sweet Dreams". ASCAP.

ALSOP, FRANCES JORDAN (ca. 1780–1821)
Last New Year's Day
Singer/popular composer, she was born in England the daughter of Mrs. Jordan, the actress. Frances composed the following songs, all arranged by A. Clifton: "Last New Year's Day", "The Poor Hindoo", and "William and Mary", with words by Mrs. Opie. Alsop made her American debut in *The Country Girl* at the Park Theatre in New York City in 1820, and died there in 1821.

AMACHER, MARYANNE (1943–)
Music for Sound-joined Rooms (1980–82)
Composer, creator of unusual mixed-media sounds for the stage, she was born on February 25th at Kates, Pennsylvania. She studied with Rochberg at the University of Pennsylvania (BFA 1964) and with Stockhausen. She also studied computer science. Her *City-Links* explored psychoacoustical sound effects consisting of microphones installed at various locations in a city and then transmitted to her sound studio. She continued her acoustic research as a Fellow at the Massachusetts Institute of Technology (1972–76), then as a Fellow at Radcliffe College, and at Harvard University (1978–79), where she transmitted sounds from a Boston pier to her performing studio.

AMOS, TORI (1963–)
Under the Pink
Pianist/singer/songwriter, she was born in North Carolina where her father, a Methodist minister, raised her on "fire and brimstone, hell and damnation, and God's vengeance." She began playing the piano at age two and a half and was composing music at age four. She was sent to the Peabody Conservatory in Baltimore, but was a temperamental student

and was expelled. Then she played Gershwin tunes in the bars of Washington, D.C. Her first album *Little Earthquakes* sold over one million copies in 1992. She sang about being raped on *Me and a Gun,* then on *Baker Baker* realized the experience made her emotionally unavailable to a lover. Her album mentioned above with her own songs details her life to some extent. On *Cornflake Girl* she examines how women can betray one another, that feminists shouldn't condemn men as a whole— we need a balance, but on the other hand with thousands of years men have taught to love your neighbor, do as we say or we'll rape your women, such as her songs "Hot Cross Buns" and "Icicle", which rejects Christian dogma and celebrates masturbation. One critic wrote "Amos is an impressive musician, capable of fragility and thunder" (Edna Gundersen in *USA Today,* 11/7/94).

ANDERSON, BARBARA ELIZABETH "BETH" (1950–)
"Revelation"—for orchestra, chamber music, mixed chorus
Composer and pianist, she was born on January 3rd at Lexington, Kentucky. Anderson studied at the University of Kentucky, then was a pupil of Austin, Cage, and Swift at the University of California at Davis (B.A. 1971), with Ashley and Riley at Mills College, Oakland (M.F.A. 1973, M.A. 1974). She wrote the opera *Queen Christina* (1973), musical *Nirvanna Manor* (1981), and *Revelation* (1981).

ANDERSON, EVELYN RUTH (1928–)
"Centering"—for four musicians and a dancer
Composer and flutist, she was born on March 21st at Kalispell, Montana. Graduated from the University of Washington in flute (BA, 1949 and composition MA, 1951), she then studied with Ussachevsky and electronic composition with Kim at Columbia and Princeton universities. After taking private lessons with Boulanger and composition with Milhaud, she studied the flute with Jean-Pierre Rampal. During the 1950s she played the flute with the Totenberg Instrumental Ensemble, the Seattle and Portland symphony orchestras, and the Boston Pops. Anderson won two Fulbright scholarships (1958–59), five MacDowell Colony Fellowships between 1957–73, and other grants. She served as director of the electronic music studio at Hunter College, CUNY. Her music displays acoustic design, psychoacoustics in electronics. "Sound Environment" was written in 1975, "Centering" in 1979, "Time and Tempo" in 1984, among other compositions.

ANDERSON, LAURIE (1947–)
United States Live
Composer of rock music and a progressive violinist/soprano/painter/ sculptor, she was born on June 5th in Chicago, the second of eight children. Her

father worked at his wife's family paint business. She studied classical violin, played in the Chicago Youth Symphony, graduated from Barnard College with a degree in history (1969), and received a master of fine arts from Columbia University (1972). She made her debut performance in *Automotive* in Rochester, Vermont, in 1972. Later she filled her violin with water so it would "weep" when she played Tchaikovsky concertos.

She started playing in SoHo clubs in New York City and composed *Americans on the Move* (1979). In 1980 she wrote the song "O Superman" (in which an answering machine receives a message of doom), which cost her $400 to produce 1,000 copies. She sold copies by mail order, and sales were slow until she received an order for 40,000 copies from England. By 1990 it had grossed over $1 million.

Other compositions were *Big Science* (1982), *United States Live* (1983) performed at the Brooklyn Academy of Music, *Mister Heartbreak* (1984), *Strange Angels* (1989), and the videos *Collected Videos* and *Home of the Brave*. She introduced *Empty Places* at a full house at the Brooklyn Academy of Music in October 1989 with projected slides asking: "Should the unborn have civil rights? Yes, because they can thank you later." A second slide reads: "Should the dead have civil rights? No, because they can't talk anymore."

ANDROZZO, ALMA B. (1912–)
If I Can Help Somebody
Composer/lyricist, she was born on October 10, 1912, in Harriman, Tennessee, and raised in Philadelphia where she was graduated from high school. She wrote songs including, "If I Can Help Somebody" for the National Tuberculosis Society. ASCAP.

ARBUCKLE, DOROTHY FRY (1910–)
The Church Where I Worship
Organist/composer/hymnist, she was born on January 23rd in Eldred, Illinois. She was educated at Northwestern University and the University of Illinois. She composed choral works including the anthem "The Church Where I Worship".

ARCHER, VIOLET BALESTERI (1913–)
Concerto No. 1 for Piano and Orchestra
Pianist/composer born on April 24th in Montreal, Quebec, Canada. After receiving her degree in composition at McGill University in Montreal (BS Mus. 1936), she studied organ at the Royal Canadian College of Organists (1938), composition on a scholarship at McGill again (1940–44), and with Bela Bartok in New York (1942). She received her M.Mus. in composition at the Yale University School of Music in New Haven, Connecticut (1949). She taught music at McGill, North Texas State

College, University of Alberta in Edmonton, etc. She has composed symphonies, orchestral and choral works, chamber music, two operas, etc. Her setting for "Caleidoscopio" consists of poems written by her sister Gisella Azzi.

ARLEN, JEANNE BURNS (1917–)
San Francisco Sketches
Composer/lyricist, she was born on February 18th in New York City and educated at the Malikan Conservatory. She wrote songs for the Cotton Club revues—*To My Beloved, I Gotta Go Places, Got a Need for You, Little Town Gal*. She also composed *San Francisco Sketches* for piano. ASCAP.

ARMATRADING, JOAN (1950–)
To the Limit
Singer/guitarist/composer, she was born on December 9th in St. Kitts, West Indies. At age seven she was brought to Birmingham, England. Her father played the guitar, and Joan loved to write songs. But she felt she had to sing them in public to get them just right. During the 1960s, instead of being influenced by the Beatles or the Rolling Stones, she preferred the music of Nat "King" Cole and Tommy Steele. She went to London with a friend to audition for *Hair,* but Joan won the role herself, which lasted for eighteen months. Her first album came out in 1973, but it was her 1976 album *Joan Armatrading* that brought her instant success. Her album reached the Top Five in England and the Dominions, and remained on the charts in the USA for 28 weeks. She switched to jazz/rock in her 1978 album *To the Limit* and appeared that year at Avery Fisher Hall in New York City. Her albums are *Hearts and Flowers, Show Some Emotion, The Key, Sleight of Hand, Walk Under Ladders, Classics 21, The Shouting Stage, Track Record.*

ASHFORD, EMMA LOUISE HINDLE (1850–1930)
Sacred cantata—"The Prince of Peace"
A composer, she was born at Newark, Delaware, on March 27, 1850, and was taught by her father, who was a music teacher. She sang in the local church choir and also played the guitar. In 1864 the family moved to Plymouth, Massachusetts, then to Seymour, Connecticut, where she became organist at St. Peter's (Episcopal) Church. In 1867 she married John Ashford and they moved to Chicago, where she was contralto in the quartet of St. James (Episcopal) Church during the time Dudley Buck was organist and director there. Later they moved to Nashville, Tennessee, where they were in charge of music in a Presbyterian Church and the Jewish Temple, simultaneously. Later she became connected with the Lorenz Publishing Company of Dayton, Ohio. She composed over 250 anthems, 50 sacred solos, 24 sacred duets, trios, and cantatas, and

over 200 organ voluntaries. She also wrote numerous gospel songs and *Ashford's Organ Instructor.* Her hymn tunes "Evelyn and Sutherland" appeared in the *Methodist Hymnal* (1911).

AUFDERHEIDE, MAY FRANCES (1888–1972)
"Dusty Rag", "The Richmond Rag", "Pelham Waltzes"
Pianist and waltz and ragtime composer she was born on May 21st in Indianapolis, Indiana. After studying with her aunt, she composed her first piano rag "Dusty Rag" in 1908, which was so successful that her father, John H. Aufderheide, became a music publisher and set up business in Richmond, Indiana, that year, whereupon May wrote "The Richmond Rag". Her piano rags attracted attention in New York City and after her "Buzzer Rag" (1909) and "The Thriller Ray" (1909), she composed 17 more pieces between 1910–1912. At this point, Aufderheide was married, became a housewife, and ceased composing. But she will go down in history as the first and most famous female ragtime composer.

AULIN-VALBORG, LAURA (1860–1928)
"Christmas Hymn"
Composer and pianist, she was born at Gävle, Sweden, on January 9, 1860, and was the sister of Tor Aulin, composer, conductor, and violinist. She studied at the Stockholm Conservatory (1877–82) and won the Jenny Lind award for two years' study in Paris with Godard and Massenet. Her "Christmas Hymn" was composed for mixed chorus and organ. She was a pianoforte teacher in Orebo, Sweden, and died there on January 11, 1928.

AUSTIN, LOVIE (1887–1972)
"Any Woman's Blues"
Pianist, leader, and composer, she was born Cora Calhoun in Chattanooga, Tennessee. After studying at Roger Williams University in Nashville and Knoxville College, she led the Serenaders in 1923. She composed "Any Woman's Blues," which was introduced by blues singer Ida Cox in 1923. Austin later was a pianist at Jimmy Payne's dancing school. She also recorded with Ma Rainey and Johnny Dodds. She died on July 10th in Chicago, Illinois.

-B-

BABITS, LINDA (1940–)
"Western Star"
Pianist/composer, she was born on July 28th in New York City and educated at the Manhattan School of Music (BM), Oberlin Conservatory, and also studied with Roger Sessions. Her works are "Clinton Corner Delancy", and the piano concerto "Western Star".

BACAL, MELAINE ELLA (1948–)
"Don't Run Away"
Composer/lyricist, she was born on March 18th in Lynbrook, New York. She wrote the songs "Don't Run Away", "I Guess, I Guess, I Guess", "Who Told You?", and "One Heart Is No Good".

BAEZ, JOAN CHANDOS (1941–)
"A Song for David"
Folksinger, guitarist, songwriter, she was born on January 9th on Staten Island, New York. She is known as the "Queen of the Folksingers". Graduated from high school, she attended Boston University but dropped out to sing in coffeehouses. She was a sensation at the 1959–60 Newport Folk Festivals and her Vanguard record "Joan Baez" was a sensation. She lived in Carmel, California, and was a crusader against the Vietnam War. Baez sang "Joe Hill" at the Woodstock, New York, Festival in 1969. Her compositions include "A Song for David", "Honest Lullaby", and "Diamonds and Rust". With Bruce Springsteen, she was on the 1988 top-ten grossing concerts.

BAILEY, MARIE LOUISE (1876–Dec'd.)
(Piano pieces)
Pianist/composer, she was born on October 24th in Nashville, Tennessee. She studied at the Leipzig Conservatory in Germany and was a pupil of C. Reinecke and Leschetizky, winning a scholarship. After making her debut at Gewandhaus in Leipzig in 1893, she served as chamber-virtuoso to King Albert of Saxony. After 1900 she toured Europe and the United States. She married a Mr. Apfelbeck. Bailey composed piano pieces.

BAINBRIDGE, KATHARINE (1863–1967)
"God answers prayer"
Composer and hymnist, she was born at Basingstoke, England, on June 30, 1863, and educated at Hardwicke College in Australia. She was a member of the National League of American Pen Women and a life member of the Poetry Society of Southern California. She composed the music for this hymn. She died on February 12, 1967 in her 104th year.

BAKER, ANITA (1957–)
"Giving You the Best I've Got"
A singer/songwriter, she was born on January 26th in Toledo, Ohio. She never knew her father and her mother abandoned her when she was two years old, at which time she went to live with her maternal grandparents. Anita was thirteen when they died, so she was raised in Detroit by a Baptist church congregation. After singing in the church choir she joined Chapter 8, a rhythm and blues group in the 1970s.

Her first album *The Songstress* was released in 1983, then *Rapture* (1986). She won a 1988 Grammy for R&B Vocalist for "Giving You the Best I've Got", won a 1990 Grammy for *Compositions,* and had a platinum video, *One Night of Rapture.* Her hit songs include "My Funny Valentine" and "Sometimes I Wonder". On her album *Rhythm of Love* (1994) she wrote or co-wrote five of the album's twelve songs. In 1988 she married Walter Bridgforth, a real estate broker, and they have two sons. Anita and her husband live in a 12-room mansion in Grosse Point, Michigan.

BALLASEYUS, VIRGINIA (1893–Dec'd.)
"California"
Composer/lyricist, she was born on March 14th in Hollins, Virginia. She studied at the University of California (BA) and studied music with Louis Persinger, Hugo Kortschak, and Darius Milhaud. She wrote "California" for the 1962 California State Fair theme song; she also wrote "Glory in the Land."

BALLOU, ESTHER WILLIAMSON (1915–)
"Capriccio for violin and piano"
Composer, pianist, and teacher, she was born on July 17th at Chichester, England. After studying piano and organ as a child, she studied composition with Luening at Bennington College in Vermont in 1937, Mills College in 1938, and with Wagenaar at The Juilliard School in New York City in 1943. Ballou toured as a pianist for dancing groups and from 1959 taught at the American University, Washington, DC. Her "Capriccio" performed at The White House in 1963 for President and Mrs. Kennedy was the first composition by a woman given in the Executive Mansion. She composed chamber music, choral works, etc.

BARKER, ELIZABETH RAYMOND HALKETT (1829–1916)
Tune—"Paraclete"
Composer, daughter of William Halkett of Aylestone Hall, Leicester, England, she studied music under G. A. Löhr. In 1853 she was married to the Rev. F. Barker of Oriel College. Later she became acquainted with Dr. John Mason Neale (1818–1866). In 1867 she joined the Roman Catholic Church. Her tune appeared in the English *Methodist Hymn-Book* (1935).

BARKIN, ELAINE RADOFF (1932–)
"Media Speak" with nine speakers, sax, slides
Composer, she was born on December 15th in the Bronx, New York City. After studying with Leo Kraft, Saul Novack, and Karol Rathaus at Queens College, CUNY (BA, 1954), she then studied with Arthur

Berger, Irving Fine, and Harold Shapiro at Brandeis University (MFA, 1954, Ph.D., 1971). Barkin taught at Queens College from 1964–70, the University of Michigan from 1970–74, and then joined the faculty of the University of California at Los Angeles. She has been a guest composer at various universities and received fellowships, honors, and commissions to produce various works. She has composed chamber music and choruses.

BARNARD, CHARLOTTE ARLINGTON (1830–1869)
  Tunes — "Brocklesbury" and "Barnard"
A composer and songwriter, she was born at London, England, on December 23, 1830 and was married to Charles C. Barnard on May 18, 1854. Between 1858 and her death in 1869, she wrote about 100 songs and ballads under the pen name "Claribel." She published *Thoughts, Verses and Songs* and *Songs and Verses*. Brocklesbury is a town near Dover, England, where she died on January 30, 1869. She is buried in the cemetery of St. James' Church. Her tune has appeared in hymnbooks with the hymn "Jesus, Tender Shepherd, hear me," and with "Savior, Who Thy flock are feeding," in *The Baptist Hymnal* (1973). Her tunes appeared in *Hymns for the Living Church* (1974). Her best-known popular song was "Come Back to Erin." One of her popular songs is worth repeating here:
  "I cannot sing the old songs,
  I sung long years ago,
  For heart and voice would fail me,
  And foolish tears would flow."

BARNES, HELEN (1908–Dec'd.)
  "Sunrise in Seville"
Composer/lyricist, she was born on November 23rd in Xmas Creek, Texas, and educated at Texas State College and the Peabody Conservatory. She wrote songs such as "White Winterland," "Will It Make any Difference?", "My Second Date," "Will You Be Mine?", "Sunrise in Seville." ASCAP.

BARNETT, ALICE RAY (1886–1975)
  "Chanson of the Bells of Oseney"
Composer, teacher of piano and violin, she was born May 26th in Lewiston, Illinois. After studying with Ganz and Boroeski at the Chicago Musical College (BM, 1906) and with Henior Levy and Adolf Weidig at the American Conservatory in Chicago, she studied composition with Wilhelm Middleschulte in Chicago and with Hugo Kaun in Berlin from 1909–10. She taught music at the San Diego High School in California from 1917–26. Barnett wrote some sixty art songs between 1906–32, in-

cluding the one mentioned above in 1924, and music for the piano and violin. She died on August 28th in San Diego at the age of 89 years.

BARRAUNE, ELSA (1910–)
"La Poesie interrompue"
Composer/musical director, she was born on February 13th in Paris, France. After studying composition under Paul Dukas, harmony with Jean Gallon, fugue with Caussade and score reading with Estyle at the Conservatorie National Superior de Musique in Paris (1919–29), she became Chief de Chant of the Orchestre National de France and musical director of Chant du Monde (1944–46), and then professor of musical analysis at the Conservatorie de Paris (1953–74). She composed symphonies, orchestral and choral works, instrumental and chamber music, etc. Her cantata mentioned above was written in 1948 for three voices and orchestra.

BASIA
"Time and Tide"
Singer/songwriter born Basia Trzetrzelewska, one of four children. As a teenager she worked with the band Perfect and was offered a six-month gig at a Polish club on Chicago's South Side. In the early 1980s she joined the jazz-funk band Bronze led by Danny White. Her first single "Time and Tide" was a hit in 1987 and her CD of the same title sold over 1,000,000 copies. Her album *London Warsaw New York* also did very well. Basia felt you had to live through experiences in order to write about them, so she visited Poland and spent some time with family members there. Her pop/jazz CD features a muted trumpet and blues guitar with Danny White's band. It's called *The Sweetest Illusion* (1994). She toured the states in 1994 and among other places appeared at the King Center for the Performing Arts in Melbourne, Florida, in August 1994.

BASSETT, KAROLYN WELLS (1892–1931)
"Little Brown Baby"
Pianist/composer, she was born in Derby, Connecticut. After taking some piano lessons, she gave her first recital at age six. Karolyn studied with Van York, Carl and Reinhold Faelton. She wrote "Yellow Butterfly," "Little Brown Baby," "The Moon of Roses," "A Child's Night Song."

BATES, KATHERINE LEE (1859–1929)
"O Beautiful for Spacious Skies,
For Amber Waves of Grain"

"Dear God, our Father, at Thy Knee Confessing,
Our Sins and Follies, Close in Thine Embrace."

Daughter of a Congregational minister, she was born at Falmouth, Massachusetts, on August 12, 1859 and was graduated from Wellesley College (BA, 1880). She taught at the high school in Natick, Massachusetts, and at Dana Hall, then at Wellesley (1886–1925). In 1893 she visited the Columbian Exposition in Chicago and decided to travel west and visit Pike's Peak, Colorado, where she was so impressed with the beauty of the view that she wrote her famous hymn, which appeared in *The Congregationalist*. She also wrote the hymn, "The kings of the East are riding" (1914) and was the author or co-author of about 20 books or collections, including a *History of American Literature* (1908) and a book of poems, *The Pilgrim Ship* (1926). She died in Wellesley, Massachusetts, on March 28, 1929. The first hymn above appeared in the *American* (1968); *Baptist* (1973); *Broadman* (1977); *Christian* (1953); *Family of God* (1976); *Joyfully Sing* (1968); *Methodist* (1966); and *Presbyterian* (1955) hymnals and *The Pilgrim Hymnal* (1958).

BATYA, NOMI (1961–)
"King of Kings and Lord of Lords"
Hymnist, she was born on April 21st, but no other information has been located. Her hymn appeared in the *Baptist Hymnal* (1986).

BAUER, MARION EUGENIE (1887–1955)
"From the New Hampshire Woods"
Composer, pianist, and teacher, she was born on August 15th in Walla Walla, Washington. After studying at Portland, Oregon, she studied in Paris and Berlin with Boulanger, Huss, Rothwell, and others. While a teacher at New York University from 1926–30 and an associate professor from 1930–51, she was also on the faculty of the Juilliard School from 1940–44. Bauer was a cofounder of the American Music Guild in 1921. Her works included pianofortes, vocal pieces, orchestral works, etc. Her piano piece above was composed in 1921. Bauer died on August 9th in South Hadley, Massachusetts.

BAYES, NORA (ca. 1880–1928)
"Shine on, Harvest Moon"
Singer/songwriter, she was born Dora Goldberg in the vicinity of Joliet, Illinois. She made her debut as a vaudeville singer, sang Harry von Tilzer's "Down Where the Wurzburger Flows" in Brooklyn (1902). She sang at the Palace Theatre in London in 1905 and in the "Ziegfield Follies of 1907". She was married five times. With her second husband, composer Jack Norworth, she wrote the lyrics for "Shine On, Harvest Moon" for the "Follies of 1908". They introduced "When It's Apple Blossom Time in Normandy" (1912) and popularized Cohan's "Over There" (1917).

BEACH, AMY MARCY CHENEY (1867–1944)
Mass with Orchestra
Born at Henniker, New Hampshire, on September 5, 1867, she was a composer, hymnist, pianist, and songwriter. She studied with her mother, also with E. Perabo, K. Baerman (piano), and Junius W. Hill (harmony). After making her debut as a pianist in Boston in 1883, she made many appearances as a soloist with various orchestras and toured Europe in 1910. She married Dr. Henry Harris Aubrey Beach, the singer. She served as president of the Board of Councillors of the New England Conservatory in Boston, Massachusetts, and composed *Mass with Orchestra, Mass in e; Gaelic Symphony* and various orchestral works, and several sacred songs. She died in New York City on December 27, 1944.

BEAT, JANET EVELINE (1937–)
Cross Currents and Reflections
Composer/horn player, she was born on December 17th in Streetly, Staffordshire, England. After studying at the University of Birmingham (MMus, 1960), she played the horn in the Midlands (1960– 65), then as a lecturer in music at Madley College, Worcester College, then became a lecturer at the Royal Scottish Academy of Music and Drama in 1972. She was a founder-member of Scottish Society of Composers (1980), Scottish Electro-Acoustic Music Society (1987), Soundstrata, an electroacoustic music ensemble (1988). She has composed orchestral and choral works, chamber music, etc. Beat owned one of the first synthesizers available in the British Isles and much of her work is a combination of instrumental and electronic sound.

BEATH, ELIZABETH MARGARET COX "BETTY" (1932–)
Piccolo Victory, Images of Colonial Australia
Pianist/composer, she was born on November 19th in Bundaberg, Queensland, Australia. After studying under Frank Hutchens at the Sydney Conservatorium and the Queensland Conservatorium of Music (Diploma in Music 1969), she studied piano at Trinity College of Music and continued her musical studies in New Guinea, Indonesia, Java, and Bali. She served as music specialist and later head of the music department at St. Margaret's Anglican Girls School since 1967. She was composer in residence at North Adams State College, Massachusetts (1987), and now resides in Queensland. She married John Beath, and they had a son and a daughter. After her divorce, she married writer and artist David Cox. She has composed choral and chamber music, three operas, etc. Her piece mentioned above for flute/piccolo, harpsichord or piano, cello, rhythm sticks, was performed on April 25, 1982 in Brisbane, Australia.

BEAUMESRIEL, HENRIETTE ADELAIDE VILLARD DE (1758–
1813)
Oratorio—*Les Israelites poursuivis par Pharaon*
Composer and singer, born at Paris, France, on 31 August 1758, she was
a pupil of C. F. Clement and made her debut in *Sylvie* (by Berton and
Trial) at the Paris Opera in 1766. Her one-act opera, *Tibrille at Delie, ou
Les Saturnales,* was the third opera by a woman performed at the Acad-
emie Royale de Musique on January 15, 1784 (*see* Mme la Guerre). Her
oratorio (above) was sung at the Concert Spirituel on December 8, 1784.
She died in Paris in 1813.

BEATTY, SUSI (1963–)
"Nobody Loves Me Like the Blues"
Guitarist/singer/songwriter, she was born in Alexandria, Virginia. She
holds a degree in business administration from the College of Charleston,
South Carolina. Later she attended dance school in California and then
performed around Nashville, Tennessee. With Dan Chauvin and Jim
Allison, she co-wrote the song "Nobody Loves Me Like the Blues" on
her album *One of a Kind* with backup guitarist Brent Rowan and saxist
Jim Horn. She also co-wrote two other songs on the album produced in
1990.

BEBERUS, VIRGINIA (1893–1964)
"Thanksgiving"
Composer/lyricist, she was born on June 30th in Mercer, Maine. She
wrote a number of songs, her "Thanksgiving" won the Medal of Honor
from the George Washington Foundation. She died on October 3rd at
Glen Mills, Pennsylvania.

BEERS, ETHELINDA ELIOT (1827–1879)
"All Quiet Along the Potomac Tonight"
Lyricist, she was born in Goshen, New York. With music by John Hill
Hewitt, she wrote the lyrics for "The Picket Guard," which contained the
lines "All Quiet Along the Potomac Tonight" in 1861, which became a
popular Civil War song.

BEHREND, JEANNE (1911–)
"Festival Fanfare: Prelude to the National Anthem"
Composer, pianist, and teacher, she was born on May 11th in Philadelphia, Pennsylvania. After studying piano with Josef Hofmann and composition with Rosario Scalero at the Curtis Institute in Philadelphia
(graduated 1934), she taught piano at The Juilliard School, the Curtis Institute, and Western College in Oxford, Ohio, and taught American music at the Philadelphia Conservatory and Temple University. She toured

South America from 1945–46 on a State Department goodwill tour upon the recommendation of Villa-Lobos. Her "Festival Fanfare" mentioned above performed by members of the Philadelphia orchestra opened the Philadelphia Festival of Western Hemisphere Music in 1960. In 1965 the Brazilian government awarded her the Order of the Southern Cross for her services to Brazilian music. She also wrote piano pieces, songs, and various chamber music.

BELLE, BARBRA (1922–)
    "A Sunday Kind of Love"
Composer/lyricist, she was born on November 22nd in Brooklyn, New York City, and educated at New York University. She wrote music for Louis Armstrong, Lucky Millinder, and Louis Prima—"A Sunday Kind of Love", "Joseph 'n His Brudders", "Early Autumn", "You Broke the Only Heart that Ever Loved You." ASCAP.

BENARY, BARBARA (1946–)
    'Sleeping Braid'
Composer and violinist, she was born on April 7th in Bay Shore, Long Island, New York. After studying at Sarah Lawrence College (BA, 1968), she received her MA and PhD in ethno-musicology at Wesleyan University in 1973. Using an ensemble of Javanese instruments, including metallophones and gongs, she composed 25 works for the *Gamelan Son of Lion* between 1975–83. Other composers in this effort were Daniel Goode, Philip Corner, and Peter Griggs. *Braid,* written for Gamelan using a 14-note sequence, and *Sleeping Braid,* mentioned above, with a female voice and gamelan string instruments from India, China, and Bulgaria, becomes the subject of a canon.

BENNETT, ELSIE M. (1919–)
    Hebrew-Jewish Songs and Dances
Accordianist/composer/lyricist, she was born on March 30th in Detroit, Michigan, and was educated at the Ganapol School of Music, Wayne State University (BM), Columbia University Teachers College (MA). Her collaborators were Ethel Mendelson, Mischa Kottler, George Cailotta, and Joe Biviano. She wrote *Hebrew-Jewish Songs and Dances* (2 volumes), *Folk Melodies for the Accordion, Chord Patterns*, etc. ASCAP.

BENNETT, JOYCE W. (1923–)
    "Honeymoon Mambo"
Pianist/composer/lyricist, she was born on July 28th in Trenton, New Jersey, and was educated at the Eastman School of Music at Rochester, York (BM). She married composer Phil Bennett. She wrote "Honeymoon Mambo", "It Isn't Surprising", etc.

BERCKMAN, EVELYN (1900–Dec'd.)
"Die Nebelstadt"

Pianist/composer, she was born in Philadelphia, Pennsylvania. A temporary attack of paralysis resulting from intensive piano practice delayed her career for seven years. She composed music for orchestra and chamber ensembles and wrote the soprano solos "Die Nebelstadt" and "Sturm" in 1924, published by M. Senart of Paris.

BERKEY, GEORGIA GUINEY
Tune—"Dwell in Me"

A composer, her tune for "Dwell in Me, O Blessed Spirit" first appeared in the *Sunday School Hymnal* for the Evangelical and Reformed Churches, Heidelberg Press, Philadelphia 1899. She married A. G. Berkey. More recently her tune appeared in the 1941 edition of *The Hymnal*. The hymn was written by Martha J. Lankton (Fanny Crosby).

BERNARD, CAROLINE RICHINGS (1827–1882)
The Duchess

Pianist/singer/composer, she was born in England and brought to America as a child. She made her debut as a pianist in Philadelphia in 1847, sang in *La Fille du Regiment* in 1852 and married the tenor P. Bernard in 1867. She organized the Old Folks Concert Company, but it was unsuccessful, so she taught piano in Baltimore. She wrote the operetta *The Duchess* and sang the leading role in Baltimore in 1881. She then taught in Richmond, Virginia, but died there of smallpox.

BERNSTEIN, SYLVIA (1924–)
"My Kindergarten Hero"

Composer/lyricist, she was born on April 5th in Milwaukee, Wisconsin. With Seymour Lefco she wrote "My Kindergarten Hero".

BIGGS, LOTTIE LOVELL (1913–)
"The White Steps of Baltimore"

Composer/lyricist, she was born on February 27th in Henry, Virginia, and educated at the Kolb Music & Singing School. She wrote "Goodbye Sweetheart", "My Country Mine", "The White Steps of Baltimore", "I Love Only You", and "Solitaire Blues".

BINGEN, HILDEGARD, ABBESS OF (1098–1179)
"You beautiful faces
Beholding God and building in the dawn
How noble you are."

Composer and hymnist, known as the "Sybil of the Rhine," she was born at Böckelheim near Kreuzmach, West Germany. While Abbess of Bingen, Rhineland-Palatinate, West Germany, she wrote 35 antiphons, 18 responses, 6 sequences, and 10 hymns. Seventy-seven of her chants were included in her cycle *Symphonia Armonic celestium revelationium* (*Symphony of the Harmony of the Heavenly Relations*), known as *Scivias*. The above is a quote from her Song No. 38, extolling women.

Thirteen of her chants were addressed to Saint Ursula and fifteen to the Virgin Mary. She is the only woman composer of the Middle Ages whose music has survived. She died at Rupertsberg, near Bingen, Rhineland. She is referred to in a number of publications as "Saint Hildegard," although she has never been created a Saint.

BITGOOD, ROBERTA (b.1908–)
    "The greatest of these is love."
Conductor, composer, hymnist, violist, and organist, she was born at New London, Connecticut, on January 15, 1908 and was graduated from the Connecticut College for Women; Columbia University (MA) in New York City; and Union Theological Seminary (MSM; SMD). She was a violist at Redlands University Community Symphony in California, the Detroit Women's Symphony in Michigan, the Saginaw (Michigan) Symphony, and then Director of Music at Bloomfield College and Seminary in New Jersey (1936–1947). Also she was organist at Temple Sharey Tefilo, East Orange, New Jersey (1943–47), and Temple Beth El in Riverside, California (1958–60). She composed the music for the above chorale. She married Bert Wiersma. In March 1982, she became the first woman President of the American Guild of Organists. She resided in Quaker Hill, Connecticut. (Information from Frances and Royal Bitgood of East Lyme, Connecticut.)

BLACK, JENNIE PRINCE (1868–1945)
    "Autumn Leaves"
Composer, she was born on October 10th in New York City and was educated at the Hudson River Music School. She wrote a number of songs—"Autumn Leaves", "Lord's Prayer", "When Arbutus Blooms", "Old Dutch Nursery Rhyme", "It Is Night." She died in New York City on September 20th.

BLACKMON, ALMA MONTGOMERY (1921–)
    Tune—"Give Me Jesus"
Conductor/arranger/organist/singer, she was born on July 25th in Washington, DC and received a college education. From age ten she was organist and singer at the First Seventh-Day Adventist Church in Washington, DC, later director of the Dupont Park Choir. She taught in Washington public schools and at Oakwood College in Huntsville, Alabama. She made an arrangement of the above tune, which appeared in *The Hymnal for Worship and Celebration* (Baptist 1986).

BLAHETKA, MARIE LEOPOLDINE (1811–1887)
"Die Rauber und die Sanger"
Pianist/composer, she was born on November 15th in Vienna, Austria, the daughter of Babette Traeg and J. L. Blahetka. She also played the physharmonica. After Beethoven left Bonn, Germany, in November 1792, he settled in Vienna. The Blahetka family knew Beethoven, who heard Marie play when she was only five years old and suggested that the girl study music under Joseph Czerny. After receiving instruction from Czerny, Kalkbrenner, and Moscheles and composition with Sechter, she composed "Die Rauber und die Sanger" produced at the Karntnertor Theatre in Vienna (1830). Her Op. 25, a concert piece for pianoforte and orchestra, was published in 1832. After touring France, she settled in Boulogne, where she died on January 12, 1887.

BLAKE, BEBE (1925–)
"Dreamy Eyes"
Composer/lyricist, she was born on May 7th in Los Angeles, California, and educated at the University of Southern California. After being discovered by Gus Edwards, she wrote songs for his shows, collaborating with Victor Young, Walter Scharf, Jimmy McHugh, Sammy Fain, and Daniele Amfitheatrof to create "Christmas in Jail", (song for the National Safety Council); "I Thank God", which won the Freedom Foundation award; "Cowboys Never Cry", "Dreamy Eyes", "Hidden in My Heart." ASCAP.

BLAKE, MYRTLE ANN (1906–Dec'd.)
"Wonderful Pal"
Composer born on January 23rd in Washington County, Maine. She had a high school education. Her songs include "So Blue", "Sweet Mary Lee", "Wonderful Pal", and "God Will Help You."

BLEY, CLARA BORG (1938–)
"Escalator Over the Hill"
Jazz composer and bandleader, she was born on May 11th in Oakland, California. She was self-taught, but had some help from her father, a church pianist/organist. In 1955 she moved to New York City and worked as a cigarette girl and sometimes as a pianist. In New York, she married Paul Bley and wrote jazz tunes for him and for Jimmy Giuffre and George Russell. Along with trumpeter Mike Mantler in 1964, she organized the Jazz Composers' Guild Orchestra and the next year changed the name to the Jazz Composers Orchestra. After she divorced Bley, she married Mike Mantler. She composed music for Charlie Haden's Liberation Music Orchestra. Bley was named Composer of the Year in 1980 by *down beat* critics poll. Albums available in 1994—*Dinner Music, Escalator Over the Hill, European Tour 1977, Fleur Carnivore, Live, Night-glo, Sextet, Social Studies, Very Big Clara Bley Band.*

BLOOM, VERA (1898–1959)
"Laredo"
Lyricist, she was born on May 17th in Chicago, Illinois, the daughter of
Congressman Sol Bloom. She was educated at the Horace Mann School.
She wrote the lyrics for *East is West*. With music by Jacob Gade and oth-
ers, she wrote the lyrics for "Jalousie", "My Message in the Stars", "Sou-
venir Waltz", "Just Keep Loving Me", "Ecstasy", "I Wish I Could Write
a Love Song", "The Only Things that Matters", "Laredo", "Yet I Know
You're Here." She died on January 10th in Baltimore, Maryland.

BLOOMFIELD-ZEISLER, FANNY (1863–1927)
(Popular at Carnegie Hall)
Concert pianist/composer, she was born on July 16th in Bielitz, Silesia,
Austria. At age two she was brought to America and played in public in
Chicago at age 10. She was a pupil of Ziehn and Karl Wolfsohn, then
of Leschetizky (1876–81). She toured America from 1883–93 as a con-
cert pianist and Europe starting in 1893. She married Sigmund Zeisler.
She composed piano pieces and songs. Zeisler died on August 20th in
Chicago, Illinois.

BOFILL, ANGELA (1955–)
"Under the Moon and Over the Sky"
Rock singer/songwriter, she was born in New York City. Her album
Something About You was on the top five on jazz charts. Her CDs are *The
Best of Angela Bofill* and *Intuition*.

BOGGUSS, SUZY (1957–)
"Letting Go"
Country singer/songwriter. With her husband Doug Crider she co-wrote
the hit "Letting Go" on the gold record *Aces* (1991), which won a Country Music Horizon award. She had a top ten single "Someday Soon", and
also wrote "Voices in the Wind" (1992), and "Drive South" (1993). She
toured with Dwight Yoakum in 1993.

BOND, CARRIE JACOBS SMITH (1862–1946)
"God Remembers When the World Forgets"
Composer, hymnist, songwriter, and publisher, she was born at Janesville,
Wisconsin on August 11, 1862. When she was only seven years old she
was badly scalded and never fully recovered from the trauma. In 1880
she married E. J. Smith and they had one son, but were later divorced.
In 1887 she married Dr. Francis Bond, who took up his medical practice in the small mining town of Iron River, Michigan. Then tragedy
struck—the mines closed, they had no income, Dr. Bond slipped on an
icy pavement and fell. He died five days later (1895). She moved to
Chicago with her nine-year-old son and for the next six years lived

on one meal a day. During this time she wrote 32 songs, although she had no musical training whatsoever. She formed the Bond Shop and printed her own songs. With an income of less than $8 per month, she managed somehow. To increase her income she sang her own songs in nightclubs in Chicago. In about 1901 she published *Seven Songs,* which included "I Love You Truly." It sold over 1 million copies. While staying at the Mission Inn at Riverside, California, in 1909 she drove up to Mount Rubidoux to see the sunset and wrote "The End of a Perfect Day", which sold over 5 million copies in its first wave of popularity. In 1932, in a fit of depression, her only child committed suicide. But despite all her tragedies, she felt she had a good life. She was entertained in The White House by President and Mrs. Theodore Roosevelt, and she was thrilled when she heard the soldiers singing "The End of a Perfect Day" in camps during World War I. She died in Hollywood, California, on December 28, 1946.

BOND, VICTORIA (1948–)
(First woman coconductor)
Conductor/composer, she was born on May 6th in Los Angeles, California. She assisted Andre Previn in leading the Pittsburgh Orchestra (1978–80), the first woman to conduct a major U.S. symphony orchestra. She composed chamber music and songs.

BONDS, MARGARET (1913–1972)
Arrangement—"Lord I just can't keep from crying"
Black composer, arranger, conductor, pianist, and writer, she was born in Chicago, Illinois, on March 3, 1913, and was educated at Northwestern University, Evanston, Illinois (BM; MM), Juilliard in New York City, and studied privately. She won scholarships from the National Association of Negro Musicians, Julius Rosenwald, the Rodman Wanamaker Award, etc. She toured as a pianist and served as chairman of Afro-American Music for the Eastern Region and on the National Association of Negro Musicians. She composed *Mass in d* and other works. She made numerous arrangements of Negro spirituals—"I'll Reach to Heaven," "Ezekiel Saw the Wheel," etc.

BONELLI, MONA MODINI (1903–)
"Four Sonnets from California Hills"
Lyricist, she was born on January 18th in Los Angeles, California, and educated at Bishop's School, Mills College (BA). With music by Charles Wakefield Cadmen, Elinor Remick Warren, Ernest Charles, Kenneth Walton, and Solon Alberti, she wrote a number of songs including "My Lady Walks in Loveliness", "White Swan", "Four Sonnets from California Hills", "My Lady Lo-Fu", and "Gifts". ASCAP.

BOOTH, CORNELIE IDA ERNESTINE SCHOCH (1864–1919)
"Bring to the Saviour thy Burden of Grief"
Composer, hymnist, and songwriter, one of three talented sisters, she was the daughter of a Dutch military colonel, and was born in The Netherlands on October 13, 1864. Upon his retirement from military service he joined The Salvation Army and was given the rank of Colonel responsible for its work in Holland. Her sisters were married to Lt. Colonel Fritz Malan and Commissioner W. Elwin Oliphant. Cornelie was married to Herbert Booth in Congress Hall, Clapton, London, England. Her compositions "A Perfect Trust" with its refrain "O for a deeper . . . O for a perfect trust in the Lord!" and "Holy Spirit, seal me I pray" appeared in *Songs of Peace and War* at the time of her marriage. Her hymn above appeared in Canadian *War Cry* (1893); *The Musical Salvationist* (April 1894); and in *The Song Book of the Salvation Army* (1930). Her hymn "Have you heard the angels singing?" appeared in the 1953 songbook.

BOOTH, EVANGELINE CORY (1865–1950)
"Dark shadows were falling, my spirit appalling"
Composer and hymnist, she was born at Hackney, England, a suburb of London on December 25, 1865, the seventh of eight children of Catherine Mumford and William Booth, founders of the Salvation Army. She was raised a Methodist, self educated in music, and was selling the *War Cry* on the streets at age fifteen. She composed several Salvation Army hymns, the best known being "The Word of God." She became Field Commander of Canada at Toronto, Ontario, in 1896 and the American commander in chief in 1904 and a United States citizen in 1923. Upon her retirement in 1939, she resided in Hartsdale, New York, until her death on July 17, 1950. Her hymns appeared in *The Song Book of The Salvation Army* (1953).

BOOTH-HELLBERG, LUCY MILWARD (1868–1953)
"Sins of Years are All Numbered"
Composer and hymnist, the youngest child of William and Catherine Booth, she was born at 1 Cambridge Lodge Villas, Hackney, London, England, on April 28, 1868. As a young woman, she suffered several periods of illness, during which time she wrote lyrics and composed the melodies for them.

After spending some time in The Salvation Army, she married Emanuel D. Hellberg, a Swedish officer in the Army. They worked together in India, Switzerland, and France. He changed his name to Booth-Hellberg. After his death in 1909, Mrs. Booth-Hellberg continued as a territorial commander in Denmark, South America, and in Norway. When her mother was dying, at Clacton-on-Sea, England, Lucy stayed up all night with her mother, who told Lucy to love backsliders and to pray for sinners. Upon returning by train to London, she wrote her hymn, and later set the words to music. She died on July 18, 1953. Her hymn appeared in *The Musical Salvationist* (November 1890) and in *The Song Book of the Salvation Army* (1899; 1953).

BOSWELL, CONNEE (1907–1976)
"You Ain't Got Nothin' "
Singer/composer/arranger, she was born on December 3rd in New Orleans, Louisiana, and studied with Otto Finck. Boswell sang with the Casa Loma Orchestra in the 1930s; then with her sisters Martha and Vet she formed the Boswell Sisters Trio. Later Connee went solo. She entertained U.S. Armed Forces during World War II. She appeared in Broadway shows *Star Time, Curtain Time,* and *Show Time* and sang on radio. She wrote "Putting it On", "You Ain't Got Nothin'," and "I Don't Mind." She died on October 11th in New York City.

BOTSFORD, TALITHA (1901–)
"Danse de Ballet"
Pianist/violinist/composer, she was born on September 21st in Millport, New York, and studied at Ithaca Conservatory on a scholarship. She was a violinist and pianist in resorts, summer theaters, concerts, and nightclubs. Her works for piano are "Frolic", "Carnival Capers", "Danse de Ballet", "Whimsical Dance", and "Jolly Dance". ASCAP.

BOULANGER, JULIETTE MARIE OLGA "LILY" (1893–1918)
La Princesse Maleine
Composer, she was born on August 21st in Paris, the younger sister of Nadia Boulanger. She studied at the Paris Conservatory, and won the Prix de Rome (1913). Boulanger composed chamber music, orchestral and choral works, and died on March 15th at Mezy, Seine-et-Oise, before she was able to complete her opera *La Princesse Maleine*.

BOULANGER, NADIA JULITTE (1887–1979)
(World-famous teacher)
Teacher/composer/conductor, she was born on September 16th in Paris. She studied at the Paris Conservatory and won first prizes in harmony, organ, and accompanying, fugue and counterpoint. Her teachers included Chapuis, Faure, Guilmant, Vidal, Vierne, and Widor. She was professor of harmony, counterpoint, and history of music at the Ecole Normale and then at the American Conservatory at Fontainebleau from 1921 and director from 1949. Her students included American composers Marc Blitzstein, Elliot Carter, Aaron Copland, David Diamond, Roy Harris, Walter Piston, Roger Sessions, and Virgil Thomson.

Boulanger composed an opera, piano pieces, orchestral works, and songs but ceased composing after the death of her sister Lily in 1918.

BOURGES, CLEMENTINE de (died 1561)
"Da bei rami"
Composer/poetess, she married organist/composer Clement de Bourges of Lyons, France. "Da bei rami", a four-part chorus included in Paix's "Orgel-Tabulatur-Buch" (1583), was taken from the works of Clement and Clementine de Bourges and signed "Clem.de Bourges". He was killed in 1560 while fighting the French Huguenots, and she died on September 30th the following year.

BOWDEN, CHRISTINE M. (1908–)
"Indianapolis"
Organist/pianist/composer, she was born on August 17th in Bedford, Indiana, and educated at the Arthur Jordan Conservatory and De Pauw University. She was a pianist on radio in Indianapolis and in Louisville, Kentucky, then a church organist and teacher. Her songs were "Why Oh Why", "Cannibal's Menu", "My Crescent Girl", and "Indianapolis", the official song of Speedway Race Day. ASCAP.

BOYD, ELSIE THOMPSON (1904–Dec'd.)
"So Grateful"
Composer/organist/singer, she was born on May 27th in St. Paul, Minnesota. While in high school, she was an organist in theaters showing silent films. She went to Brooklyn, New York, in 1929 and was a singer and organist in Paramount Theaters, and later a staff organist for CBS. She wrote "So Grateful". ASCAP.

BRACKEN, JOANNE (1938–)
Fifi Goes to Heaven
She was born Joanne Grogan in Ventura, California. During the late 1950s-60s she worked with Dexter Gordon, Woody Shaw, and others, during the 1970s with Art Blakey, Joe Henderson, Stan Getz, and others. She played at Gulliver's Place in West Paterson, New Jersey, in 1978 and at Salt Peanuts in New York City in 1980. As of 1994 her available albums and CDs were *Breath of Brazil, Fifi Goes to Heaven, Havin' Fun, Live at Maybeck Hall, Special Identity, Where Legends Dwell.*

BRAMBILLA, MARIETTA (1807–1875)
Vocalizzi
Contralto/composer/teacher, she was born Cassano d'Adda on June 6th in Milan, Italy. After studying at the Milan Academy, she made her

debut as Arsace in Rossini's *Semiramide* (1827) in London. She sang in London, Italy, Vienna (1837–41), and in Paris. She published books on musical exercises and vocalizzi. Brambilla died on November 6th in Milan.

BRANSCOMBE, GENA (1881–1977)
Chorale—*The Lord is our fortress*

Composer, conductor, educator, and songwriter, she was born in Picton, Ontario, Canada, on November 4, 1881, and was educated at the Chicago Musical College (BM), Whitman College (hon. MA), and studied privately with Engelbert Humperdinck among others, in Germany. She headed the piano department of Whitman College Conservatory (1907–09), and married John F. Tenney. She conducted the Branscombe Choral, State Chorus of New Jersey, Contemporary Club Choral in Newark, New Jersey, MacDowell Choral in New Jersey, etc. She composed *Pilgrims of Destiny* (a cantata, 1928) and other pieces. She died in New York City on July 26, 1977.

BREWER, TERESA (1931–)
"I Love Mickey"

Singer/songwriter, she was born on May 7th in Toledo, Ohio, and educated at Waite High School. She toured on the *Major Bowes' Amateur Hour* from age five to twelve, then on the *Pick and Pat Show;* appeared on *Eddie Dowling's Big Break*. She married Bill Monahan; later she appeared on the *Perry Como Show* and the *Ed Sullivan Show*. With music by others, she wrote "I Love Mickey", "Down the Holiday Trail", "Hush-a-Bye, Wink-a-Bye-Do", "Imp", "There's Nothing as Lonesome as Saturday Night".

BRICKELL, EDIE
"What I Am"

Singer/songwriter. Folk-pop singer, in the late 1980s she formed the New Bohemians. She married composer/songwriter Paul Simon. Brickell wrote "Philosophy is the stuff on a cereal box/Religion is the smile of a dog". Her albums are "Ghost of a Dog", "Shooting Rubberbands", "Picture Perfect Morning" (1994).

BRIDGES, ETHEL (1897–Dec'd.)
"Hawaiian Lullaby"

Composer, she was born on November 10th in San Francisco, California, and was educated at Miss Hamilton's Finishing School. As a child she won the Portola Festival songwriting contest. Later she lived in Hawaii and wrote songs—"Hawaiian Lullaby", "Here You Are", "Ching a Ling's Jazz Bar", "Just Like a Rose", and a Hawaiian love song—"Whispering". She married Richard N. Winfield. ASCAP.

BRIEL, MARIE (1896–1960)
Ritual music for *The Holy Communion*
Composer and organist, she was born at Peru, Illinois, on February 14, 1896, and was educated at Northwestern University School of Music (Mus.B., 1919; Mus.M., 1925), Evanston, Illinois. She taught at Marionville College in Missouri, at Iowa Wesleyan College at Mt. Pleasant, Iowa; Columbia School of Music in Chicago; American Conservatory of Music in Chicago; and at the National College of Education in Evanston, Illinois. She was organist-director of the Methodist Episcopal Church in Wilmette, Illinois. Her music appeared in the *Methodist Hymnal* (1935). She was married to J. William Humphries and she died on May 24, 1960. (Information from Patrick M. Quinn, University Archivist, Northwestern University Library, Evanston, Illinois.)

BRINSON, ROSEMARY GREENE (1917–Dec'd.)
"My First Love"
Composer/songwriter, she was born on September 8th in East St. Louis, Illinois, and was educated at the University of Illinois (BS), Northwestern University (MA), Indiana University, St. Louis University. She became a choral director at St. Louis University, then was a producer and music director for CBS and NBC-TV. Her songs include "My First Love", "Am I the Guy?" ASCAP.

BRITAIN, RADIE (1899–1994)
'Suite for Strings'
Composer, she was born on March 17th at Silverton, Texas. Educated at Clarendon Junior College, Texas, she was graduated from the American Conservatory, Chicago (BM piano 1924). After studying composition and theory in Munich with Albert Noelte and organ in Paris with Marcel Dupre, she returned to the states and studied piano with Godowsky and organ with Yon. She taught at Clarendon College, at the Girvin Institute of Music, Chicago from 1930–34, and at the Chicago Conservatory from 1934–39, then taught privately in Hollywood, California, from 1940–60. Her "Epic Poem" won first prize in the National Contest of American Pen Women in 1927; and "Suite for Strings" won first prize from the American Women Composers. For "Heroic Poem", she became the first woman to receive the Juilliard Publication Award in 1945; "Nirvana" took first prize from the Texas Confederation of Music Clubs.

BROCK, BLANCHE KERR (1888–1958)
"He's a Wonderful Savior to Me"
Composer and pianist, she was born at Greenfork, Indiana, on February 3, 1888, and was educated at the American Conservatory of Music in Chicago, Illinois, and at the Indianapolis Conservatory in Indianapolis,

Indiana. She was a solo pianist with evangelistic preachers. Her husband, Virgil P. Brock, wrote hymns and she composed the music for them. She died in Winona Lake, Indiana, on January 3, 1958.

BROOKE, JONATHA (1964–)
"Missing Person Afternoon"
Composer/cellist/violinist, educated at Amherst College, Amherst, Massachusetts. With Jennifer Kimball (b. 1963) on album *The Story*. Brooke also composed "Fatso".

BROOKS, ANNE SAVOY (1911–)
"Calypso Love"
Composer/singer/songwriter, she was born on July 21st in Leeds Point, New Jersey, and has a high school education. She sang in church choirs, with glee clubs, etc. With Charles King and Sol Marcus, she wrote a number of songs such as "Calypso Love", "Across the Border", and "The Best in Trinidad".

BROOKS, KAREN
"A Simple I Love You"
Country singer/songwriter/guitarist. With singer/songwriter/guitarist Randy Sharp she had a hit single, "A Simple I Love You", and an album *That's Another Story* (1992).

BROWN, BARNETTA (1859–1938)
"Cradle Song"
Songwriter, she was born on January 7th in New York City, and was educated at Miss Bean's Boarding School in New York. She taught school in Brooklyn. She wrote the lyrics for "Cradle Song", "Ride of the Cossacks", and published an *Anthology of Classics,* which she translated and for which she wrote original lyrics.

BROWN, MARGARET WISE (1910–1952)
"Where Have You Been?"
Songwriter, she was born on May 23rd in New York City, and was educated at Hollins College (BAEd.). She wrote children's books and lyrics for songs such as "Where Have You Been?", "I Like People", and books with records for children like *The Golden Egg, Five Little Firemen, Little Brass Band, Little Fat Policeman*. She died on November 1st in Nice, France.

BROWN, MARILYN MCMEEN (1938–)
"Thy Servants are Prepared"
Hymnist born in Denver, Colorado, and educated at Brigham Young University. She married William Brown and they have six children. She

has written short stories, poems, and novels. Her hymn above appeared in the Mormon hymnal (1985).

BROWNE, AUGUSTA (1820–1882)
"The Warlike Dead in Mexico"
Composer, born in Dublin, Ireland, she was brought to America as a child and during the 1840s–50s was organist at the First Presbyterian Church in Brooklyn, New York. Browne was known for her salon piano pieces and parlor songs. Her songs were influenced by the Mexican War—"The Volunteer's War Song" 1846, "The Warlike Dead in Mexico" 1848—and piano—"The Mexican Volunteer's Quickstep", etc. She was an early advocate of women's rights. Her married name was Garrett.

BROWNE, MARY ANNE (1812–1844)
Tune—"Plymouth" or "Browne"
A composer, she was born in England and was a relative of the noted poet Felicia Browne Hemans. She composed her tune "Plymouth" for the hymn "The Breaking Waves Dashed High" by Hemans about the Pilgrims landing at Plymouth, Massachusetts, in 1620. Her tune appeared in *New Hymn and Tune Book* (Unitarian, 1914).

BRUBECK, IOLA WHITLOCK (1923–)
"Blow Schatmo"
Songwriter, she was born on August 14th in Corning, California, and was educated at Shasta Union High School in Redding, California, and the University of the Pacific (BA). She married composer/songwriter Dave Brubeck and wrote the lyrics for some of his compositions of cantatas, oratorios, and songs. They have six children. Her songs are "Blow Schatmo!", "Easy As You Go", "In the Lurch", "Since Love Had Its Way", "Summer Song", "Too Young for Growing Old", "Trav'lin' Blues."

BRUSH, RUTH J. (1910–)
"Street Singers"
Composer, she was born on February 7th in Fairfax, Oklahoma, and was educated at the Kansas City Conservatory, and studied with Wiktor Labunski. She was also a concert pianist and organist at St. Luke's Episcopal Church in Bartlesville, Oklahoma. Her works are "6 Suites for Strings", "2 Expressive Pieces for Organ", "Valse Joyeuse" for violin and piano; and an opera "Street Singers". ASCAP.

BRYANT, FELICE (1927–)
"Rocky Top"
Songwriter, she was born on August 7th at Milwaukee, Wisconsin. While on tour, country singer and guitarist Boudleaux Bryant met Felice in

Milwaukee in 1945, and sometime later they were married. The two wrote songs, and in 1949 Little Jimmy Dickens recorded their "Country Boy". They moved to Nashville, Tennessee, and recorded their own material but with little success. Their career was launched by the Everly Brothers with "Bye Bye Love", "Wake Up Little Susie", "All I Have to Do is Dream", and "Bird Dog". "Rocky Top" is considered a Tennessee state song by some. In 1978 James Taylor and Carly Simon recorded their "Devoted to You". In 1981, Joe Sampley and Moe Bandy recorded their song "Hey Joe, Hey Moe".

BUCHANAN, ANNABEL MORRIS (1888–1983)
Tune—"Land of Rest"
A composer, she was born at Groesbeck, Texas, on October 22, 1888, and was graduated from the London Conservatory of Music in Dallas (1907) and attended the Guilmant Organ School in New York City. She taught music in Oklahoma and Texas for eight years, then at Stonewall Jackson College in Abington, Virginia, for three years. In 1912 she married John Preston Buchanan. She was president of the Virginia Federation of Music Clubs (1927–30), cofounder of the Virginia State Choral Festival, and director of the White Top Music Festival and Conference (1931–41). Her tune is a harmonization of an old Scottish or North English tune and was the setting for the hymn "Jerusalem, my happy home," in *The Pilgrim Hymnal* (1958). She died in Paducah, Kentucky, on January 6, 1983, where she resided, and was buried in Marion, Virginia. (Letter from Mack H. Sturgill of Marion, Virginia.)

BUCKLEY, HELEN DALLAM (1899–Dec'd.)
"Earth in Cycle"
Pianist/singer/composer, she was born in Chicago, Illinois. After studying at the American Conservatory of Music in Chicago and at the Academy of Allied Arts in New York City, she returned to Chicago to teach at the American Conservatory there. Her works are "Quartet for Strings", "Piano (Chicago News prize), "An Indian Legend" (Chicago News prize), "The Slave", "Temple Song", "Earth in Cycle" (soprano, harp, strings, and quartet).

BUNDY, EVE M. (1910–)
"Po Ling, Ming Toy"
Songwriter, she was born on September 12th in Seattle, Washington, and was educated at the University of Washington. With music by Rudolf Friml, she wrote "Po Ling, Ming Toy", etc.

BURKALOW, ANASTASIA VAN (b. 1911–)
"Almighty God, who made all things"
Composer and hymnist, daughter of Mable R. Ramsay and James T. van Burkalow, she was born in Buchanan, New York, on March 16, 1911, and was educated at Hunter College (BA, 1931) and Columbia University

(PhD, 1934) in New York City. She was a member of the faculty of Hunter College in New York City (1938–75) and was professor of geology and geography. "I have been organist and choir director in several New York City churches, though I gave up that work in 1965 because of the pressure of my college duties. For my choir I made numerous special arrangements and some original compositions, but none of these have been published. . . . Four of my hymns have been published by The Hymn Society of America." (Letter dated 4/29/82 from Miss van Burkalow from New York City. Her article, "60 Years of The Hymn Society of America 1922–82", was published in *The Hymn* (January 1982), pages 12–15. "High time it is to seek the Lord" was published in *15 New Bible Hymns* (1966), two hymns in *16 New Hymns on the Stewardship of the Environment* (1973), and the above hymn in *New Hymns for America* (1976), all published by The Hymn Society of America. She is a Methodist.

BURNETT, JUNE (1914–Dec'd.)
   "She Was Five and He Was Ten"
Comedienne/songwriter, she was born on March 25th in Philadelphia, Pennsylvania. She was a child performer in theaters, then in nightclubs. With music by Mike Di Napoli, she wrote songs such as "She Was Five and He Was Ten". ASCAP.

BURNS, ANNELU (1889–1942)
   "Shadows on My Heart"
Songwriter, she was born on November 12th in Selma, Alabama and was educated at Judson College, Boston Conservatory, Brenau College, and the Leopold Auer School. She resided in Pleasantville, New York, where she taught school and gave private lessons. With music by Ernest Ball and others, she wrote the words to the songs "For the Sake of Auld Lang Syne", "I'll Forget You", "Little Brown Shoes", "Little Spanish Villa by the Sea", and "Shadows on My Heart". She died on July 12th in Mt. Kisco, New York.

BUSEY, BERNICE BLAND (1918–)
   "Love Tears"
Composer, she was born on April 29th in Washington, DC and was educated at Howard University. With Eubie Blake, she wrote a number of songs. Her songs include "It's Almost Christmas", "Look What I Found", "Love Tears", "Paragon", and "Sharing". ASCAP.

BUSH, KATE (1958–)
   The Kick Inside
Ballad singer/songwriter, she was born on July 30th in London, England. Her single "Wuthering Heights" was a hit in 1978. After her guitarist Alan Murphy died, Bush did her recording alone. But for the past two and

a half years she has invited other artists to record with her, and they have accepted—Eric Clapton, the artist formerly known as Prince, and ex-Procal Harum keyboardist Gary Brooker. Her albums and CDs are *The Kick Inside* (Pregnant), *The Dreaming, Hounds of Love, Lionheart, Never Forever, Sensual World, The Whole Story*. Her laser discs/videos are *Live at Hammersmith* and *Sensual World: The Videos*. Her latest CD is *The Red Shoes* with two top singles: "Why Should I Love You?" and "Rubberband Girl" (1994).

BYLES, BLANCHE DOUGLAS (1892–1979)
    Tune—"Thy Great Bounty"
A composer, daughter of Mary Baker and Enoch A. Douglas, she was born in Sterling, Connecticut, on August 14, 1892, and was educated at Brown University, Providence, Rhode Island (AB, 1914) and became a school-teacher at the Norwich Free Academy in Norwich, Connecticut. As a composer and organist, she had no formal training, but played the organ at a small Baptist church where she was raised, and later sang in choirs of the Madison Avenue Methodist Church and the Episcopal Chapel of the Intercession in New York City. Later she was a church organist in Los Angeles for six years. Ten of her hymns were published in the *Modern Youth Hymnal*. She was married to Howard T. Byles, who was serving as a lieutenant colonel in the U. S. Army at Fort Douglas, Utah, in 1945. They had one son and one daughter. Her hymn tune appeared in the *Evangelical and Reformed Church Hymnal* (1941). She died on May 10, 1979. (Letter from Sandra Clifford Valletta, Brown University, Providence, Rhode Island.)

-C-

CACCINI, FRANCESCA (1588–1640)
    Sacred opera—*Il martirio di Sant' Agata*
Composer, singer, and harpsichordist, the daughter of Giulio Caccini, singer and composer, she was born in Florence, Italy, on September 18, 1588, and studied under her father. She was married to Giovanni Battista Signorini, and they had two daughters. She collaborated with Giovanni Battista da Gagliano on her sacred opera (above), which was produced in Florence on February 10, 1622. She was the first woman composer of an opera-ballet, *La liberazione di Ruggiero dall' isola d'Alcina* (words by Ferdinando Saracinelli), which was produced at the Tuscan court at the Villa Poggio Imperiale, near Florence, on February 2, 1625. She died at Lucca, Italy, in about 1640.

CAESAR, SHIRLEY (1930–)
    "He's Working It Out for You"
Gospel singer/composer, she was born in Durham, North Carolina. She recorded on *Jubilation* Great Performances Vols. 1 and 2 issued in 1992.

"He's Working It Out for You" on the Stellar Awards TV Show, won a Grammy in January 1993. "Stand Still" won Soul Gospel Grammy in 1994.

CAHOON, MATILDA ROZELLE WATTS (1881–1973)
"The Light Divine"
Hymnist born in Murray, Utah. She taught school in Utah and in Nevada and coached boys' choirs. In 1900 she went to Chicago for further music study. After the death of her husband, she obtained her bachelor's degree from the University of Utah. Her hymn above appeared in the Mormon hymnal (1985).

CALDWELL, ANNE (1867–1936)
"Three cheers"
Librettist/songwriter, she was born on August 30th in Boston, Massachusetts, and was educated in the public schools. She wrote or co-wrote the words for the following Broadway musicals: *The Canary, The City Chap, Pom-Pom, She's a Good Fellow, The Sweetheart Shop, Good Morning Dearie, Chin Chin, Jack o'Lantern, Tip Top, Hitchy Koo of 1921, Three Cheers,* and many more. With music by Jerome Kern, Vincen Youmans, and others, she wrote the words for "In the Dark", "Temple Bells", "Wait Till the Cows Come Home", "Come and Have a Swing With Me", "Blue Danube Blues", "Left All Alone Again Blues", "Raggedy Ann", and many more songs. She died on October 22nd in Hollywood, California.

CALDWELL, MARY ELIZABETH GLOCKLER (b. 1909–)
"Tell us shepherd maids"
Conductor, organist, hymnist, and composer, she was born in Tacoma, Washington, on August 1, 1909, was graduated from the University of California at Berkeley (AB, 1930), and studied at the Munich Conservatory (1930–31). On October 14, 1932, she married Philip G. Caldwell. She served as organist and choir director at the Scotia (N.Y.) Reformed Church (1933–40), First Baptist Church of Pasadena, California (1941–44), and San Marino Community Church from 1948. She composed cantatas, and her hymn above had two recordings listed in *Phonolog Reports* (1978) of Los Angeles, California. "I have to admit that your letter provided a bit of comic relief to our otherwise very businesslike weekly staff meeting at church! Yes, I'm still very much alive and am finishing my 34th year as organist at the San Marino Community Church—I'm still a size 8 and climb mountains in the summertime as you may see by the enclosed article which I am sending." (Letter of February 17, 1982.) Her first published anthem, *The Carol of the Little King,* has sold 700,000 copies, and her second opera, *The Gift of Song,* about Franz Gruber, the

composer of "Silent Night," has been performed over 200 times in America, England, and Australia, and her third opera, *The Night of the Star,* is about a young shepherd boy who stayed behind to help an angel with a broken wing.

CALLOWAY, BLANCHE (1902–1978)
"Rhythm on the River"

Singer/composer, she was born in Baltimore, Maryland, the older sister of bandleaders Cab and Elmer Calloway. She began her career as a singer in shows in Baltimore and Chicago in the 1920s and helped her brother Cab get into show business. She sang in the broadway musical *Shuffle Along* by Eubie Blake and Nobble Sissle in 1921. She sang in Cab Calloway's band in the early 1930s, then led her own jazz band in Philadelphia. In the 1950s, she bacame the first black woman disk jockey in the South at radio station WMBM in Miami Beach, Florida, and then became the station's director a few years later. As a songwriter, she wrote "Rythm on the River", "I Need Loving", "Growling Dan." She died on December 16, 1978.

CAMERON, CATHERINE ARNOTT (1927–)
"God, Who Stretched the Spangled Heavens"

Hymnist, she was born on March 27th in St. John, New Brunswick, Canada, and was educated at McMaster University (BA) and the University of Southern California (MA and PhD). She married Dr. Stuart Oskamp, and she has been professor of psychology at the University of La Verne, California, since 1971. Her hymn appeared in the Baptist Hymnal (1986).

CAMP, MABEL JOHNSON (1871–1937)
"Lift up your heads, Pilgrims aweary."
Tune — "Camp"

Composer, hymnist, and pianist, the daughter of a banker, she was born in Chanute, Kansas, on November 25, 1871, and attended a girl's school in Steubenville, Ohio. She was an accomplished pianist, had a beautiful contralto voice, and was also a composer of hymns. She married Norman H. Camp, an attorney, who, after attending one of Dwight L. Moody's Union Bible classes taught by William R. Newell, was converted to Christianity, as was his wife. He became an envangelist teacher. Her hymns and hymn tunes were published by the leaders of the Moody Memorial Church in Chicago. She died in Chicago, Illinois, on May 25, 1937. Her hymns and tunes appeared in the *American Service* (1968); *Great Hymns of the Faith* (1972); and *Hymns for the Living Church* (1974).

CAMPBELL, LUCIE EDDIE (1885–1963)
"Something Within Me—"
Composer, pianist, and teacher, she was born on April 30th in Duckhill, Mississippi. The family moved to Memphis, Tennessee, when she was four years old. As a child, she studied piano and music theory. After graduating from Booker T. Washington High School in 1899, she taught there for the next 44 years. Attending classes at Rust College, Holly Springs, Mississippi, in the summer time, she earned her BA there and her MA at the State University in Nashville. In 1919 she was one of the founders of the National Baptist Training Union where she served as music director. Campbell wrote 45 gospel songs, mostly for the annual National Baptist Conventions, and most of them began with the words "Something within me". Her other songs include "He'll Understand and Say, Well Done" (1933), "In the Upper Room", and "My Lord and I", both composed in 1947, and "Footprints of Jesus" (1949).

CAPERS, VALERIE (1935–)
"Sing about Love"
Pianist/conductor/composer, she was born on May 24th in the Bronx, New York, the daughter of Alvin Capers, who played the stride piano and was a friend of Fats Waller. At age six she suffered a streptococcus infection, which started as a strep throat, then entered her bloodstream and affected her optic nerve, which blinded her. Her younger brother, the late tenor saxist Bobby Capers, who worked with Mongo Santamaria and others, got her interested in jazz. But her dad wanted her to study classical music. While at the New York Institute for the Education of the Blind, she earned a reputation as a classical pianist. After earning her bachelor's and master's degrees at Julliard in New York City, she taught at the Manhattan School of Music. In 1970 she won a Creative Artists Public Service Fellowship to write a full Christmas cantata running two hours and fifteen minutes, which was first performed in 1974 at the Central Presbyterian Church in New York City. The cantata was also performed the next two years at the Cutahoga Community College in Cleveland, Ohio. Her cantata "Sing About Love" was full of gospel/pop/jazz/ Latin rhythms and was performed for the fourth time under the aegis of the New York Jazz Repertory Company at Carnegie Hall in New York City on December 18, 1978.

CARA, IRENE (1959–)
"Flashdance"
Actress, soprano, and songwriter, she was born March 18th in the Bronx, New York. As a child she appeared on Spanish-language television and as a teenager in films, television series, and Broadway shows. She wrote the

lyrics and sang the title song in *Flashdance,* she also sang the title song in the film *Fame* in 1980. She received a Grammy Award for Best Female Pop performance and an Academy Award for the Best Song of the Year.

CARDONI, MARY (1938–)
"Love in a Mist"
Songwriter, she was born on March 21st in Cleveland, Ohio, and was educated at the Collinwood High School. With music by Frank Cardoni, she wrote "Love is a Mist" and other songs.

CAREY, JOSIE (1930–)
"Around the Children's Corner"
Actress/songwriter, she was born on August 20th in Pittsburgh, Pennsylvania, and was educated at the University of Pennsylvania in Philadelphia. She appeared on the WQED TV Show *The Children's Corner* and was named "Woman of the Year" by the Pittsburgh *Post Gazette* in 1965. With music by Fred Rogers, Johnny Costa, and others, she wrote the lyrics for "Around the Children's Corner", "Goodnight God", "It's Morning", and "Tomorrow on the Children's Corner". ASCAP.

CAREY, MARIAH (1970–)
"Dreamlover"
Singer/songwriter, she was born on March 27th in Huntington, Long Island, New York, the daughter of Alfred Carcy, a black aeronautical engineer from Venezuela, and Patricia, an aspiring Irish-American opera star from Indiana. When Mariah was only two years old, her parents separated and Mariah went to live with her mother, who gave her musical training. When Mariah was not yet three years old, her mother was rehearsing at home for her New York City Opera debut as Maddalena in Verdi's *Rigoletto,* then hesitated, missing her cue. Whereupon Mariah broke in and sang the song in Italian at exactly the right pitch. Mariah had no formal musical training and while in high school she wrote songs. After graduating from Harborfield High School in 1987, Mariah moved to New York City and worked as a waitress. She met Sony music mogul Tommy Mattolla at a party and gave him her music demo tape, whereupon he signed her to a contract. Her 1990 debut album *Mariah Carey* sold 6 million and won two Grammys. *Emotions* (1991) sold 3 million, *Unplugged* (1992) 2 million, and *Music Box* (1993) spent two months as No. 1 on the top ten. She received the American Music award for pop/rock vocalist in 1993 and a Grammy in 1993. After divorcing his wife of 20 years, Mattolla married Mariah in June 1993, attended by guests Robert DeNiro, Barbra Streisand, and Bruce Springsteen. On her

album *Merry Christmas* (1994), Carey co-wrote three songs, including "All I Want for Christmas Is You".

CARLSON, MABLE DOSIA (1930–)
   Tune—"God's Glory"
Composer/hymnist born on January 11th in Huron, South Dakota, and educated at De Pauw University, Greencastle, Indiana; Oberlin College in Ohio; University of Toledo in Ohio (B.Ed.); Hartford Seminary in Connecticut (MA); University of Pittsburgh in Pennsylvania (PhD). She served as faculty member of Defiance College in Ohio from 1960–74; Beatitudes Campus of Care, Phoenix, Arizona from 1974–81; director, Beautitudes Center from 1981–93; pastor of Caring Ministries, Church of the Beautitudes since 1993. "God's Glory" includes 50 hymns and tunes of which Carlson composed the tunes and wrote the words for 40 of them, the title hymn being #17, "God's Glory". Her hymns and tunes have also been published by the Pilgrim Press in 1969 and 1981, Choisters Guild 1975, United Methodist Publishing House in 1977 and 1981, American Baptist Churches in the USA in 1979, The Geneva Press in 1979, United Church Press in 1990, and Hope Publishing in 1992.

CARNES, KIM (1945–)
   "The Heart Won't Lie"
A singer/songwriter, she was born July 20th in Hollywood, California. With a deep raw voice, she sang in Christy Minstrels, and her hit "Bette Davis Eyes" won a Grammy (1981). Her albums and CDs are *Best of Kim Carnes, Mistaken Identity,* and *Gypsy Honeymoon* (1993). With Donna Weiss, she wrote "The Heart Won't Lie" (1994).

CARNEY, JULIA ABIGAIL FLETCHER (1823–1908)
   "Think Gently of the Erring One"
Born at Lancaster, Massachusetts, on April 6, 1823, she began writing verses as a child and at age fourteen was contributing poems to juvenile magazines. She became a primary schoolteacher in Boston in 1844 and there wrote her famous poem:
   Litle drops of water,
   Little grains of sand,
   Make the mighty ocean,
   And this beauteous land.
It was first published in the *Boston Primary School Reader* in 1845 and more recently in *Songs of Praise* (1931). In 1849, she married Rev. Thomas J. Carney, a Universalist minister. She was also a Universalist, and died at Galesburg, Illinois, on November 1, 1908. Her hymn above appeared in the *Methodist Hymnal* (1911). More recently her hymn

appeared in the *Methodist* (1955); *Evangelical United Brethren*, and the *Union Hymnal* (Jewish).

CARPENTER, IMOGENE (1919–Dec'd.)
"Born to Sing the Blues"
Composer/pianist/singer, she was born on February 2nd in Hot Springs, Arkansas, and was educated at the Chicago Musical College on a scholarship, and at the Boguslawski School of Music. She was a concert pianist, then led her own orchestra. With Lenny Adelson and Kim Gannon, she wrote a number of songs, including "Anytime, Anywhere", "Born to Sing the Blues", "Don't Change Your Mind About Me", "If Winter Comes", "Say So". ASCAP.

CARPENTER, MARY-CHAPIN
"Down at the Twist, and Shout"
Country guitarist/singer/songwriter, she was raised near Washington, DC, and was graduated from Brown University, Providence, Rhode Island. She wrote the song mentioned above. Her hits were "When Halley Came to Jackson" (about Halley's Comet in Mississippi), for which she won Female Vocalist at the 1992 Country Music awards; "Come On, Come On" in 1992; "I Feel Lucky" won a 1993 Grammy. She appeared on the CBS Special *Women of Country* in January 1993; she won the Country Music Female Vocalist award in 1993; sang on the *Christmas in Washington* show on NBC-TV in 1993; sang "Passionate Kisses" and won Country Vocal Female Grammy in 1994. Her albums and CDs available in 1994 included *Come On, Come On, Hometown Girl, Shooting Straight, State of the Heart*.

CARR, MARGIE (1900–)
"A Lonely Cowboy"
Composer, she was born on May 15th in Shelbyville, Indiana, and was educated at the Arthur Jordan Conservatory, the Indianapolis Central College, and studied with Otto Cesana. She taught piano and organ and was a singer with orchestras. With her husband Billy Heuston, they wrote "A Lonely Cowboy", "I'm Headin' for the West Again", "It's Back to the Plains for Me", "Yippee Ti Yea, Ti Yea", "Put Your Trust in Jesus", "I Am a Child of God", "Cupid", "It's a Date".

CARREAU, MARGARET (1899–)
"Sea Nocturne"
Organist/pianist/composer, she was born on January 23rd in Bedford, Pennsylvania, and was educated in public schools. She studied with Oliver Denton and Kate Chittenden. She was a rehearsal pianist for Irving Berlin, Sam Harris, and an accompanist for John Charles Thomas.

With Frederick Martens, she composed a number of songs and instrumentals, such as "Comparison", "Eventide", "Query", "Rapture", "Sea Nocturne", "Pastures of the Soul", "You and I Together". ASCAP.

CARREÑO, MARIA TERESA (1853–1917)
String Quartet in B Minor
World-famed pianist and composer, she was born on December 22nd in Caracas, Venezuela. She was taken to New York City when she was eight years old where she studied with Louis Moreau Gottschalk. After giving her first recital in New York on November 25, 1862, she toured the United States. In 1863 she gave a recital in The White House for President Lincoln and played "Listen to the Mocking Bird" (by Septimus Winner, 1855), but the piano was out of tune and she refused to play another piece. After 1866 she lived in Europe and studied with George Mathias and Anton Rubinstein. She married violinist Emile Saurer in 1872 and divorced him a while later. She then married baritone Giovanni Tagliapietra in 1875, whereupon they lived in Venezuela for almost two years during which time she organized an opera company in which she sang and conducted. She returned to the States in 1876 to study in Boston. In 1892 she married Eugen d'Albert and divorced him a while later. In 1902 she married Arturo Tagliapietra, the younger brother of Giovanni. Most of her works were for the piano. Edward A. MacDowell was her student, and she played his piano pieces at Saratoga, New York, in 1883 and at Chicago in 1884. She played the piano with the New York Philharmonic on December 8, 1916, her last public performance, and died in New York on June 12, 1917.

CARROLL, BARBARA (1925–)
"Lost in a Crowded Place"
Pianist/composer, she was born on January 25th in Worcester, Massachusetts, and was educated at the New England Conservatory. As a member of an instrumental trio, she toured for the USO; she was also a pianist in nightclubs. Her songs and instrumentals are "Barbara's Carol", "Fancy Pants", "Just Plain Blue", "Lost in a Crowded Place". ASCAP.

CARROLL, GEORGIA LILLIAN (1914–)
"Reach for the Moon"
Composer/singer/songwriter, she was born on September 15th in Weed, California, and was educated at a junior college. She sang with Fanchon and Marco; wrote, directed, and appeared in the radio show *Phyllis & Don*. She wrote songs such as "Reach for the Moon". ASCAP.

CARSON, MARTHA (1921–)
"I Can't Stand Up Alone"
Country/gospel singer/songwriter/guitarist, she was born in Neon, Ken-

tucky. When she was eighteen, she sang on radio station WHIS in Blue-
field, West Virginia, then in Atlanta, Georgia, and Knoxville, Tennessee.
She joined the Grand Ole Opry in 1952. Carson wrote "Satisfied, I'm
Gonna Walk and Talk with My God" and "I Can't Stand Up Alone".

CARTER, CARLENE (1957–)
"Every Little Thing"
Guitarist/country singer/songwriter, she was born in Madisonville, Ten-
nessee, the daughter of June Carter and the stepdaughter of Johnny Cash.
Her hit was "I Fell in Love" (1991). With Al Henderson, she wrote
"Every Little Thing" (1994).

CARTER, JUNE (1929–)
"Ring of Fire"
Autoharpist/singer/songwriter, she was born on June 23rd in Maces
Springs, Virginia, the daughter of Mother Maybelle Carter. With her sisters Helen and Anita, the trio became know as The Carter Sisters (1943)
and were featured on radio stations in Charlotte, North Carolina, Richmond, Virginia, and Knoxville, Tennessee. With Johnny Cash she wrote
"The Matador" (1963), with Merle Kilgore "Ring of Fire" (1963), and
with Cash and Kilgore "Happy to Be With You" (1966). She then teamed
up with Cash and married him, but they later divorced. Then she wrote
"He Don't Love Me Anymore".

CARTER, MOTHER MAYBELLE (1909–1978)
"A Jilted Love"
Autoharpist/singer/songwriter, she was born in Nickelsville, Virginia.
Sister-in-law of Alvin Pleasant Carter, with Carter's wife Sara Carter,
they formed the Carter Family Singers, cut their first record in Bristol,
Tennessee (1927), and became famous folk singers. Sara divorced A. P.
Carter in 1932. A. P. Carter with Mother Maybelle sang on radio station
XERA, Mexico, near Del Rio, Texas (1938–41), then on station WBT,
Charlotte, North Carolina (1941–43). Mother Maybelle's daughters
Helen, June, and Anita Ina formed the Carter Sisters singing trio. After
she broke up with A. P. Carter in 1943, Mother Maybelle joined her
daughters singing on station WRVA Richmond, Virginia, in 1943.
Mother Maybelle wrote "A Jilted Love" and "Walk a Little Closer". Her
LP records included *Songs of the Famous Carter Family, Mother May-
belle,* and *Mother Maybelle Carter.* A postage stamp was issued in 1993
honoring A. P., Sarah, and Maybelle Carter.

CARTER, RUTH (1900–1982)
"For Your Holy Book We Thank You"
Hymnist, she was born on August 22nd in Upper Clapton, London, Eng-

land, the daughter of Ethel and James Carter. She was educated at West-hill Training College and was a schoolteacher in Chelmsford, Essex. Her hymn above appeared in the Baptist Hymnal 1986.

CASSEL, FLORA HAMILTON (1852–1911)
Tune—CASSEL—"I Am A Stranger Here, Within a Foreign Land"
Tune—LAMBDIN—"From Over Hill and Plain"
Composer, pianist, singer, daughter of the Rev. B. B. Hamilton, a Baptist pastor, she was born at Otterville, Jersey County, Illinois, on August 21, 1852, and raised at Whitehall, Illinois, where her father was pastor. At age sixteen she went to live with an aunt in Brooklyn, New York, where she studied voice with Madame Hartell. Later she was sent to Maplewood Institute at Pittsfield, Massachusetts, where she studied piano, harmony and composition. After graduation she took charge of the department of music at Shurleff College in Upper Alton, Illinois, and while there married Dr. E. T. Cassel of Nebraska City, Nebraska. While in Nebraska, Dr. Cassel practiced medicine in South Bend, Ashland, Edgar, and Hastings. She published a songbook, *White Ribbon Vibration* (1890), which included her song, "Around the World"; it became a Women's Christian Temperance Union Song. In 1902 the Cassels decided to move to Denver, Colorado, where her tragic death occurred. (Information from Linda M. Rea, Hastings Public Library, Hastings, Nebraska.) As she placed her foot on the step of her buggy, her dress got caught in the step. Something frightened the horses, and she was dragged to her death on November 17, 1911. Her hymn tunes appeared in the *Baptist Hymnal* (1956). Her husband wrote the words to her hymn tunes.

CAWTHORN, JANIE M. (1888–1975)
"In that Beautiful Home Above"
Composer and hymnist, she was born at Mt. Carmel, South Carolina, on November 27, 1888, and was educated at Harbison College and Teachers' Normal School. She was superintendent of the Apostolic Church Sunday School for 27 years and an evangelist. Other hymns she wrote were "I See Him," "Won't You Come and See the Man?," "Somebody He Can Use," and "Call Heaven." She died on May 21, 1975.

CHAMINADE, CECILE LOUISE STEPHANIE (1857–1944)
Callirhoë
Pianist/composer, she was born on August 8th in Paris. At age eight she composed some pieces of church music and studied with Le Couppey, Godard, Marsick, and Savart, and gave her first concert at age eighteen. She composed pianoforte pieces, orchestral works, and songs. Her ballet *Callirhoë* was performed at Marseilles in 1888. She died at Monte Carlo, Monaco, on April 18th.

CHAPLIN, MARIAN WOOD (1914–)
"Open Your Heart to Spring"
Composer/songwriter, she was born on July 5th in Defiance, Ohio, and was educated at Defiance College. She wrote songs with Cynthia Medley, such as "Open Your Heart to Spring". ASCAP.

CHARLESWORTH, FLORENCE M. (1885–Dec'd.)
"I'm Drifting Back to Dreamland"
Composer/songwriter, she was born on January 26th in New York City. She wrote songs, including, "I'm Drifting Back to Dreamland". ASCAP.

CHEATHAM, CATHERINE SMILEY BUGG "KITTY" (1864–1948)
(Concert singer)
Mezzo-soprano/songwriter, she was born in Nashville, Tennessee. She gave numerous concerts of folk music and children's songs. She wrote a number of songs herself. She died in Greenwich, Connecticut.

CHERDAK, JEANNE (1915–)
"I'll Leave the Door Open"
Songwriter, she was born on December 2nd in Newark, New Jersey, and received a high school education. With Richard Loring, Jack Manus, and Guy Wood, she wrote the lyrics for the songs "Do Me a Favor", "I'll Leave the Door Open", "Jump Through the Ring", "Maid of Honor", "No Money Can Buy", "Say Hello for Me." ASCAP.

CHERRY, EDITH ADELINE GILLING (1872–1897)
"We Trust in You, Our Shield"
Hymnist, she was born on February 9th in Plymouth, Devonshire, England. Her hymn above appeared in *The Anglican Hymn Book* (1965) and in the *Baptist Hymnal* (1986). She died on August 29th in Plymouth.

CHILDS, TONI
"Walk and Talk Like Angels"
Singer/songwriter raised in Orange, California and now living in Los Angeles. Her albums include *House of Hope* and *Union* (1988) which includes the rock flavored "Don't Walk Away", the warm "Walk and Talk With Angels" and the Caribbean samba "Stop Your Fussin" written with David Ricketts, as well as the earthy ballad "Let the Rain Come Down" written by Childs, Ricketts, and David Batteau of the group David and David.

CHRISTOPHER, MAY (1912–)
"Too Late"
Composer/songwriter she was born on August 28th in Benwood, West Virginia, and received a public school education. With Ted Rosen, she wrote "Too Late" and other songs.

CLARK, AMY ASHMORE (1882–1954)
"And So Your Soul Was Born"
Composer/hymnist/songwriter, she was born on May 6th in Toronto, Ontario, Canada. She toured in vaudeville and was advertising director of the Junior League magazine for ten years. With Ernest Ball, Frederick Vanderpool, and others, she wrote a number of songs, including, "And So Your Soul Was Born", "In a Little Town Nearby", "If Thoughts Be Prayers","I Am Lost Without The Lovelight in Your Eyes", "My Rosary for You", "The Heart of You", "With Love He Cleanses Every Sin".

CLARK, MATTIE MOSS (1928–)
"Salvation Is Free"
Composer and gospel singer, she was born at Selma, Alabama. As a young woman, she moved to Michigan, where in 1958 she helped form the Southwest Michigan State Choir of the Churches of God in Christ with 300 members. The choir sang at the annual conventions of the church in Memphis and attracted nationwide attention. In 1973 the International Churches of God in Christ appointed her as music director. Her brother, Bill Moss, is leader of the Cestials, a gospel singing group. Her daughters are members of a gospel group known as the Clark Sisters. Mrs. Clark has written some 100 gospel songs. The one mentioned above was written in 1963.

CLARK, PETULA (1932–)
"Just Say Goodbye"
Singer/songwriter, she was born on November 15th in Ewell, Surrey, England. She had a hit single, "Downtown" (1965). With Tony Hatch and Pierre Delance, she wrote "Just Say Goodbye and Let Me Walk Away". Albums and CDs are *Greatest Hits, Live at Royal Albert Hall.*

CLARKE, REBECCA THACHER (1886–1979)
Sonata For Viola
Composer and violist, she was born on August 27th at Harrow, England, of German-American parentage. After studying composition with Charles Sanford at the Royal College of Music in London, she studied the viola privately with Lionel Tertis. In 1912 the Queen's Hall Orchestra asked Clarke to join, one of the first women to be asked. Her viola sonata mentioned above in 1919 tied for first place with Bloch's *Viola Suite,* but the award was given to Bloch. She continued writing string pieces. In 1944 she married composer and pianist James Friskin and they settled in New York City. She died there on October 13, 1979. As of 1994 her album *Sonata for Viola* is available for purchase.

CLARKSON, EDITH MARGARET (b. 1915–)
"So I send you to labor unrewarded,
To serve unpaid, unloved, unsought, unknown."

"So I send you, by grace made strong to triumph
O'er hosts of hell, o'er darkness, death and sin."
Composer and hymnist, she was born in Melville, Saskatchewan, Canada,
on June 8, 1915, and is Presbyterian. She taught in public schools in
Toronto, Ontario, from 1942. A member of the Knox Presbyterian
Church, Toronto, Ontario, she also served on the board of the Church Re-
newal Foundation and was active working for the Inter Varsity Chris-
tian Fellowship. She wrote *Let's Listen to Music* (1944); *The Creative
Classroom* (1958); *The Wonderous Cross* (1966); *God's Hedge* (1968);
and *Grace Grows Best in Winter* (1972). She also wrote books of verse,
Clear Shining After Rain (1962); *Rivers Among the Rocks* (1968); and
Conversations with a Barred Owl (1975). Her hymns appeared in the
American Service Hymnal (1968); the *Baptist Hymnal* (1975); and
Hymns for the Family of God (1976). Three other hymns she wrote ap-
peared in *Hymns for the Living Church* (1974). As of February 1983 she
was living in Willowdale, Ontario, Canada.

CLONINGER, CLAIRE (1942–)
"If My People's Hearts Are Humbled"
Composer/hymnist/songwriter, she was born on August 12th in Lafayette,
Arkansas, the daughter of psychologist Virginia and attorney Charles de
Gravelles. She was educated at Louisiana State University and the University of Southwestern Louisiana (BA and MA). She lives with her husband in Baldwin County, Alabama and has composed 15 choir musicals,
anthems, and praise choruses, and has written dozens of hymns. Her hymn
above and "Good Shepherd, Take This Little Child" appeared in the *Baptist Hymnal* (1986).

COATES, DOROTHY MCGRIFF LOVE (1928–)
"He May Not Come When You Want Him, But He's Right on Time"
Composer and gospel singer, she was born on January 30th in Birmingham, Alabama. At age ten she was playing the piano in her local church
and as a teenager she sang with the Royal Travelers. At age seventeen
she joined the Original Gospel Harmonettes of Birmingham. Other
members were pianist Evelyn Starks and singers Odessa Edwards, Mildred Miller Howard, Vera Kilb, and Willie Mae Newberry. The group
sang most of the original gospel songs by Dorothy Coates. The song
above was written in 1953. As of 1994, her album *Best of Dorothy Love
Coates, Volume 2* was available.

COCCIA, MARIA ROSA (1759–1833)
Dixit Dominus
Composer, born at Rome, Italy, on January 4, 1759, she wrote a *Mag-
nificat* for four voices and organ, dated October 2, 1774, and was exam-

ined by four professors of the Roman Accademia di Santa Cecilia, and later was admitted as a member of the Accademia Filarmonica of Bologna, according to reports of the time, a most unusual honor for a woman. She also wrote a cantata for four voices (1783), and died in Rome in November 1833.

COELHO, TERRYE (1952–)
Tune—"Maranatha"
Composer/hymnist, she lives in Walnut, California, and is married to Jim Strom. They have four children. She wrote the tune and words for the above tune as well as "Father I Adore You, Lay My Life Before You" (1972), which appeared in *The Hymnal for Worship and Celebration* (Baptist–1986).

COLLINS, JUDY MARJORIE (1939–)
True Stories and Other Dreams
Singer, guitarist, and songwriter, she was born on May 1st in Seattle, Washington. She studied piano with Antonia Brico in Denver, Colorado, from 1949–56, but at age sixteen played the guitar and became interested in folk music. After studying at MacMurray College, Jacksonville, Illinois, and at the University of Colorado, she began singing in nightclubs. Collins made her folk concert debut at New York's Town Hall in 1964, where she was greeted with wild applause. Her LP record *The Judy Collins Concert* in 1969 was a hit of the year. As of 1994 18 of her albums were available, including, *In My Life* (1966), *Wildflowers* (1967), *Who Knows Where the Time Goes* (1968), *Whales and Nightingales* (1970), *Hard Times for Lovers* (1979), *Running for My Life* (1980), *Times of Our Lives* (1982), *Bread and Roses, Best of Colors of the Day, Fires of Eden, Home Again, True Stories and Other Dreams.*

With the help of words from the children of Sarajevo, Yugoslavia, she wrote "Song of Sarajevo" on her CD *Come Rejoice* (1994).

COLTRANE, ALICE MCLEOD (1937–)
"Turiya Aparna"
Jazz harpist, pianist, organist, and composer, she was born on August 27th in Detroit, Michigan. After touring with vibist Terry Gibbs from 1962–63, she married saxist John Coltrane in 1964. She then joined Coltrane's quintet, which included tenor saxist Pharaoh Sanders, bassist Jimmy Garrison, and drummer Rashied Ali in 1966, replacing pianist McCoy Tyner. The group recorded the album *Coltrane—Live at the Village Vanguard Again.* Her husband died in 1967, Mrs. Coltrane went to India, studied Buddhism, and took the name Turiya Aparna. As of 1994, there were dozens of albums by John Coltrane available and one by Alice, *Journey in Satchidananda.*

COMDEN, BETTY (1915–)
"Bells are Ringing"
Librettist and lyricist, she was born on May 3rd in New York City. She attended New York University, then teamed with Adolph Green to write the book and lyrics for *On the Town* in 1944, Leonard Bernstein's first Broadway show based on his music from his ballet *Fancy Free*. Working with composer Jule Styne, they produced *Two on the Aisle* (1951), *Peter Pan* (1954), *Bells are Ringing* (1956), and other Broadway shows. They also wrote the screenplays for *Singin' in the Rain* (1952) and *The Band Wagon* (1953). Comden and Green wrote Broadway shows in the 1960s and 1970s.

COOPER, ROSE MARIE (1937–)
"This is the day"
Composer, she was born on February 21st in Cairo, Illinois, and was educated at Oklahoma Baptist University (BM), and Teacher's College, Columbia University (MA). She wrote the songs, "Great Is the Lord", "This Is the Day", "Plainsongs and Carols". ASCAP.

COOPER, WILMA LEE LEARY (1921–)
"Heartbreak Street"
Singer/guitarist/banjoist/organist/songwriter, she was born in Valley Head, West Virginia. After graduation from Davis and Elkins College, West Virginia, she sang with the Leary Family. Wilma married singer/fiddler Stoney Cooper, and they became a team, singing on radio stations in Fairmont and Wheeling, West Virginia, and in Harrisonburg, Virginia. They joined the Grand Ole Opry, Nashville, in 1957. She wrote (some jointly with Stoney Cooper) "Cheated Too" (1956), "I Tell My Heart", "Loving You","My Heart Keeps Crying" (1957), "He Taught Them How" (1958), "Heartbreak Street", "Tomorrow I'll Be Gone", and "Big Midnight Special" (1959). Their top records were "Come Walk With Me", "There's a Big Wheel", "Wreck on the Highway"(1961). Her husband died in 1977.

COPELAND, JULIA VIOLET (1916–)
"God Gave Me You"
Songwriter, she was born on January 22nd in Elvins, Missouri, and was educated in public schools. She wrote the lyrics for "God Gave Me You" and other songs.

CORNABY, HANNAH LAST (1822–1905)
"Who's on the Lord's Side?"
Hymnist born in Suffolk, England. She married Samuel Cornaby. After receiving Mormon literature and anti-Mormon literature, they sailed for

America in 1853 and settled in Spanish Fork, Utah. Her hymn above appeared in the Mormon hymnal (1985)

CORNETT, ALICE (1911–)
"You're Everything I Dreamed You'd Be"
Composer/singer, she was born on July 21st in Plant City, Florida, and was educated at Florida State College for Women (BM). She taught voice and piano in Lakeland, Florida, and had her own radio program. She wrote "My Serenade", "Cool Blue Waters", "I Found a Bit of Heaven", "Tic-toe", "Who Said There's No Santa Claus", and "You're Everything I Dreamed You'd Be". ASCAP.

CORRI, SOPHIA GIUSTINA (1775–1847)
(Harp and pianoforte pieces)
Harpist/pianist/singer/composer, she was born on May 1st in Edinburgh, Scotland, the daughter of singer/composer Domenico Corri, and was trained by her father. After the family moved to London, she was a principal singer at professional concerts there. In 1792, she married composer Jan Ladislav Dussek. After Dussek went into the music business with his father-in-law and failed, in 1800 he fled to Hamburg to escape his creditors. He was in the employ of several princes, then of Prince Tallyrand in Paris in 1808. Corri taught her daughter Olivia Dussek to play the harp and the piano. After Sophia's husband died in 1812, she married viola player John Alvis Moralt. Corri composed harp and pianoforte pieces.

CORWIN, BETTY L. (1920–)
"Going Back to School"
Songwriter, she was born on November 19th in New York City, and was educated at Adelphi University (BA). With Andre Wuhrer, Harriet Bailin, and others, she wrote several songs, including, "Going Back to School" and "Love's a Snap".

COSTEN, MELVA WILSON (1933–)
Tune—"Balm In Gilead"
Teacher/arranger, she teaches worship and music at the Interdenominational Theological Center in Atlanta, Georgia, and was chairwoman of the committee that created a new hymnal for Presbyterians in 1990. Costen adapted the following hymn tunes from African-American spirituals: "Go Tell It" (1987), "Were You There?" (1987), "Let Us Break Bread" (1988); and the following in 1989: "He Is King," "Pentecost", "Go Down Moses", "Balm In Gilead", "Great Day, My Lord", "What a Morning". Her arrangements appeared in *The Presbyterian Hymnal* (1990). Costen also wrote *African American Christian Worship* published in 1993.

(Information from Mary Louise VanDyke, Project Librarian/Coordinator, Dictionary of American Hymnology.)

COTTEN, ELIZABETH "LIBBA" (1893–Dec'd.)
    "Freight Train"
Guitarist, folk singer, and songwriter, she was born near Chapel Hill, North Carolina. She was only twelve years old when she wrote "Freight Train", often attributed to others. She then composed a number of rags and dance tunes. Cotten earned her living as a housekeeper for a number of different families. She went to work in Washington, DC for teacher and writer Charles Seeger (1886–1979), who recognized her talents. "Freight Train" was recorded and became successful in 1962. She toured the nation in 1983 at age 90 and received a National Heritage Fellowship from the National Endowment for the Arts in 1984.

COX, IDA PRATHER (1896–1967)
    "Ida Cox's Lawdy Lawdy Blues"
Blues singer and songwriter, she was born on February 25th in Toccoa, Georgia, or Cedartown, Georgia. At age fourteen she joined the Rabbit Foot Minstrels, later with Silas Green's Minstrels from New Orleans. She married her accompanist, pianist Jesse Crump of Paris, Texas, who was seventeen years younger than she was. She recorded with cornetist Tommy Ladner and Pianist Lovie Austin on Black Swan disks and also with the Pruett Twins. Her blues mentioned above was recorded in 1923, "Coffin Blues" (1925), "Jail House Blues" (1929), "Four Day Creep" (1939), and "Blues for Rampart Street" (1961). She died on November 10th in Knoxville, Tennessee.

CRAWFORD, JANE VILATE ROMNEY (1883–1956)
    Tune — "Romney"
Composer/organist born in Salt Lake City, Utah, and educated at the University of Utah, she had private music study. She was married and went on a church mission to England. She composed the music for the hymn by Parley P. Pratt, "Father in Heaven, We Do Believe", which appeared in the Mormon hymnal (1985).

CRAWFORD, RUTH PORTER (1901–1953)
    "Three Songs"
Composer, she was born on July 3rd in East Liverpool, Ohio. After studying piano at the School of Musical Art, Jacksonville, Florida, she studied piano with Henior Levy and Louise Robyn, and theory and composition with John Palmer and Adolf Weidig in the early 1920s at the American Conservatory in Chicago. In 1929, she moved to New York and studied composition with Charles Seeger. She received a Guggenheim Fellowship

to study in Berlin and Paris in 1930. After her return to the States, she married Charles Seeger in 1931. Her "Three Songs" (with words by Carl Sandburg), "Rat Riddles" (New York, 1930), "In Tall Grass" (Berlin, 1932), and "Prayers of Steel" (Amsterdam, 1933) were chosen to represent the United States at the International Society for Contemporary Music Festival in 1933. She died on November 18th in Chevy Chase, Maryland.

CREED, LINDA (1949–1986)
"The Greatest Love of All"
With Michael Masser this singer/songwriter wrote the song "The Greatest Love of All" with the words "I Believe the Children are the future". With Tom Bell she wrote the hits "Could It Be I'm Falling in Love"(1973), and "You Make Me Feel Brand New" (1974). She died on April 10th in Amber, Pennsylvania.

CROCKER, ELISABETH (1950–)
Tune—"Uplifted Eyes"
Composer, born on April 15th in Torquay, Devonshire, England, and educated at Manchester University, Royal Manchester College of Music, and Royal College of Music, London (MusB, ARMCM, GRSM). She sang for seven years with the British Broadcasting Corporation Singers. She has been collaborating with Michael Baughen at the Holy Trinity Church, Rusholme, Manchester. She wrote the tune "Uplifted Eyes", which appeared in *The Hymnal for Worship & Celebration* (Baptist 1986).

CROCKETT, EFFIE J. (1857–1940)
"Rock-a-Bye Baby"
Songwriter, born at Rockland, Maine. To the music of an old song, she wrote the song above. She also wrote "Baby is sleeping so cozy" in about 1887.

CROSBY, FANNY (1820–1915)
"Blessed assurance, Jesus is mine!"
"Jesus, keep me near the cross."
"Pass me not, O gentle savior."
"All the way my Savior leads me."
Frances Jane Crosby was born in South East, Putnam County, New York, on March 24, 1820. She lost her eyesight when she was six weeks old and was blind for the rest of her life. At the New York Institute for the Blind she was a pupil of composer George F. Root and wrote lyrics for some of his popular songs, in addition to writing over 4,000 hymns. She was a Methodist and was married to a blind musician, Alexander van

Alystyne. She died in Bridgeport, Connecticut, on Feburary 12, 1915. The popularity of her hymns is shown by the fact that *Phonolog Reports* (1978) of Los Angeles, California, lists 32 different recordings of "Blessed Assurance," 21 of "Jesus keep me near the cross," 18 of "Pass me not, O gentle Savior," 8 of "All the way my Savior leads me," 8 of "I am thine, O Lord, I have heard Thy Voice," etc., and by the fact that many of her hymns have appeared in *Baptist* (1973); *Methodist* (1966); and *Presbyterian* hymnals (1955) now currently in use.

CROW, SHERYL (1964–)
"All I Wanna Do"

Singer/songwriter born on February 11 in Kennett, Missouri, she is the third of four children. She received her music training from her mother, Bernice, who played the piano, and from her father, lawyer Wendell Crow, who played the trumpet on weekends in local bands. Sheryl graduated from the University of Missouri (1984) with a degree in music and piano, then moved to Los Angeles (1986). When she heard that Michael Jackson was looking for backup singers for his 1987 World Tour, Crow crashed the closed auditions and was selected. She was on tour with Jackson for 18 months. Later, she wrote songs for Eric Clapton and Wynonna Judd, then was a backup singer for Don Henley. She had a hit with "Leaving Las Vegas" from her debut album *Tuesday Night Music Club* (1994), which went gold. After appearing at the 1994 Woodstock Music Festival, her single "All I Wanna Do" hit the charts. This song was written with David Baerwald, Bill Bottrell, Wyn Cooper, and Kevin Gilbert and won a Grammy award (1995). She also won Grammys as best new artist and female pop vocalist.

CUMMINGS, PATRICIA HAGER (1924–)
"Crocodile Chile"

Songwriter, she was born on November 1st in Springfield, Illinois, and was educated at Northwestern University (BA). She wrote a newspaper column, children's books, and songs including, "Law Ma'am", "Crocodile Chile." ASCAP.

CURRAN, PEARL GILDERSLEEVE (1875–1941)
"The Best Is Yet To Be"

Composer, she was born on June 25th in Denver, Colorado, and was educated at Denver University. She studied with Otto Pfeffercorn, Flora Hunsicker, M. Miner Richards, and Stella Alexander. She was a member of the Westchester County (NY) Music Festival. She wrote "A Picture", "Contentment", "Gratitude", "Holiday", "Two Magicians", "The Nest Is Yet To Be", "To the Sun", "Blessing", "Dawn", and "Ho Mr. Piper." She died on April 16th in New Rochelle, New York.

CURRIE, NANCY FORD (b. 1938–)
Tune—"While Angels Sang"
Composer. In 1959 she composed the music for the Christmas Carol, "While angels sang in praises glorified" by Gene Claghorn, the author of this book. At the time, Currie's husband was a student at Yale University, New Haven, Connecticut. It was first sung by Barbara Burger (later Mrs. Ossorio) at the Manger Service at the First Congregational Church, Old Greenwich, Connecticut, Christmas Eve, 1959 under the direction of Gerry Mack, choir director, and Richard Rosan, organist. It was sung again on Christmas Eve, 1960 at the church by Nancy Rosan (later Mrs. Richard O. Roblin, Jr.). At the Christmas Eve services in 1962 and 1965 it was sung by Louise "Bonnie" Hatch (later Mrs. John Harrison). The original title used was "Come to Him", later changed to "While Angels Sang" (taken from the first lines). The Christmas Carol was first sung in Florida at the Riverside Presbyterian Church of Cocoa Beach by soprano Mary Harvell with Glenn A. Arnold, organist and choir director, on December 18, 1983.

CUSHING, CATHERINE CHISHOLM (1874–1952)
"L'amour, Toujours, l'amour"
Composer/lyricist/playwright/librettist, she was born on April 15th in Mt. Perry, Ohio. With music by Rudolf Friml, she wrote "L'amour, Toujours, l'amour". She died in Mt. Perry on October 19th.

CUTHBERT, ELIZABETH HOWARD (1800–1857)
Tune—"Howard"
A composer, she was born in Dublin, Ireland. Her tune is used for the hymn on "Love to Christ" by Philip Doddridge and appeared in the *Methodist Hymnal* (1911). It was also used with the hymn "O thou my soul, bless God the Lord," taken from Psalm 103 and appeared in the Presbyterian *Hymnbook* (1955).

-D-

DALE, H. JEAN (1904–)
"Christmas Eve by the Fireside"
Composer/singer/songwriter, she was born on December 8th in St. Louis, Missouri, and was educated at the Kroeger School of Music and at the Hyneck School of Music. She was a member of the singing group the "Dale Sisters" and sang on KWK and KFVO radio in St. Louis for ten years. She wrote many songs, including, "Around the Christmas Tree", "Christmas Eve by the Fireside", "Rock, Rock, Rock", "Gateway to the West", "Little Admiral", and "Coast Guard March.

DALE, VIKKI (1931–)
"Ulcer Alley"
Songwriter/dancer, she was born on August 19th in New York City, and was educated at Queens College. She wrote the lyrics for several songs, including, "A Dangerous Game", "Like in Love", "The Ladies", and "Ulcer Alley". ASCAP.

DALLAS, MITZI EVANS (1928–)
"Humanity's insanity"
Composer/songwriter she was born on November 22nd in Evanston, Illinois, and was educated at Wellesley College (BA). She worked for advertising agencies and record companies. With Dave Lambert, she wrote the lyrics for "Hang the Mistletoe", "Humanity's Insanity", "I Walk and Sing". ASCAP.

DANIELS, MABEL WHEELER (1878–1971)
Sacred chorus a capella—*The Christ Child*
Composer, she was born at Swampscott, Massachusetts, on November 27, 1878, and educated at Radcliffe College (BA, 1900), Cambridge, Massachusetts, and was educated privately. She was director of the Radcliffe Glee Club (1911–13) and musical director at Simmons College, Boston (1913–18). She received an Hon. Mus. Doc. from Boston University (1939). She wrote *An American Girl in Munich* (Boston, 1905), and died in Cambridge, Massachusetts on March 10, 1971.

DANZIG, EVELYN (1902–)
"Warm Hearted Woman"
Composer/pianist, she was born on January 16th in Waco, Texas, educated at the Academy of Holy Name Cross in Albany, New York, and studied with Sari Biro and Sigismund Stojowski. She composed the music for the stage production of *The Scarlet Letter* and with other musicians wrote "Midnight in Manhattan", "Half a Heart", "A Face in the Crowd", "I Miss the Boy", "Teddy Bear", "Scarlet Ribbons", "Simple, Simple, Simple", "Where I May Live with My Love", "We're All Kids at Christmas". ASCAP.

DAUNCH, VIRGINIA OBENCHAIN (1919–)
"Uncle Billy's Candy Shop"
Composer, she was born on April 26th in Ohio and was educated at the St. Louis Institute of Music; she also studied privately. Her works include "Organ Originals" (instrumental) and "Uncle Billy's Candy Shop" (an operetta), and songs.

DAVIDSON, KAREN LYNN (1943–)
"Each Life That Touches Ours for Good"

Hymnist born in Glendale, California, and educated at Brigham Young University (BA, MA); University of Southern California (PhD); USC dean's exchange fellowship at Cambridge University, England; year's study at University of Chicago on a National Endowment for the Humanities fellowship. Professor of English at Brigham Young University for a time, she married David A. Davidson and they live in southern California. Her hymn above and also "O Savior, Thou Who Wearest a Crown" appeared in the Mormon hymnal (1985).

DAVIS, GENEVIEVE (1889–1950)
"The Shepherd and the Echo"
Composer/pianist/singer, she was born on December 11th in Falconer, New York, and studied with Adolph Frey at Syracuse University and with Ruth Burham, Arthur Stahlschmidt, and Edwin Swain. She was a soloist at the First Presbyterian Church in Irvington-on-Hudson, New York. Her works include "The Shepherd and the Echo" (for piano), and the songs "Children of Light", "Caprice", "Eventide", "I Am Joy", "Love at Dusk", "A Maid and the Moon", and "The River in Spring". She died on December 3rd in Plainfield, New Jersey.

DAVIS, HAZEL (1907–)
"Lady With a Torch"
Composer/songwriter, she was born on February 14th in Bucklin, Kansas, and was educated at Kansas State Teachers College. With Lyon Perry Wilbur, Jr., she wrote a number of songs, including "America, America Return to God", "An Unknown Soldier", "I Would Cry a Million Tears", "Lady with a Torch", "This Flag I Love", "Through God", "Voices of Truth and Freedom".

DAVIS, KATHERINE KENNICOTT (1892–1980)
Tunes — "Massachusetts", "Surette", and "Wachusett"
Composer and hymnist, she was born at St. Joseph, Missouri, on June 25, 1892, and was educated at Wellesley College (BA, 1914), Wellesley, Massachusetts, where she later taught. After studying composition with Stuart Mason at the New England Conservatory of Music in Boston, she studied with Nadia Boulanger in Paris and studied choral music with Thomas Whitney Surette at his Concord Summer School of Music in Concord, Massachusetts. Later she taught voice and piano in Philadelphia until 1930, when she devoted her full time to composing and arranging. She was a member of the Congregational Church, then a Christian Scientist, then an Episcopalian. Her hymn, "Let all things now living," was published in the *United Methodist Book of Hymns* (1966); *The Covenant Hymnal* (1973); *Baptist Hymnal* (1975); and the *Lutheran Book of Worship* (1978). The three tunes above were included in the

Methodist Hymnal (1964). She died at Concord, Massachusetts, on April 20, 1980. She is best known as the composer of "The Little Drummer Boy," that perennial Christmas favorite.

DAVIS, SHEILA (1927–)
    "Keep Cool"
Composer/songwriter, she was born on August 6th in New York City, and was educated at Dominican Academy and Marymount College. She wrote "Keep Cool", "Fly by Night", and other songs. ASCAP.

DAVIS, SKEETER (1931–)
    "My Last Date"
Singer/songwriter, she was born Mary Frances Penick in Dry Ridge, Kentucky. She joined with Betty Jack Davis as the Davis Sisters (1949–53), and then went solo. With Boudleaux Bryant and Floyd Cramer, she wrote "My Last Date—One Hour and I'll Be Meeting You". She also co-wrote "Home Breaker". Her recording hits were "Set Him Free" (1959), "I'm Falling Too" (1960), "Optimistic" (1961), "Where I Ought to Be" (1962), "The End of the World" (1963), "Gonna Get Along Without You Now" (1964), "Singin' in the Summer Sun" (1966), "My Heart's in the Country" (1967), and "She Sings, They Play".

DEACON, MARY CONNOR (1907–)
    "Beside Still Waters"
Composer/organist/pianist/songwriter, she was born on February 22nd in Johnson City, Tennessee, and was educated at Virginia Intermont College, East Tennessee State College, and studied with Frank La Forge, Ernest Berumen, William Stickles, Stuart Ross, and Carl Deis. She taught piano at the Royal Conservatory in Toronto, Ontario, Canada. Her songs are "Ocean Lore", "Beside Still Waters", "I Will Lift Up Mine Eyes", "Hear My Prayer", "Follow the Road", "Call of the Sea", "Your Cross".

DE CEVEE, ALICE (1904–)
    'Coney Island'
Composer/pianist, she was born on February 25th in Harrisburg, Pennsylvania, and was educated at the Harrisburg Conservatory and the Juilliard School of Music in New York City, with Ernest Hutcheson and she also studied with Harvey Gaul, Henry Hadley, and Harry Shelley. She was head of the music department and director of the Harrisburg Conservatory. She made her piano debut at Town Hall in New York City in 1936. Her works are *Coney Island* (ballet), *Boogie Woogie Goes High Hat* (piano), *Holland Tunnel* (2 pianos), *Love In a Bottle* (musical drama), *Memorabilia* for the Harrisburg Symphony, and *Blue Ridge Ballads* (song cycle).

DEE, SYLVIA (1914–)
"Too young"
A songwriter, she was born Josephine Moore on October 22nd in Little Rock, Arkansas, and was educated at the University of Michigan. She was an advertising copywriter for a Rochester, New York, newspaper. With music by others, she wrote the lyrics for many songs: "After Graduation Day", "Chickery Chick", "I', thrilled", "It Couldn't Be You", "Have You Changed?", "My Sugar Is So Refined", "Angel Lips", "Angel Eyes", "Pushcart Serenade", "Laroo Laroo Lili Bolero", "Too Young" (won the Michael TV Radio award), etc. Her married name was Proffitt. ASCAP.

DELUGG, ANNE RENFER (1922–)
"Gee I'm Glad I Married You"
Composer/songwriter, she was born on April 22nd in Wenatchee, New York, and received a college education. A pianist, she taught dancing and married composer/songwriter Milton Delugg. With her husband and Sammy Gallop she wrote a number of songs, "The Little White Horse", "The Big Beat", "Honolulu", "Gee I'm Glad I Married You". ASCAP.

DENNI, GWYNNE (1882–1949)
"Mystery of Night"
Actress/director/songwriter, she was born on May 24th on Green Island, New York, and was educated at the New England Conservatory. She appeared in Broadway musicals, was a director, and wrote songs for the radio. With Lucien Denni, she wrote "Mystery of Night", "Memory's Garden", "Forgotten Perfume", "I Gave a Rose to You", "Sing a Little Song."

DENNIS, GINNY MAXEY (1923–)
"Snuggle Up, Baby"
Singer/songwriter, she was born on September 4th in Indianapolis, Indiana, and was educated in public schools. She sang with the orchestras of Tony Pastor, Charlie Barnett, Ziggy Elman, and with the Modernaires. With her husband composer/pianist Matt Dennis, she has written several songs, such as "We've Reached the Point of No Return", "You Can Believe Me", and "Snuggle Up, Baby." ASCAP.

DENTON, SANDY "PEPA"
"Shoop"
Singer/songwriter and member of rap group SALT-N-PEPA with Cheryl "Salt" James and Dee Dee "Spinderella" Roper. "Pepa" Denton is divorced, has lost 40 pounds, has a son, and exercises. She wrote the sassy hit "Shoop" (1994). Her album is *Black's Magic*. Her hit songs are "Push It", "Expression", "Let's Talk About Sex".

DEPPEN, JESSIE L. (1881–1956)

"Japanese Sunset"

Composer/pianist, she was born on July 10th in Detroit, Michigan, and was educated at the American Conservatory in Chicago. She studied with Victor Garwood, Leopold Godowsky, and Adolph Weidig. At age fifteen she made her piano debut at Steinway Hall in New York City. With George Graff, she wrote a number of songs and also composed instrumentals of her own, including "Japanese Sunset", "Chinese Fantasy", "Joli Bleuet", "Remembrance", "Eleanor", "In the Garden of Tomorrow", "On Wings of Memory", "Come Back Home", "Red Hair and Freckles". She died on January 22 in Los Angeles, California.

DE ROSA, CARMELLA MILLIE (1914–)

"Get With It"

Composer/songwriter, she was born on July 26th in Paterson, New Jersey, and has a high school education. She has written a number of commercials for TV. She wrote the song "Get With It". ASCAP.

DES'REE (1970–)

"You Gotta Be"

Her parents migrated from the West Indies to London where Des'ree was born and rasied. Growing up, she listened to reggae, calypso and jazz, then switched to rock, then folk-island, modern rhythm. She didn't sing in night clubs; she spent her time writing music and lyrics, singing to herself and friends. She made her first album, *Mind Adventures,* in 1991. Her song "You gotta be bad, You gotta be bold—You gotta be wiser" hit the Top Ten on the charts in 1994 and 1995. In 1995 she performed in New York City, and appeared on the "David Letterman Show" and on "Good Morning America." After New York City she toured the USA.

DICK, DOROTHY (1900–Dec'd.)

"A Star is Born"

Songwriter, she was born on November 29th in Philadelphia, Pennsylvania, and was educated at the Sternberg School of Music in Philadelphia, the Academy of the Arts, and the Academy of Design. With various composers she wrote the lyrics for a number of songs, such as "A Star is Born", "Call Me Darling", "By My Side", "The Kiss that You've Forgotten", "Remember Tonight", "Until We Meet Again Sweetheart". ASCAP.

DICKINSON, JUNE MC WADE (1924–)

"Glass Balls on a Christmas Tree"

Composer of songs, she was born on June 26th in Rochester, New York. With Edward Dickinson, she wrote "Glass Balls on a Christmas Tree", "High School Memories" (March). ASCAP.

DIEMER, EMMA LOU (1927–)
"Symphonie antique" (Symphony No. 3)
Composer, organist, and teacher, she was born on November 24th in Kansas City, Missouri. She began writing pieces for the piano at age seven and as a teenager had composed several piano concertos. After studying under Donovan and Hindemith at Yale University (BM 1949, MM 1950), she studied at the Royal Conservatory in Brussels on a Fulbright Scholarship (1952–53), then earned her PhD at the Eastman School in Rochester, New York, in 1960. Over 130 of her compositions have been published. She has taught at the University of Maryland and the University of California at Santa Barbara. Her symphony no. 3 was composed in 1961. Her tune "Huntsville", composed in 1986, appeared in *The Presbyterian Hymnal* (1990).

DILLON, FANNIE CHARLES (1881–1947)
Birds at Dawn
Composer and pianist, she was born on March 16th in Denver, Colorado. After graduating from Pomona College, Claremont, California, she studied piano with Leopold Godowsky, composition with Hugo Kaun, and theory with Heinrich Urban in Berlin from 1900–06. After studying with Goldmark in New York, she made her debut as a pianist in 1908 in Los Angeles. She taught at Pomona College from 1910–13, then in Los Angeles public schools from 1918–41. She composed several orchestral works and a number of piano pieces, including the one mentioned above in 1917. Dillon died on February 21st in Altadena, California.

DITTENHAVER, SARAH L. (1901–1973)
"Carolina Cakewalk"
Composer/pianist, she was born on December 16th in Paulding, Ohio, and studied with May Laukart Cat at the Cosmopolitan Conservatory in Chicago, and Oberlin College (Mus.B). She taught piano in Asheville, North Carolina. Her works for piano are "Carolina Cakewalk", "Lyric to the Moon", "Mardi Gras", "Pied Piper's Tune", "Tumbling Creek", "Night Wanderer", "Where Go the Clouds?", "Witches Ride", "Toccata in d". She died on February 4th.

DLUGOSZEWSKI, LUCIA (1934–)
"Fire Fragile Flight"
Composer and pianist, she was born on June 16th in Detroit, Michigan. While studying physics at Wayne State University from 1949–52, she developed the timbre piano, so-called, with strings stuck by beaters and played with bows and plectra. She studied piano with Suktan and music analysis with Salzer at Mannes College, New York City from 1952–53, and composition with Varese. She composed a number of scores while associated with the Erick Hawkins Dance Company and invented and

developed a new percussion and friction instrument with tangent rattles. In 1977 her "Fire Fragile Flight" won the Koussevitzky International Recording Award, the first woman so honored. She composed dance scores, "Archaic Music" for her timbre piano, and other compositions.

DOLAN, LIDA (1912–)
"Waiting for Joe"
Composer/songwriter, she was born on July 2nd in Vancouver, British Columbia, Canada, and educated at a business college. With Paul Wierick and Mary Lacey, she wrote a number of songs, including, "Break It to Me Gently", "One Wild Oat", "Ocean of Tears", "Waiting for Joe".

DONELLY, TANYA (ca. 1968–)
"Feed the Tree"
Singer/songwriter, she sang with the Throwing Muses band for six years and five albums and then helped form the Breeders. She then formed Belly with brothers Chris Gorman and Tom Gorman in 1994. The trio's first album *Star* contained all pop songs written by Donelly. Her hit song was "Feed the Tree".

DONNELLY, DOROTHY (1880–1928)
"Drinking Song"
Lyricist, born in New York City. With music by Sigmund Romberg, she wrote the words for "Deep in My Heart, Dear", "Song of Love—You Are My Song of Love, Melody Immortal" (1921), "Drinking Song—Drink, Drink, Drink to Eyes that are Bright as Stars When They're Shining on Me" in the *Student Prince* (1924), "Serenade", "Silver Moon", "Students March Song", "Your Land and My Land Will Be our Land Someday". She died in New York City.

DOOLEY, EDNA MOHR (1907–)
"My Garden State"
Composer/songwriter, she was born on August 11th in Brooklyn, New York, and was educated at Teachers College of Columbia University (BS) and at Wyoming University. She was a teacher in the New York public schools (1929–50), in Newcastle and Casper, Wyoming (1950–58), and in Morris Plains and Millburn, New Jersey. With Dave Ringle and Jimmy Selva, she wrote a number of songs, including "Graduation Day", "Two Little Pink Ballet Slippers", and "My Garden State".

DORAN, CAROL (1936–)
Tunes—"Carol's Gift," "Christpraise," "Inward Light," "Revision"
Composer, organist, hymnist, and teacher. She holds her DMA in Music Literature, Church Music, and Organ from the Eastman School, Rochester, New York. Doran has served as organist and choir director in

Episcopal and Presbyterian churches. Currently she is associate professor of Church Music and director of Community Worship at Colgate Rochester Divinity School, Bexley Hall Crozer Theological Seminary. She has served as president of the Association of Anglican Musicians and dean of the Rochester Chapter of AGO and as a Board member of the Hymn Society of America. Fifty-two of her hymns settings were published in 1986 as *New Hymns for the Lectionary*. Doran and her husband have four children. The four hymn tunes mentioned above appeared in *The Presbyterian Hymnal* (1990).

DORAN, ELSA (1915–)
    "Free and Easy"
Songwriter, she was born on February 11th in Chicago, Illinois, and received a business school education. With Sol Lake, she wrote the lyrics for a number of songs, including, "Blond Hair Blue Eyes and Ruby Lips", "Falling Star", "Free and Easy", "Crawfish", "Love was Born", "Roly Poly". ASCAP.

DOUGHERTY, ANNE HELENA (1908–Dec'd.)
    "Castle of Dreams"
Composer/songwriter, she was born on March 24th in Wilmington, Delaware, and educated at St. Joseph Academy and Maryland National Park College. She wrote the songs "Castle of Dreams", "Old Fashioned Christmas", and "Who's Who".

DOUGHERTY, GENEVIEVE "JENNY" (1888–Dec'd.)
    "Just a Year Ago"
Composer/songwriter, she was born on September 8th in Philadelphia, Pennsylvania. She wrote a number of songs: "Dear Little Mother in Gray", "Just Another Dream", "Just a Year Ago", "Just Another Way to Break My Heart", "Let Me Be the One to Love You."

DRURY, MIRIAM LEYRER (b.1900–)
    "O thou whose favor hallows all occasions."
Composer and hymnist, daughter of Otto and Edith Leyrer, she was born in Santa Ana, California, on January 27, 1900. She married Clifford M. Drury, and while he was studying for his PhD in Edinburgh, Scotland, she took work in music at the University. She began writing songs for little children when he was pastor of the First Presbyterian Church in Moscow, Idaho (1928–38), and while there she received her BA degree at the University of Idaho. "Thirty-three of her pieces—music, words, or both—appeared in *When a Little Child Went to Sing,* issued by the Presbyterian Board of Christian Education in 1935. She also had some songs included in the Board's songbook for the primary and junior departments. Several of her anthems have been printed. Two of her hymns

(words only) were printed in the *Worship Book* (1970) of the Presbyterian Church. She is not well now and has not been doing any writing." (March 1982 letter from her husband, Dr. Drury, from Pasadena, California.) Her hymn "Bless Thou Thy Chosen Sons" appeared in *Hymns on the Ministry,* published by The Hymn Society of America (1966), "Within the Church's Hallowed Walls" in the Society's booklet *The Mission of the Church,* and the hymn above appeared in *Marriage and Family Life Hymns* published by The Society (1961) and in *Hymns for Christian Worship* (1970).

DUNCAN, ROSETTA (1900–1959)
"The Moon Am Shinin'"
Composer/songwriter, she was born on November 23rd in Los Angeles, California. With her sister Vivian they formed the Duncan Sisters, entertainers. Rosetta played Topsy in the Broadway musical *Topsy and Eva,* and the sisters wrote the songs "Do Re Me," "I Never Had a Mammy," "The Moon Am Shinin'," "Someday Soon". She died on December 4th in Chicago, Illinois. ASCAP.

DUNCAN, VIVIAN (1902–Dec'd.)
'Topsy and Eva'
Composer/songwriter, she was born on June 17th in Los Angeles, California, the younger sister of Rosetta. They performed in vaudeville and in Broadway shows. In *Topsy and Eva* Vivian was Eva. They also appeared in *Doing our Bit, She's a Good Fellow,* and *Tip Top.* Besides the songs mentioned above written with her sister, she also wrote "Los Angeles", "Hollywood Belongs to the World", "United We Stand".

DUNGAN, OLIVE (1903–)
Tropical Night Suite
Composer/pianist, she was born on July 19th in Pittsburgh, Pennsylvania, and was educated at the Pittsburgh Institute of Musical Art, the Miami Conservatory in Florida, the University of Miami, and the University of Alabama. She made her piano debut at age seven with the Pittsburgh Festival Orchestra. During World War II, she entertained wounded and ill soldiers in hospitals. She composed the *Tropical Night Suite* for piano, "White Jasmine", "Enchantment", and "Magnolias in Moonlight". Also *Tropical Tunes* for children and many songs. ASCAP.

DUNN, BONNIE (1920–)
"Hazel Eyes"
Composer/singer/songwriter, she was born on June 9th in New York, and was educated in a convent. She sang in Al Donahue's, Paul Baron's, and Carl Ravazza's orchestras. With her husband Michael Dunn they

wrote a number of songs: "Dearest Santa", "Hazel Eyes", "Only the Mocking Bird Heard", "There's No Happiness for Me", "That's How It Feels to Love." ASCAP.

DUNN, HOLLY
"I'm Not Through Loving You Yet"
With Chris Waters and Tom Shapiro, this singer/songwriter wrote "I'm not through loving you yet—You've got that lookin' around look in your eye, don't turn your back on me". Her hit albums are *Blue Rose of Texas, Heart Full of Love, Getting It Dunn,* and *Milestones* (1992).

DUNN, REBECCA WELTY (1890–Dec'd)
Purple on the Moon
Composer/pianist/songwriter, she was born on September 23rd in Guthrie, Oklahoma, and was educated at Washburn College (BA), Kansas State University, Wichita University, and Southwestern College. She composed the operetta *Purple on the Moon* and an operetta called *Sunny* for children, as well as a number of songs.

DUSSEK, OLIVIA (1801–1847)
(Harp and pianoforte pieces)
Pianist/harpist/organist/composer, she was born on September 29th in London, the daughter of composer Sophia Giustina Corri and composer Jan Ladislav Dussek. Sophia trained Olivia on the harp and pianoforte. Olivia married a Mr. Buckley and she was organist at the Kensington Parish Church in the 1840s. She composed pieces for the harp, piano, and some songs.

DUSSEK, VERONICA ANNA DUSIKOVA (1769–1833)
(Pianoforte works and concertos)
Singer/harpist/pianist/composer, she was born on March 8th in Caslav (now the Czech Republic), the daughter of Jan Dussek and the sister of composer Jan Ladislav Dussek. She studied under her father and mother, harpist Veronika Stebetova Dussek. She performed in London in around 1795 and married music dealer Francesco Cianchettini. Dussek composed two concertos and solo piano works. Her son Pio Cianchettini was a pianist/composer. She died in London, England.

-E-

EAKIN, VERA (1890–1977)
"Oh come, let us sing unto the Lord"
Composer, hymnist, pianist, and organist, she was born in Emlenton, Pennsylvania, on August 6, 1890, and was educated at Slippery Rock

Teachers' College in Slippery Rock, Pennsylvania, and at the New England Conservatory of Music in Boston, Massachusetts. She composed music for the original hymn, which had appeared in the *Scottish Psalter* (1650). She died on June 4, 1977.

EASTES, HELEN M. (1892–Dec'd.)
"Dreams Were Made for Lovers"
Composer/songwriter, she was born on April 21st in Galesburg, Illinois, and was educated at the Knox College Conservatory of Music (BM). With J. Fred Coots she wrote a number of songs, including, "April Came Across the Hill", "Can You Sing a Song?", "God Grant Us Peace", "The Little Lamb that Followed", "Thou Lovely Spring."

EBERHART, NELLE RICHMOND (1871–1944)
The Willow Tree
Librettist/songwriter, she was born on August 28th in Detroit, Michigan. With composer Charles Wakefield Cadman, she wrote the librettos for the operas *Garden of Mystery, A Witch of Salem, Shanewis,* and *The Willow Tree* produced on radio. She died on November 15th in Kansas City, Missouri. ASCAP.

EBSEN, KIKI (1959–)
Red
Singer/songwriter, she is the daughter of actress Nancy Wolcott and actor Buddy Ebsen (Jed Clampett on the "Beverly Hillbillies"). Her parents were divorced in 1983. Her debut album (1993) *Red* consists of jazzy love songs she wrote. She lives in the Malibu mountains with her husband.

ECKER, JUDITH KOCH (1933–)
"Full Moon Above"
Songwriter, she was born on December 27th in Louisville, Kentucky, and was educated at Western Kentucky State College (BA) and Iowa State University (MA). With her husband composer Thomas R. Ecker, she wrote the lyrics for several songs, including, "Full Moon Above", "Beware", "Crocodile Hop", "Who Is He?". ASCAP.

EDDY, MARY BAKER (1821–1910)
"Blest Christmas Morn, Though Murky Clouds"
"Brood O'er Us with Thy Shelt-ring Wing"
She was born in Bow, New Hampshire, on July 16, 1821, and had three brothers and two sisters. She became a member of the Congregational Church in 1838, then married George W. Glover in 1843, who died the next year. In 1853 she married Daniel Patterson, an itinerant dentist, but they were divorced in 1873. Then she met Asa Gilbert Eddy, a traveling

sewing-machine salesman, and they were married on New Year's Day, 1877. He died in 1882. She founded the Church of Christ, Scientist, Boston. Mary Baker Eddy died in Chestnut Hill, Massachusetts, on December 3, 1910. Six of her hymns appeared in the *Christian Science Hymnal* (1937).

EDWARDS, ALICE PURDUE (1878–1958)
"Saviour, My All I'm Bringing to Thee."

Composer, hymnist, pianist, she was born at Battersea, London, England, in October 1878 and was converted to Christianity as a child of twelve at a Salvation Army meeting in Notting Hill, and later became a soldier of the corps. She studied theory, harmony, and the pianoforte with a London musician, and then also the mandolin and advanced musical lessons with an Italian professor. She would play the piano while a soldier at Notting Hill as an accompanist to Lt. Colonel Slater's musical parties. She once wrote that the inspriation for the song was her act of surrender to God's will. At first her soul rebelled against what she felt to be God's unreasonable demands. But after serious prayer, her heart was put to rest. Alice entered the Training Home to become an officer in December 1896. Then in 1899 she married Major Robert Edwards, who had been a Household Trooper in the Salvation Army. Later he served in the Public Relations Department. He died in 1945 and she died on October 22, 1958. Her hymn appeared in *The Musical Salvationist* (July 1893) and in *The Song Book of the Salvation Army* (1899; 1953). She also composed the music for her hymns.

EDWARDS, CLARA GERLICH (1887–1974)
"When Jesus Walked on Galilee"

Composer, pianist, and singer, she was born on March 18th in Mankato, Minnesota. After studying singing in Vienna, she returned to the states in 1914 and was active composing ballads and gospel songs and playing the piano and singing. Her songs included "With the Wind and the Rain in Her Hair" (1930), "By the Bend in the River", and "Into the Night", which was sung by Ezio Pinza on several occasions. She died on January 17th in New York City.

EDWARDS, JOAN (1919–1981)
"Darn It Baby, That's Love"

Singer/songwriter, she was born on February 13th in New York City. With Lyn Duddy she wrote "Darn It Baby, That's Love" and "I Love Bosco". She costarred with Frank Sinatra on the radio show "Your Hit Parade" (1941–46). ASCAP.

EICHHORN, HERMENE WARLICK (1906–)
"First Corinthians"

Composer/organist/conductor, she was born on April 3rd in Hickory, North Carolina, was educated at the University of North Carolina (BSM) and had private music study. She was organist at the Holy Trinity Episcopal Church in Greensboro, North Carolina. She composed the cantatas *First Corinthians, Mary Magdalene, Song of the Highest.*

ELLIOTT, CHARLOTTE (1789–1871)
"Just As I Am, Without One Plea"
"O Holy Savior, Friend Unseen"
"My God, My Father, While I Stray"
She was born in Clapham, London, England, on March 17, 1789, and never married. She became an invalid in about 1820 and devoted her time to writing verses and corresponding with the evangelist, César Malan of Geneva (for 40 years). She was editor of the *Christian Rembrance Pocket-book* (1834–1859) and wrote some 150 hymns. Her *Hymns for the Week* (1839) sold 40,000 copies. Her hymns were also published in *The Invalid's Hymn Book* (1836); her brother Henry's *Psalms and Hymns for Public, Private and Social Worship* (1835–48); and *Thoughts in Verse and Sacred Subjects* (1869). She died in Brighton, East Sussex, England on September 22, 1871. More recently her hymns appeared in *The American Service Hymnal* (1968); *Baptist* (1973); *Broadman* (1977); *Christian Worship* (1953); *Christian Science* (1937); *Episcopal* (1940); *Family of God* (1976); *Lutheran* (1941); *Methodist* (1966); *Presbyterian USA* (1955); *The Pilgrim Hymnal* (United Church of Christ, 1958); and others.

ELLIOTT, EMILY ELIZABETH STEELE (1836–1897)
"Thou didst leave Thy throne and Thy kingly crown, When Thou camest to earth for me."
Daughter of the Rev. E. B. Elliott and a niece of hymnist Charlotte Elliott, she was born at Brighton, England, on July 22, 1836. Anglican, Low, she edited the *Church Missionary Juvenile Instructor* for six years, contributed to *Additional Hymns* (1866) for use in St. Mark's Church in Brighton, and 48 of her hymns were published in *Under the Pillow,* a book with tunes for people hospitalized and those in infirmaries or sick at home. In addition, 70 of her hymns were published in *Chimes of Consecration* (1873) and 71 hymns in *Chimes for Daily Service* (1880). She died in Mildmay Park, London, England, on August 3, 1897. Her hymn appeared in the *American* (1968); *Baptist* (1973); *Christian* (1953); *Episcopal* (1940); *Family of God* (1976); *Presbyterian* (1955) hymnals, and *The Pilgrim Hymnal* (1958).

ELSER, ROSALEE (1925–)
"Hymns of the Saints"

Composer/organist/arranger, she was born in Independence, Missouri, and educated at the Kansas City Conservatory of Music (University of Missouri, BA); Graceland College in Lamoni, Iowa; and Willamette University in Salem, Oregon. She had the major responsibility for hymn harmonizations in "Hymns of the Saints" for the Reorganized Church of Jesus Christ of Latter-day Saints. She is the great-granddaughter of the Prophet Joseph Smith.

ETHERIDGE, MELISSA (1961–)
"Bring Me Some Water"
Folk/jazz/rock/R&B guitarist/singer raised in Leavenworth, Kansas. She attended Berklee College of Music in Boston but dropped out and moved to Los Angeles. She wrote "Bring Me Some Water", a hit from her album *Melissa Etheridge* (1988) and then *Brave and Crazy* (1989); *Never Enough* (1992) won a 1993 Grammy and *Yes I Am* (1994) with "Come to My Window" and "I'm the Only One" hit the Top Ten singles. At the 1994 Woodstock Festival, she paid tribute to Janis Joplin by singing "Try", "Move Over", and "Piece of My Heart". Etheridge is a lesbian and lives in Los Angeles with her lover, Julie Cypher, a film director and ex-wife of actor Lou Diamond Phillips.

EVANS, DALE (1912–)
"Happy Birthday Gentle Savior"
Country-music singer, songwriter, and pianist, she was born Frances Octavia Evans on October 31st in Uvalde, Texas. After studying piano, singing, and dancing in Osceola, Arkansas, she sang on the radio in Memphis, Dallas, and Louisville, then in 1940 she joined CBS radio in Chicago. By 1943 she was singing in western films with Roy Rogers, whom she married in 1947. During the 1950s the couple performed in rodeo shows and had their own show on television. She wrote the lyrics for gospel and country-western songs and also composed the music, such as "San Antone", "Happy Trails", and the gospel song mentioned above. Both Dale and Roy appeared occasionally on television in the 1980s–90s.

EZELL, HELEN INGLE (1903–)
"Oklahoma Windmill"
Composer/pianist, she was born on May 18th and was educated at Juilliard in New York City, Columbia University, University of Oklahoma (BFA), and she studied with Clarence Bing, Jacques Abram, Digly Bell, Faye Trumbull, Lyle Dowling, Henry Cowell, Otto Luening, Spencer Norton, and Violet Archer. She composed the following piano pieces: "Oklahoma Windmill", "Louisiana Levee", "Ghost Town", "A Lovely Day", "Pollyanna", "River Boat", "Square Dance", "Two Pigeons". ASCAP.

-F-

FAITHFULL, MARIANNE
Twentieth Century Blues

Blues singer/songwriter. Her albums include *A Child's Adventure, Blazing Away, Broken English, Greatest Hits, Strange Weather*. Her one-woman variety show *Twentieth Century Blues* with a mixture of pop, rock, and songs of Kurt Weill and other well-known composers is scheduled to be performed at a Broadway or off-Broadway theater in New York City in the spring of 1996.

FAIRCLOTH, ALTA COOK (b. 1911–)
Tune—"Dunwoody"

Composer and hymnist, she was born in Valley Mills, Texas, on November 8, 1911, and was educated at Louisiana College (BA), Pineville, Louisiana. She taught at public schools in Memphis, Tennessee, and was the supervisor of music at the Louisiana Baptist Children's Home in Monroe, Louisiana (1942–1951). During this time she was also choir director and pianist of the College Place Baptist Church, and accompanied and directed an opera club music chorus. She joined the Baptist Sunday School Board in 1951 in the Church Music Department as an assistant editor and continued working there until her retirement in 1976. Her tune above appeared in the *Baptist Hymnal* (1975).

FARGO, DONNA (1949–)
"Happiest Girl in the Whole USA"

Country singer/songwriter, she was born on November 10th in Mt. Airy, North Carolina. She wrote the song above with the lines "Good morning, morning, hello, sunshine". She also wrote "Funny face, I love you funny face and I need you". Her albums available in 1994 were *The Best of Donna Fargo* and the *Happiest Girl in the Whole USA*.

FARMER, BESS (1919–)
"For I Love You"

Organist/accordionist/arranger/songwriter, she was born in Hegira, Kentucky. After graduating from Tennessee Tech., Cookesville, Tennessee (1956), and Eastern Kentucky State College, Richmond, Kentucky (MA, 1959), she joined the Renfro Valley Barn Dance team in Renfro Valley, Kentucky, in 1963. She arranged music for this group and wrote "For I Love You".

FARRAR, GERALDINE (1882–1967)
Oh Thou Field of Waving Corn

Soprano/songwriter, she was born on February 28th in Melrose, Massachusetts, and was educated in public schools. Her music study was with

Mrs. J. H. Long, Trabadello, Emma Thursby, Lilli Lehman, and Graziani. She made her debut at the Royal Opera House in Berlin, Germany, as Marguerite in *Faust* 1901. She sang with the Metropolitan Opera in New York City 1906–22. She was active with the Red Cross during World War II. With music by Rachmaninoff she wrote the lyrics for "Ecstasy of Spring", "The Dream", "Here Beauty Dwells", "The Tryst", "The Alder Tree", "Oh, Thou Field of Waving Corn", "The Mirage", "The Fountain", "Morning". With music by Fritz Kreisler, she wrote the lyrics for "Dear Homeland", "The Whole World Knows", "Love Comes and Goes", and "Fair Rosemary". With music by Moussorgsky she wrote "Tears". ASCAP.

FENNER, BEATRICE (1904–Dec'd.)
Suite for Piano
Composer/songwriter, she was born on April 15th in Los Angeles, California, and was educated at Juilliard, Master Intitute of United Arts, and she studied with T. Tertius Noble. She composed *Suite for Piano* and the words and music for several songs, including, "Night Song", "The Man with the Jelly Bean Nose", "Reciprocation", "When Children Pray", and "Weep Little Mary".

FERRELL, RACHELLE (1961–)
"I Know You Can Love Me"
Singer/pianist/composer, she was raised near Philadelphia. With guitarist Kevin Eubanks of the "Tonight Show", she sang her compositions "Welcome to My Love", "I'm Special", "I Know You Can Love Me" while on tour. Her jazz albums are *First Instrument, Too Late* (1992), and *Rachelle Farrell*.

FIELDS, DOROTHY (1904–1974)
"I Can't Give You Anything But Love, Baby"
Lyricist and librettist, she was born on July 15th in Allenhurst, New Jersey, the daughter of Lew Fields of the vaudeville team of Weber and Fields. With composer Jimmy McHugh, she wrote the words for "Diga, Diga, Doo", "I Can't Give You Anything But Love" (1927), "On the Sunny Side of the Street" (1930), "I'm in the Mood for Love" (1935); with Jerome Kern, she wrote "Lovely to Look at" in *Roberta* (1935) and "The Way You Look Tonight" in *Swing Time* (1936) and won an Academy Award. She also wrote lyrics for Sigmund Romberg, Irving Berlin, Cole Porter, and others. She died on March 28th in New York City.

FINCH, RUTH GODDARD (1906–)
"Sing Me a Song"
Songwriter born September 27th in Boston, Massachusetts, she was educated in public schools. She wrote several songs, including, "Bound",

"I Found You in Another's Arms", "Knockin' on the Door to Heaven", "Sing Me a Song", "I Found the Key", and "Riding Along with You." ASCAP.

FINE, VIVIAN (1913–)
Drama for Orchestra
Composer and pianist, she was born on September 28th in Chicago, Illinois. At the age of five she was awarded a scholarship to the Chicago Musical College and later studied piano with Diane Lavoie-Herz, composition with Ruth Crawford and Adolf Weidig. She moved to New York City in 1931, where she continued her studies and played professionally. Fine taught at New York University, the Juilliard School, and Bennington College, Vermont. Her compositions include "The Race of Life" (1937), "Opus 51" (1938), "The Great Wall of China" (1947), "A Guide to the Life Expectancy of a Rose" (1956), "Morning" (1962), etc. Her commissioned *Drama for Orchestra* was performed by the San Francisco Symphony Orchestra conducted by E. de Waart on January 8, 1983.

FINLEY, LORRAINE NOEL (1899–Dec'd.)
Persian Miniature
Composer, she was born on December 24th in Montreal, Ontario, Canada, educated at Wellesley College, Juilliard, and Columbia University in New York City, and studied with J. J. Goulet, Ada Richardson, Louise Heritte-Viardot, Frank La Forge, Percy Goetschius, Rubin Goldmark. She married composer/conductor Theodore Fitch. Her works include: *Persian Miniature* (ballet), *Symphony in D, 3 Portraits, Brave Horse of Mine* (male chorus), a clarinet sonata and two violin sonatas, and many songs.

FIRESTONE, ISABELLE (1874–1954)
"You Are the Song in My Heart"
Composer/songwriter, she was born on November 10th in Minnesota City, Minnesota, and was educated at Alma College, Ontario, Canada. She wrote "Bluebirds", "Do You Recall?", "Melody of Love", "You Are the Song in My Heart". She married Harvey S. Firestone. She also wrote the theme songs for the "Voice of Firestone" radio and TV programs, "In My Garden" and "If I Could Tell You". She died on July 7th in Akron, Ohio. ASCAP.

FIRSOVA, ELENA OLEGOVNA (1950–)
The Nightingale and the Rose
Composer, she was born on March 21st in Leningrad, Russia. She studied composition under Alexander Pizumov at the Moscow Conservatory

(1970–75) and married composer Dimitri Smirnov on Augsut 19, 1972. They have one son and a daughter. She has composed symphonies, choral and instrumental works, chamber music, two operas, etc. Her opera above is based on the writings of Oscar Wilde (1991).

FISHER, CLETA MARIANNE JOHNSON (1932–)
Tune—"Abiding Peace"
Composer/hymnist, she was born totally blind in Las Vegas, Nevada. She attended the School for the Blind in Ogden, Utah, and won a scholarship to the Perkins School for the Blind in Massachusetts; Brigham Young University (BA); University of Utah (MA in music and MA in audiology). She also wrote the words for the hymn above—"As I Search the Holy Scriptures" in the Mormon hymnal (1985).

FISHER, DORIS (1915–)
"Into Each Life Some Rain Must Fall"
Singer/songwriter, she was born on May 2nd in New York City. With Fred Fisher she wrote "Whispering Grass" and with Allan Roberts, "Into Each Life Some Rain Must Fall", "You Always Hurt the One You Love", and "You Can't See the Sun When You're Crying." ASCAP.

FISHER, JESSIE (1909–)
"Dance of the Wooden Shoes"
Composer/violinist/songwriter, she was born on July 16th in Brielle, New Jersey, and was educated at the Philadelphia Conservatory, studied with Boris Koutzen and at Trenton State University (BS). She gave violin concerts and was first violinist of the Riverhead Long Island Friends of Music. She also was a music supervisor in New Jersey and New York schools. Her songs and instrumentals include "Dance of the Wooden Shoes", "Joyous Tidings", "Mysterious Forest", "Shades of Song". ASCAP.

FISHER, MARJORIE WILLIAMS (1916–)
"Letters from You"
Composer/songwriter, she was born on October 27th and received a college education. She wrote songs for college productions, including, "Letters from You" and "Op". ASCAP.

FITZGERALD, ELLA (1918–)
"My One Bad Habit"
Singer/songwriter, she was born on April 25th in Newport News, Virginia. She is known for her easygoing scat singing with snippets of lyrics. After being discovered on an amateur show in Harlem, New York, in 1934, she joined Chick Webb's show when she was only sixteen and stayed with him until his death in 1939, then became leader of the band.

She wrote "A-Tisket, a-tasket, a Green and Yellow Basket", based on a 19th-century song. She also wrote "My One Bad Habit" with Dave and Iola Brubeck—"I neither smoke, nor drink, nor swear, my one bad habit is falling in love."

Fitzgerald toured Canada, Europe, South America, Japan, and Australia during the 1950s–60s. She also made many tours with Norman Granz's Jazz at the Philharmonic. She won three Grammys in 1958, recorded with Duke Ellington (1965–66), sang with the Boston Pops Orchestra (1972), toured Europe with Count Basie and Oscar Peterson (1975), with Tommy Flanagan Trio at the Music Hall in Detroit (1979), at the Atlantic City Jazz Festival in New Jersey (July 1980), at Grant Park Jazz Festival, Chicago (August 1981). She has won eight Grammy awards. She sang at the Infiniti Jazz Festival at the Hollywood Bowl, California, in July 1992. As of 1994, there were over sixty different albums and CDs of hers available for purchase.

FLACK, ROBERTA (1940–)
"Reverend Lee"

Pianist/singer/songwriter, she was born on February 10th at Black Mountain, North Carolina. Her rendition of "Reverend Lee" was a sensation at the 1971 Newport Jazz Festival in Rhode Island. She also sang at the 1972 Newport Jazz Festival in New York City and in concert at Carnegie Hall (1972). Her album *First Take* won a 1972 Grammy for "The first time ever I saw your face" and another Grammy in 1973 for "Killing Me Softly with His Song". She sang at Wolf Trap in Vienna, Virginia (June 1980), and at the Front Row Theater, Cleveland, Ohio (August 1980). She married bassist Steve Novosel, but they later divorced. She sang at the JVC Jazz Festival in Newport, Rhode Island, in August 1992. As of 1994, her albums and CDs available were *Best of Roberta Flack, Blue Lights in the Basement, Chapter Two, First Take, I'm the One, Killing Me Softly, Oasis, Quiet Fire, Set the Night to Music.*

FLORES, ROSIE
After the Farm

Country/rock singer/songwriter/guitarist, she lives in Los Angeles. She led the the Screaming Sirens, a West coast all-girl cowpunk outfit in the 1970s–80s. She went solo in the 1990s. Her album is *After the Farm* (1992).

FLOWER, ELIZABETH "ELIZA" (1803–1846)
Anthem—*Adoration*

Composer, daughter of Benjamin Flower, she was born in Harlow, England, on April 19, 1803 and was the elder sister of hymnist Sarah Flower

Adams. Her musical compositions were published in *Fourteen Musical Illustrations of the Waverly Novels* (1831); *Songs of the Seasons,* "Now we pray for our country" (1842); *Hymns and Anthems, the words Chiefly from the Holy Scriptures,* etc. in 5 parts; *Adoration* (1841); *Aspiration, Belief, Heaven Upon Earth* (1846); and *Life after Death,* which were composed for the congregation of South Place Chapel, Finsbury. She also composed music for her sister's hymns "Darkness clouded Calvary" and "Nearer, my God, to Thee." Sixty-three of her hymn tunes were published in W. J. Fox's *Hymns and Anthems* (1840–41). She died of tuberculosis in London, England, on December 12, 1846 and was buried in Harlow.

FODY, IIONA (1920–)
"Angel Face"
Composer/songwriter, born July 13th in Elizabeth, New Jersey, she was educated at St. Mary's Convent and Drake Business School. With Frank Oliva and others she wrote a number of songs, including, "Angel Face", "A Woman", "Ask for Me", "Green Is the Color", "Legend of the Cowboy Saint", "Ring of Virgin Gold", "You Are My Love".

FONTYN, JACQUELINE (1930–)
Scurochiaro
Composer, she was born on December 27th in Antwerp, Belgium. After studying piano under Ignace Bolotine and Marcel Maas; harmony, counterpoint, fugue, orchestration, and composition under Marcel Quintet in Brussels; composition with Max Deutsch and Hans Swarowski, she studied at the Academy for Music and Arts in Vienna and was graduated in composition from the Royal Chapel of Queen Elizabeth in Belgium. On July 18, 1961, she married Camille Schmitt and they had one son and a daughter. She served as professor of counterpoint at the Royal Conservatory in Antwerp (1963–70), then at the Royal Conservatory in Brussels (1970–79). She has won a number of international prizes in music. She has composed dozens of symphonies, instrumental and choral works, chamber music. Her *Scurochiaro* for flute, clarinet, bassoon, piano, violin, cello, double bass, was first performed in Baltimore, Maryland in 1989. Her husband died in 1976.

FORD, JOAN (1921–)
"Give the Little Lady a Great Big Hand"
Songwriter, she was born on December 12th in Denver, Colorado, and was educated at Loretta Heights College (BA) and Catholic University (MA). With Jean Kerr and Walter Kerr, she wrote the lyrics for a number of songs. "Give the Little Lady a Great Big Hand", "The Pussy Foot", and "Who's Been Sitting in My Chair?". ASCAP.

FORD, LENA GUILBERT (ca. 1870–1918)
    "Keep the Home Fires Burning"
Lyricist, she was raised in Elmira, New York. While living in London, and using music by Ivor Novello, she wrote "Keep the Home Fires Burning". She was killed in a German Zeppelin raid on London.

FORD, LORI (1928–)
    "Choo Choo Cha Cha"
Composer/singer/songwriter, she was born on February 11th in Chicago, Illinois, and received a high school education. She married composer/songwriter Carl Ford and they wrote songs, including "Choo Choo Cha Cha". ASCAP.

FORSTER, DOROTHY (1884–1950)
    "Myfanwy"
Composer/pianist, she was born on February 20th in London, England, and was educated at the Royal Academy of Music. She studied with Walter Macfarren, Frederick Corder, Frank Arnold, and she was a concert pianist in Great Britain. Her songs and instrumentals include "Myfanwy", "Perhaps", "Dearest, I Bring You Daffodils", "A Psalm of Love", "I Wonder If Love Is a Dream", "Some Day Soon". She died on December 25th in England. ASCAP.

FORSYTH, JOSEPHINE (1889–1940)
    Setting for the *Lord's Prayer*
A composer, she was born in Cleveland, Ohio, on July 5, 1889, and married R. A. Meyers on April 29, 1928. She wrote the setting to the *Lord's Prayer* for her wedding and it was sung at Easter sunrise cerermonies at the Hollywood Bowl in California for many years. She died in Cleveland on May 24, 1940.

FORT, ELEANOR HANK (1914–)
    "Save your Confederate money, boys, the South will rise again"
Composer/singer/songwriter, she was born on June 19th in Nashville, Tennessee, and was educated at the Peabody Demonstration School. She has written many songs, including, "Lady Bird", "I Love Connecticut", "Protocol", "Put Your Shoes on Lucy", "I Didn't Know the Gun Was Loaded", "The Boardwalk", "Cherry Blossom Spring", "Southern Cookin'", "Tall Tales of Texas", etc. ASCAP.

FOSTER, FAY (1886–1960)
    "The place where I worship"
Pianist, hymnist, and composer, she was born at Leavenworth, Texas, on November 8, 1886. She was head of the voice department at the Ogontz

School in Rydall, Pennsylvania for ten years. She died in Bayport, New York on April 17, 1960. One recording of her hymn is listed in *Phonolog Reports* of Los Angeles, California. She also composed music for hymns by Florence Tarr, and she composed piano pieces and five operas.

FOWLER, JENNIFER (1939–)
Sculpture in Four Dimensions
Composer, she was born on April 14th in Bunbury, Western Australia. After receiving honors in music at the University of Western Australia (BA, 1960–B.Mus. 1967), she studied electronic music at the University of Utrecht in The Netherlands and composition under John Exton. She taught at the Bunbury, Bentley, and Cannington High Schools in Western Australia, then at the Wykeham Secondary School in London (1969–72). On December 18, 1971, she married Bruce Paterson and they have two sons. She has won several international prizes and has composed orchestral and choral works, chamber music, etc. Her *Sculpture in Four Dimensions* (1969) was first performed in Perth, Australia, in 1970.

FOX, ERIKA (1936–)
Shir
Composer, she was born on October 3rd in Vienna, Austria. With the persecution of the Jews by the Germans, the family fled to London in 1939. After studying piano under Angus Morrison and composition under Bernard Stevens at the Royal College of Music in London, she married Manfred Fox on September 3, 1961, and they had a son and a daughter. She continued studying composition under Jeremy Dale Roberts, Peter Maxwell Davies, and Harrison Birtwistle (1968). She has composed orchestral and choral works, operas and chamber music. Her *Shir*, composed in 1983, was written for the flute, oboe, clarinet, bassoon, horn, trumpet, trombone, percussion, piano, two violins, viola, cello, and double bass.

FOX, GLORY M. (1918–)
"The Best Is Yet to Come"
Songwriter, she was born on May 30th in Chicago, Illinois, and was educated at St. Scholastics Academy in Chicago, Mundelein College for Women, and Columbia School for Speech and Drama. With composer/pianist Lew Douglas, she wrote the lyrics for a number of songs, including, "Boston Bounce", "The Best Is Yet to Come", "Clay Idol", "Turn Around Boy", "Let a Little Sunshine in Your Heart", "Love on the Rocks", "Love Works Miracles", and "With Love".

FOX, LUACINE CLARK (1914–)
Tune—"Love One Another"

Composer/pianist born in Washington, DC, the daughter of Luacine An-
netta Savage and J. Reuben Clark, Jr. She lived in Salt Lake City, Utah,
and in Mexico City, Mexico; she was educated at the University of Utah;
had piano study with Florence Bennion, Mabel Borg Jenkins, and Jose
Velasquez; studied harmony and composition with Tracy Y. Cannon.
She married Orval C. Fox and they have three children. She composed
the tune and wrote the words for the above hymn, "Love One Another",
which appeared in the Mormon hymnal (1985).

FRANCES, PAULA (1924–)
   "Christmas Roses"
Songwriter, she was born on June 3rd in Hoboken, New Jersey, and re-
ceived a high school education. She married composer/songwriter Gary
Romero. They wrote "Christmas Roses", "Buzzy, the Bumble Bee", "I
Blew Out the Flame", "My True Carrie, Love". ASCAP.

FRANCIS, ANNETTE (1928–)
   "Wishing Well"
Composer/pianist/songwriter, she was born on December 12th in Waco,
Texas and was educated at Sophie Newcomb College, Tulane University, and the College of Music in Cincinnati. She was a pianist on radio
in Waco and on both radio and TV in Cincinnati. She also wrote the
songs "Wishing Well" and "My Heart's Desire". ASCAP.

FRANCIS, CONNIE (1938–)
   "Italian Lullaby"
Composer/singer/songwriter, she was born Constance Franconero on
December 12th in Newark, New Jersey, and was educated at the Arts
High School. She studied music with her father and at age eleven played
the accordion on "George Scheck's Startime", a juvenile variety show
and then on the "Arthur Godfrey Talent Show". She toured the USA,
Australia, New Zealand, South Africa, and Europe. By 1973 she had
eight gold records. Songs she wrote include "Italian Lullaby" and "Senza
Mama". As of 1994 her albums available were *Christmas in my Heart,
The Very Best of Connie Francis*. ASCAP.

FRANK, CAMILLA MAYS (1899–Dec'd.)
   "Song of the Women's Army Corps"
Composer/songwriter she was born on April 22nd in Blacksburg, South
Carolina, and received a high school education. She was a captain in the
WACs, Army Special Services in the European Theater in World War II
and wrote songs with Jane Douglass. She wrote the official WAC song,
"Song of the Women's Army Corps". ASCAP.

FRANK, RUTH VERD (1899–Dec'd.)
"Down Hoosier Way"
Composer/organist/pianist/songwriter, she was born on August 28th in Bristol, Indiana, and was educated at the Moyer Music School in Freeburg, Pennsylvania. With Eddie Ballantine she wrote a number of songs, including, "Down Hoosier Way", the ABC network theme song, "Alone In a Fog", "Above the Sun", "Allegheny March", and "Stay Away".

FRANKLYN, BLANCHE (1895–Dec'd.)
"Mississippi Missy"
Composer/songwriter, she was born on January 27th in Los Angeles, California, and was educated in public schools. She wrote songs for Eddie Cantor, Frank Crumit, Al Jolson, Sophie Tucker, and Bert Williams. She collaborated with Nat Vincent. Her songs include "China Toy", "I'm Tired of Building Castles", "Pretty Little Cinderella", "Pucker Up and Whistle", and "Mississippi Missy". ASCAP.

FREEMAN, CAROLYN R. (b. 1895–)
"Never fear tho' shadows around your path may fall."
Composer, hymnist, pianist, and songwriter, and the daughter of Fred A. and Lenora G. Freeman, she was born at Taylor Center, New York, on October 22, 1895. About 1902 they sold their farm and moved to Taylor, New York, where they operated a large general store. Upon her father's death, the family moved to Cortland, New York. She was an active Methodist.

She wrote her high school graduation song (1912), and later became a staff writer for the *Teacher's Magazine*. She established the Freeman Music Company in Cortland to publish her own songs and the music of others. She published *Very Best Christmas Helps* (1938), which included recitations, dialogues, tableaus, etc.; *Very Best Easter Entertainment* (1939) for primary children and tiny tots; *The Coming of the Christ-Child* (1939), a pageant; also the words and music of *The Heart of America* (1942) and other songs. Her hymn "Back of the Clouds" was recorded on the record *I Believe,* Chapel Records (Mountain View, California) and appeared in *Rodeheaver's Gospel Solos and Duets No. 3*. She is now crippled with arthritis but can still play the piano, which was moved into the nursing home where she is residing in Cortland. (Letter from her sister, Mrs. Freda M. Miner of Cortland, New York, June 8, 1982.)

FREER, ELEANOR EVEREST (1864–1942)
Sonnets from the Portuguese
Composer and singer, she was born on May 14th in Philadelphia, Pennsylvania, the daughter of singer Amelia Clark and organist/teacher Cor-

nelius Everest. Freer played the piano at age five, was singing in local Gilbert and Sullivan operettas and composing music in her teens. She studied singing with Mathilde Marchesi and composition with Benjamin Goddard in Paris in the 1880s. After she married Archibald Freer in 1891, they lived in Chicago. Freer composed eleven operas and some 150 songs. Her forty-four *Sonnets from the Portuguese* (1939) were based on the poems of Elizabeth Barrett Browning. She died on May 14th in Chicago, Illinois.

FRICKER, SYLVIA (1940–)
"You Were on My Mind"
Singer/songwriter, she was born in Chatham, Ontario, Canada. She married Ian Tyson in 1964 and they formed the country duo of Ian and Sylvia. She wrote the above song in 1966 and "A Love Song". With her husband she wrote "Mr. Spoons". Albums available in 1994 were *4 Strong Winds, Greatest Hits,* and *Northern Journey.*

FRYXELL, REGINA CHRISTINA HOLMEN (b. 1899–)
Arrangement of Tune—"Skara"
Composer, arranger, pianist, and organist, she was born at Morganville, Kansas, on November 24, 1899, and educated at Augustana College (BA and BMus 1922) in Rock Island, Illinois, and taught there (1922–25). She studied at Juilliard in New York City (1925–27) with Leo Sowerby, Dr. Luther D. Reed, and others. In 1928 she married Fritiof M. Fryxell, who later was professor of geology at Augustana College. She taught organ at Knox College (1956-58) in Galesburg, Illinois, then at Black Hawk College in Moline, Illinois. She composed numerous solos and anthems. Her music appeared in the *Lutheran Service Book and Hymnal* (1958). In April 1982 she was living in Rock Island, Illinois. (Information from Augustana College.)

FUCHS, LILLIAN (1903–)
Fantasy Etudes
Violist, composer, and teacher, she was born on November 18th in New York City. She was the sister of violinist Joseph Fuchs. After studying violin with Svecenski and Kneisel, and composition at the New York Institute of Musical Art, she made her debut as a violinist in New York in 1926. She then played the viola and was a member of the Perole String Quartet from 1925 to the mid-1940s. She then toured Europe and the states as a violist. She also taught at the Manhattan School of Music, the Aspen Music School from 1964, and at Juilliard from 1971. Her works for solo viola include 12 *Caprices* (1950), *Sonata pastorale* (1956), 16 *Fantasy Etudes* (1961), and 15 *Characteristi Studies* (1964). She was the first to perform and record the six cello suites by Bach on the viola.

FULLER, ESTHER MARY (1907–1969)
Unison Anthems for Children
Composer, conductor, organist, and pianist, she was born in Amboy, Indiana, on November 7, 1907, and was educated at Taylor University (BM) in Upland, Indiana; Fletcher College (BM), and the University of Michigan. She taught music in public schools for 15 years and was church organist, choir director, and director of music for the Paoli Methodist Church in Paoli, Pennsylvania, Lucy Lewis wrote the words for her music, and she also collaborated with Doris Paul. Her works include *A Child's Book of Anthems; Chapel Bells; We Bow Our Heads; Altar of Christmas; Little Children Sing*. She was married to Roy Fuller. She died on March 28, 1969.

-G-

GABRIEL, ANA
"Evidencias"
Singer/songwriter, her hit "Evidencias" was on top of the Latin singles chart. She sang at the James L. Knight Center in Miami in 1992.

GAIL, EDMEE SOPHIE GARRE (1775–1819)
"Celui Qui Toucher Mon Coeur"
Singer/songwriter, she was born on August 28th in Paris, France. At age fifteen her songs were published in *La Chevardiere & Baillex* and at eighteen she married philologist Jean Baptiste Gail, but some years later they separated. After studying singing with Mengozzi, she studied musical theory with Fetis, Peine, and Neukomin. She composed the one-act operas *Les Deux Jaloux* (March 1813), *Mlle. de Launay a la Bastille* (December 1813), *Angela, au L'atelier de Jean Cousin* with Boieldieu (June 1814), and *La Serenade* (1818) produced at the Theatre Feydeau. In 1816 Gail sang in London and with Marie Calalini toured Austria and Germany in 1818. She died of tuberculosis on July 24th in Paris.

GAITHER, GLORIA (b. 1942–)
"God sent his Son, they called him Jesus."
Born at Battle Creek, Michigan on March 4, 1942, she was educated at Anderson College (BA; MA), Anderson, Indiana, majoring in English, French, and Sociology. During her college days she met William J. Gaither of Alexandria, Indiana whom she married. They both taught at the Alexandria High School. He founded the Gaither Music Company, which publishes his compositions and other musical works. Gloria and her husband, Bill, together with his brother Dan, formed the Gaither Trio, famous Gospel singing group. Her hymns appeared in the *Baptist* (1975); *Broadman* (1977); and *Family of God* (1976) hymnals. Her

hymn "There's something about that name" listed nineteen recordings for the song by *Phonolog Reports* of Los Angeles (1978). Her husband composed the music for her hymns.

GALAJIKIAN, FLORENCE GARLAND (1900–)
Symphonic Intermezzo
Pianist/composer, she was born in Maywood, Illinois. At age six she studied the piano. After she was graduated from Northwestern University School of Music and the Chicago Musical College, she taught at the Chicago Conservatory of Music. Her *Symphonic Intermezzo* won the National Broadcasting Company's orchestral award in 1932. She wrote *Tragic Overture* in 1934.

GALAS, DIAMANDA (1955–)
"Wild Women with Steak Knives"
Jazz pianist, singer, and composer, she studied piano and played in the San Diego orchestra at age fourteen. After studying biochemistry and experimental musical performance at the University of California at San Diego, she took private singing lessons. She was known as a jazz pianist and singer and performed at the Moers Jazz Festival in Germany and in Paris. Her works, such as "The Litanies of Satan" (1982) and the one mentioned above (1981–83), often use electronics and prerecorded tapes.

GALLICO, GRACE LANE (1921–)
"Birmingham Rag"
Composer/singer, she was born on July 6th in Fairfield, Connecticut, and received a high school education. She sang with her sisters on radio, then with dance bands, including Tony Pastor and Vaughn Monroe. With Tom Glazer, Earl Shuman, and Leon Carr, she wrote a number of songs, "Believe in Me", "Birmingham Rag", "Darling You Make It So", "Clinging Vine", "Fontainebleau", "Pass the Plate of Happiness Around". ASCAP.

GANNINO, RUTH LILLIAN (1916–)
"Heavenly Hawaii"
Composer/songwriter, she was born on October 17th in Lynn, Massachusetts, and was educated at Salem Hospital School of Nursing. She was a private nurse for three years, operated a nursing home from 1941–47, and then was founder and administrator of Saugus General Hospital from 1947–57. She wrote "Heavenly Hawaii".

GARDNER, RUTH MUIR (1927–)
"Families Can Be Together Forever"

Hymnist born in Salt Lake City and educated at the University of Utah, she married Lyall J. Gardner and they have four children. She wrote the hymn above and also "Go Forth with Faith", which appeared in the Mormon hymnal (1985).

GAY, ANNABETH McCLELLAND (b. 1925–)
Tune—"Shepherds' Pipes"
A composer and daughter of a Presbyterian minister in Ottawa, Illinois, she was born there and was graduated from Knox College (BME, 1947) in Galesburg, Illinois, and attended the School of Sacred Music of Union Theological Seminary in New York City (MSM, 1949), where she met the Rev. William Gay, who gained his BD at the Seminary. They were married in 1949, and he served Congregational Churches in Jefferson, Ohio, three rural churches in Brown county, then at Pleasant Hill, Ohio, from 1958. She served as leader of the Ohio Women's Fellowship of Congregational Christian Churches in hymn-singing. The tune with the hymn "The Lord is rich and merciful" appeared in *The Pilgrim Hymnal* (1958).

GAYNOR, JESSIE LOVEL SMITH (1863–1921)
"Shepherd of Tender Youth"
Composer/songwriter, she also wrote a "Thanksgiving Song".

GENTRY, BOBBIE (1942–)
"Ode to Billy Joe"
Guitarist/singer/songwriter, she was born Roberta Streeter on July 27th in Chickasaw County, Mississippi. She was raised in Greenwood, Mississippi, and in Palm Springs, California. She studied at the Los Angeles Conservatory of Music. Gentry wrote "Ode to Billy Joe—It was the third of June, another sleepy, dusty delta day" (1967), which was adapted to film and won three Grammy awards in 1976. She also wrote "Tuesday's Child", "Lazy Willie", "Chickasaw County Child", "Papa won't let me go into town with you". Her available album as of 1994 was *Greatest Hits*.

GIBBS, ADA ROSE (1865–1905)
Tune—"Channels"
A composer, she was born in England and was married to William J. Gibbs, who was superintendent of the Central Hall (Methodist) at Bromley, Kent. She was an active member in the Keswick Convention movement and was the mother of one of the directors of Marshall, Morgan, and Scott, Ltd., London. She published *Twenty-four Gems of Sacred Song* (1900), and her tune was used with the hymn "How I praise Thee,

precious Savior", which appeared in *Hymns for the Living Church* (1974).

GIBSON, DEBORAH "DEBBIE" (1970–)
Body Mind Soul
Singer/songwriter born on August 31st in New York City, she was raised in Merrick, Long Island, New York. At age seventeen she wrote "Foolish Beat", which reached Number One on the Charts. Her pop album *Out of the Blue* was on the Top Ten in 1988 and sold 2 million copies, she was named 1988 Female Artist of the Year, and had a platinum video *Live in Concert—The Out of the Blue Tour* (1989); her album *Electric Youth* sold over 2 million copies (1989), she also had a video, *Live in Concert* (1990). She co-wrote the songs on her album *Body Mind Soul* (1993).

GIDEON, MIRIAM (1906–)
"Ayelet Hashakhar"
Composer and teacher, she was born on October 23rd in Greeley, Colorado. She was taught music as a child in Boston by her uncle, organist/choir director Henry Gideon. After studying music at Boston University (BA, 1926) she studied musicology at Columbia University (MA, 1946) and composition at the Jewish Theological Seminary of America (DSM, 1970). She taught at Brooklyn College from 1944–54, Jewish Theological College, Manhattan School, and City College. She has composed an opera, numerous choral and orchestral works, and songs and song cycles. Her song mentioned above was available on an album in 1994.

GIFFORD, HELEN MARGARET (1935–)
Regarding Faustus
Composer, she was born on September 5th in Hawthorn, Victoria, Australia. After receiving a scholarship she studied piano under Roy Shepherd, and harmony under Dorian La Gallienne at the Melbourne University Conservatorium of Music (Mus.Bac.1958). She was composer for the Melbourne Theatre Company (1970–82). She has composed choral and orchestral works, operas, chamber music, etc. Her opera *Regarding Faustus* with tenor, chorus, and 14 instruments (1983) was first performed at Adelaide, Australia, in 1988.

GILBERTSON, VIRGINIA M. (1914–)
"Johnny, Come Kiss Me"
Composer/pianist/songwriter, she was born on December 4th in Memphis, Tennessee, and was educated at the De Shazo College of Music (BM), Memphis State University, and Winthrop College, she studied music with Edwin Hughes. She wrote the stage score for *One Bronze Feather* for the New Jersey Tercentennial. With Edward Eager, she

wrote the songs: "Johnny, Come Kiss Me" and "The Loneliest Boy About Town." ASCAP.

GILBRIDE, CLAIRE (1919–)
"Mississippi Moonlight"
Songwriter, she was born on January 25th in New Orleans, Louisiana, and was educated at a business college. She married composer/conductor Julian Genella. With her husband she wrote the lyrics for "Mississippi Moonlight".

GILL, CAROLYN (1918–)
"Sweetheart Waltz"
Composer/singer/songwriter, she was born on December 24th in Royalton, Minnesota, and received a high school education. She appeared on the radio show "National Barn Dance", the "Eddy Arnold Show", and at the Grand Ole Opry. With her composer husband Ralph Gill she wrote a number of songs, "A Happy Serenade", "Dancing the Polka", "Polka Go Around", "Swiss Kiss Polka", "Sweetheart Waltz", and "Windmill Waltz". ASCAP.

GILLES, ELOISE (1929–)
"Too Many Tear-drops"
Composer/guitarist/singer/songwriter, she was born on December 29th in River Rouge, Michigan, and was educated in the public schools. She sang with the Melody Mountaineers and wrote the songs "Every Moment I'm With You", "Till I Met You", and "Too Many Tear-drops".

GILLESPIE, MARIAN (1889–1946)
"Ashes of Dreams"
Composer/pianist/songwriter, she was born on January 26th in Muncie, Indiana, and was educated at Columbia University, studied with Clarence Carson and Georgia Galvin, then with Kathryn Lively at the St. Louis Conservatory. She wrote "Ashes of Dreams", "Bring Back the Golden Days", "Assurance", "Japanese Garden", "When You Look in the Heart of a Rose", "The Want of You", "Soul of a Rose", "Twilight Lullaby", "Doubts". She died on December 26th in New York City.

GILMORE, ELIZABETH MC CABE (1874–1953)
"Love Is Calling You"
Songwriter, she was born on September 20th in Tipton, Iowa, and studied nursing at Drake Sanitarium in Des Moines, Iowa, and at the Women's Hospital in New York City. She wrote the songs "Skies are Dark When You're Away", "Because I Walk with Thee", "It Is You", "Love Is Calling You." She died on March 14th in Long Beach, California.

GILMOUR, EDITH (1896–Dec'd.)
"Land of Sunshine"
Composer/songwriter, she was born on October 12th in Tripp, South
Dakota, and received a high school education. She wrote "Land of Sunshine" and "Minnehaha Laughing Water".

GIPPS, RUTH (b. 1921–)
Choral work—*The Temptation of Christ*
Composer, oboist, and pianist, she was born at Bexhill-on-Sea. Sussex,
England, on February 20, 1921, and studied at the Bexhill School of Music where her mother, Mrs. Bryan Gipps, was principal. Later she studied composition with R. O. Morris, Gordon Jacob, and Vaughan
Williams, and piano with Arthur Alexander and Kendall Taylor at the
Royal College of Music in London (1937–43). Her choral work for soprano, tenor, chorus, and small orchestra was based on the gospel according to St. Matthew. In 1942 she married Robert Bake, first clarinettist in the City of Birmingham Orchestra, where she became second
oboist and English horn player in 1944. She received her Doctor of Music degree from Durham University in 1948.

GITECK, JANICE (1946–)
A'agita
Composer and pianist, she was born on June 26th in New York City. After studying with Milhaud and Subotbick at Mills College, Oakland, California (BA, 1968; MA, 1969), at the Paris Conservatory with Messiaen
(1969–70), and the Aspen School, she studied Javanese gamelan privately, also electronic music and West African percussion. She taught at
Hayward State in California, University of California at Berkeley, and
then from 1979 at Cornish Institute in Seattle, Washington. The opera
A'agita is based on Pima-Papago mythologies of the Pimic Indians of
Arizona and the State of Sonora, Mexico. Many of her other works are
based on Indian dances and traditions.

GLANVILLE-HICKS, PEGGY (1912–)
The Transposed Heads
Composer, she was born on December 29th in Melbourne, Australia, and
at age fourteen she was studying composition with Fritz Hart at the
Melbourne Conservatorium. She studied composition with Vaughan
Williams, piano with Benjamin, and conducting with Lambert and Sargent from 1931–35, then with Wellesz in Vienna and with Nadia
Boulanger in Paris. In 1948 she became a US citizen. While a director of
the New York Composers Union, she helped organize a series of concerts (1950–59). She lived in Athens, Greece from 1959–76, then returned to Australia. Her opera *The Transposed Heads,* based on a novella

by Mann, was commissioned by the Louisville Orchestra and performed there in April 1954, in New York in 1958, and in Sydney, Australia, in 1970. She composed operas, vocal, and instrumental pieces.

GLASER, VICTORIA (b. 1918–)
Arrangement—*Cradle Song of the Shepherds*
Composer, arranger, conductor, and teacher, she was born in Amherst, Massachusetts, on September 11, 1918, and was educated at Radcliffe College (BA; MA), Cambridge, Massachusetts, and studied privately with Walter Piston and others. She was a music instructor at Wellesley College (1943–45), choral director and chairman of the Theory Department at Dana Hall School (1944–59) and at the New England Conservatory in Boston from 1957. Her works include arrangements for the *Twelve Days of Christmas* and *To Mary We Sing Praises*.

GLEASON, MARY M. (1931–)
"Forgive a Fool"
Songwriter, she was born on May 16th in Chicago, Illinois, and was educated at the University of Chicago (BA). She wrote lyrics for songs like "Forgive a Fool".

GLEN, IRMA (b. 1908–)
"This I Know. . . ."
Composer and hymnist, she was born in Chicago, Illinois, on August 3, 1908, and was educated at the American Conservatory in Chicago, Sherwood Music School in Illinois, Golden State University, and Institute of Religious Science, Los Angeles (Mus. D.). She was Minister of Music at the Beverly Hills Church of Religious Science in Beverly Hills, California, (1946) and ordained (1955). Later she was a minister in Palm Springs, California, and La Jolla, California. As of March 1982 she was enjoying her retirement.

GLESS, ELEANOR M. (1908–)
"I Wish I Were a Christmas Tree"
Composer/songwriter, she was born on February 7th in Willoughby, Ohio, and educated in public schools. With Ray Rivera, Charlie Buck, and Harry Stride, she wrote a number of songs, including "I Wish I Were a Christmas Tree".

GOETSCHIUS, MARJORIE (1915–)
'Tango del Ensueno'
Composer/pianist/cellist/singer, she was born on September 23rd in Raymond, New Hampshire, the granddaughter of professors Maria Stefany and Peter Goetschius. She was educated at Georgian Court College

and by her grandparents and Bernard Wagenaar, James Friskin, and Joseph Schillinger at the Juilliard School in New York City. She was a solo cellist and pianist in orchestras and on radio. Works (for piano) are *Sonata in B, Theme & Variations, Scherzo in Thirds, Rondo, Poetique, Rhapsody in G;* (violin): *Lament, Tango del Ensueno, Valse Burlesque, Nebuleuses.* She also wrote songs. ASCAP.

GOLD, ANITA (1932–)
"Another Heart Ache"

Composer/songwriter, she was born on December 25th in Chicago, Illinois, and went to art school. She wrote plays, short stories, and songs, including, "Another Heart Ache" and "Zoom Bali Oh". ASCAP.

GOLLAHON, GLADYS (1908–)
"Our Lady of Fatima"

Composer/songwriter, she was born on April 8th in Cincinnati, Ohio, and was educated in parochial schools. She wrote "Our Lady of Fatima" and other songs. ASCAP.

GOODLIFFE, BONNIE LAUPER (1943–)
Tune—"Sisterhood"

Composer/organist/pianist, born in San Francisco, California, and educated at the San Francisco Conservatory of Music; Brigham Young University (BA and MA in music); studied with J. J. Keeler at BYU and with Oskar Peter at the Mozarteum in Salzburg, Austria. She married Glade P. Goodliffe and they have seven children. She has served as associate Salt Lake Tabernacle Organist since 1984. She composed the music for the above, "We Meet Again as Sisters" in the Mormon Hymnal (1985).

GOODMAN, LILLIAN ROSEDALE (1887–1972)
"My Shepherd is the Lord"

Composer and hymnist, she was born in Mitchell, South Dakota, on May 30, 1887, and educated at Columbia University in New York City, Juilliard, Boguslawski College (hon. Mus. D.), and then taught there. She was vocal coach at Desilu Workshop in Hollywood, California (1958), and wrote hymns with her husband, Mark Goodman. She died on January 23, 1972.

GOULD, ELIZABETH (1904–)
"Trumpet Concerto"

Composer, she was born on March 4th in Toledo, Ohio, and was educated at the Oberlin College and Conservatory, University of Michigan (BA and BM), and studied piano with Guy Maier and Artur Schnabel. She gave concerts in the US, Europe, and Puerto Rico and also played with the Detroit Symphony, Chicago Symphony, Toledo Orchestra, and Littel Orchestra Society in New York City. Her works are *4 Piano Preludes, Tocata* (Mu Phi Epsilon piano prize), *2 String Quartets, Trumpet Concerto* (Philadelphia Orchestra comm.), *Piano Sonata, Declaration for Peace, Escapade for Orchestra, Sonata for Violin, Piano, Concertino for Clarinet, Trumpet, Strings, Sonata for Cello, Piano.* She received several Mu Phi Epsilon prizes. ASCAP.

GRAHAM, RUTH LILLIAN HERSCHER (1924–)
"In the Park"
Composer/songwriter, she was born on April 4th in Philadelphia, Pennsylvania, the daughter of composer Louis Herscher. She was educated at the University of California and New York University. She worked for CBS in New York City and wrote songs with her father: "The Best Years in Our Lives", "Baby, I'm the Greatest", "Break the Chain", "I Didn't Believe I'd Fall in Love", "In the Park", "Fifty Games of Solitaire", "Mama Never Said a Word About Love", "Orange Blossoms", "Where Were You?".

GRANDVAL, MARIE FELICIE CLEMENCE DE REISET (1830–1907)
Oratorio—*St. Agnes*
A composer, she was born in Saint-Remy-des-Monte, Sarthe, France, on January 21, 1830, and studied composition with Saint-Saëns and von Flotow. Her oratorio was performed in Paris on April 13, 1876. She also wrote six operas and died in Paris, France, on January 15, 1907.

GRANT, AMY (1960–)
"Tennessee Christmas"
Soul/rock singer/songwriter, she was born on November 25th in Augusta, Georgia. Her album *Age to Age* (1983) sold 1 million copies; she had a hit in a song she wrote with Michael W. Smith, "Find a Way" on her album *Unguarded* (1985). She lives in Nashville, Tennessee, with her husband songwriter Gary Chapman. They wrote "Tennessee Christmas—Come on weather man, give us a forecast snowy white". She won a 1988 Grammy as Gospel Vocalist for *Lead me on,* hit single "I Will Remember You" (1992), chosen Gospel Music Artist of Year 1992, video "Heart in Motion" sold 3 million copies.

GRANT, MICKI (1941–)
Don't Bother Me, I Can't Cope
Composer, singer, and actress (Minnie Perkins McCutcheon) she was born on June 30th in Chicago. While in her senior year at the University of Illinois in 1962, she left Chicago to sing in the Broadway musical *Fly*

Blackbird. Her musical mentioned above was performed on Broadway in New York City in 1972 in collaboration with Vinette Carroll and it received the Outer Circle Critics Best Musical award. Grant also perfomed in the show. She composed music for several other shows.

GRAZIANO, ANN (1928–)
"It Didn't Take Me Very Long"
Composer/ songwriter, she was born on January 18th in New York City, and received a high school education. She wrote "It Didn't Take Me Very Long" and other songs.

GREEN, CAROLEE CURTIS (1940–)
Tune—"Emerson"
Composer/organist/pianist, born in Salt Lake City, Utah, and educated at the University of Utah. She married Jack L. Green and they have seven children. She wrote the tune above for the hymn "Awake and Arise" for the Mormon hymnal (1985).

GREGG, MARY LOUISE (1921–)
"Forget Me Not Polka"
Composer/organist/pianist, she was born on May 30th in Pike County, Ohio, and was educated at a business college, and received a BM in music. She wrote "Forget Me Not Polka" and other songs.

GRIFFITH, NANCI (1954–)
"From a Distance"
Singer/songwriter, her songs have been popularized by such singers as Bette Midler for "From a Distance", Bob Dylan for "Boots of Spanish Leather", Tom Patton for "Can't Help But Wonder Where I'm Bound", Townes Van Zandt for "Tecumseh Valley", and Woody Guthrie for "Do Re Me". She sang at Carnegie Hall in New York City in March 1993. Her albums available in 1994 are *Late Night Grand Hotel, Little Love Affairs, Lone Star State of Mind, Once in a Very Blue Moon, One fair Summer Evening, Poet in My Window, Storms, True Believers,* and *Flyer*. She won the Contemporary Folk Album Grammy for *Other Voices, Other Rooms* (1994).

GUBAIDULINA, SOFIA ASGATOVNA (1931–)
'Garten von Freuden und Traurigkeiten'
Pianist/composer, she was born on October 24th in Chistopol, Tartar, Russia. After studying theory under Nazib Zhiganov, piano under Maria Piatnitskaya at the Kazan Music Academy (1946–49), piano under Leopold Lukomsky and Grigory Kogan, and composition under Albert Leman at the Kazan Conservatory (1949–54), she studied composition

under Nikolai Peiko and Vissarion Shebalin at the Moscow Conservatory (1954–63). She was composer of Documentary Films and composer at the Studio of Art Films in Odessa (1964–69) and continued her research at the Electronic Music Studio in Moscow from 1968. From 1970, she was composer at the Moscow Soviet Theatre. She has composed symphonies, choral and orchestral works, ballets, and chamber music. Her work mentioned above—"The Garden of Joys and Sorrows", or where East meets West—was influenced by her heredity—her mother was Polish-Jewish and her father was a Tartar.

GUGLIEMI, BERNADINE (1907–)
"Can't Sleep for Dreaming"
Singer/songwriter, she was born on August 10th in Kansas City, Missouri, and received a high school education. She was a singer on radio and with dance orchestras. She wrote "Can't Sleep for Dreaming" and "Sabetta".

GUSTAFSON, VERA (1918–)
"Christmas Polka"
Composer/songwriter, she was born on July 21st in Sweden and was educated in high school. She wrote stories and songs for her own marionette show: "Christmas Polka", "Hawaii", "Scrubbing the Steps to Heaven".

GUYNES, CHARLSA ANNE (1933–)
"I Love Lucy"
Songwriter, she was born on January 21st in El Paso, Texas, and was educated at Tulane University. She wrote "Everlovin'", "I Love Lucy", "I Want a Girl", and "Just Wishing".

-H-

HADDEN, FRANCES ROOTS (1910–)
'The Hurricane'
Composer/pianist/songwriter, she was born on August 24th in Kuling, Kiangsi, China, was educated at the Kuling American School, Mt. Holyoke College (BA), and studied with E. Robert Schmitz. She toured the US, Europe, and the Far East as a concert pianist from 1932–40. She married composer/pianist Richard M. Hadden and they toured together. She wrote the music for the dramatic fantasy *A Statesman's Dream,* the revues *The Good Road* and *Take It to the World,* the play *The Hurricane,* which was later filmed as the *Voice of the Hurricane,* a play *Jotham Valley,* a musical play *The Crowning Experience,* and an Asian musical *Turning of the Tide.* She wrote a number of songs with her husband. ASCAP.

HALL, ALICE (1924–)
"The Little Tune"
Composer/accordionist she was born on June 26th in Detroit, Michigan and received a high school education. She led her own trio in Chicago and Detroit and toured. She wrote "The Little Tune" and other songs. ASCAP.

HALL, GERTRUDE "SUGAR" (1912–)
"Survival Stomp"
Composer/songwriter, she was born on June 6th in Sparta, Georgia, and received a high school education. With Edgar Redmond she wrote a number of songs, such as, "Day Train", "It's a Doggone Shame", "School Day Blues", "Sadie Lou", "Survival Stomp", and "That's Why I Cried." ASCAP.

HAMILTON, NANCY (1908–Dec'd.)
"How High the Moon"
Singer/songwriter she was born on July 27th in Sewickley, Pennsylvania, and educated at the Sorbonne in Paris and at Smith College. She appeared in Broadway plays and wrote material for Beatrice Lillie from 1934–36. With Morgan Lewis, she wrote the lyrics for a number of songs, including "Barnaby Beach", "My Day", "How High the Moon", "I Only Know", "I Hate Spring", "If It's Love", "Lazy Kind of Day", and "Teeter Totter Tessie." ASCAP.

HAMMERSTEIN, ALICE (1921–)
"Creole Song"
Songwriter born on May 17th in New York City, the daughter of songwriter Oscar Hammerstein, II. She wrote the lyrics for a number of songs, including, "Creole Song", "Give Me Room", "I've Never Been Away", "Ramblin'", "Results are Just the Same", and "What I Say Goes." ASCAP.

HAMMOND, MARY JANE (1878–1964)
Tune—"Spiritus Vitae"
A composer, she was born in England and died at the Hillingdon Nursing Home on Hillside Road in St. Albans, Herts, England, on January 23, 1964. Her tune with the hymn "O Breath of Life" appeared in *Hymns for the Living Church* (1974).

HANAFORD, PHOEBE A. COFFIN (1829–1921)
"Cast Thy Bread Upon the Waters"
Hymnist and lyricist, she was born on Nantucket Island, Massachusetts, on May 6th, the daughter of Captain George W. Coffin and a descendant

of Tristram Coffin, an early settler of the island. After being tutored by an Episcopal priest in Latin, she began teaching school at age sixteen and married a Mr. Hanaford when she was twenty. In 1862 she wrote the lyrics for "The Empty Sleeve", with composer John W. Dadum, about a Civil War amputee, and it was published by George W. Bagby in *The Southern Literary Messenger*. Her hymn above appeared in *Laudes Domini* (1884) and other hymnals.

In 1868 Phoebe Coffin Hanaford was ordained a Universalist minister and served the Universalist Church in Hingham, Massachusetts. She was the first woman ordained a minister in New England, the first woman to offer an ordaining prayer; the first woman to exchange pulpits with her own son, both being pastors; the first woman to officiate at the marriage of her own daughter; the first woman to serve as chaplain of the Connecticut legislature, which she did in 1870 and 1872, the first woman to give the charge to a male minister, the Reverend W. G. Haskell of Marblehead, Massachusetts; the first woman to attend a Masonic Festival and to respond, by invitation, to a toast.

In 1870 she was installed as pastor at New Haven, Connecticut, was pastor of a church in New Jersey, then returned to New Haven in 1883. She died in Rochester, New York.

HANNA, IONE T. MUNGER (1837–1924)
Tune—"My Ain Countree"

Composer, eldest of the eight children of Martha S. Whitney and Lyman Munger, a druggist in Penn Yan, New York, she was born there. Later the family moved to Galva, Illinois. She married John Rowland Hanna, a banker, and they moved to Denver, Colorado, in 1871. She was a member of the First Congregational Church in Denver, and wrote the music for Mary Demarest's hymn, which appeared in Sankey's *Sacred Songs and Solos* (1881) and later in the *Methodist Hymnal*. She was elected to the Denver School Board in 1893 and was the first woman to hold such office. She was a member of the Daughters of the American Revolution. She died in Los Angeles, California, on August 6, 1924, and funeral services were held in the First Congregational Church in Denver. (Information from Catherine T. Engel, Reference Librarian, Colorado Historical Society, Denver, Colorado 80203.)

HANNA, KATHLEEN
"Spinster"

Singer/songwriter with Bikini Kill. With Joan Jett, she wrote "Spinster" and four of the 12 songs on Jett's album *Pure and Simple* (1994).

HARADON, VIRGINIA (1913–)
"When Are You Comin' Home, Joe?"

Composer/songwriter, she was born on July 27th in Redfield, South Dakota, and received her MA and M.Ed. in college. She wrote "When Are You Comin' Home, Joe?" and other songs. ASCAP.

HARDELOT, HELEN GUY d' (1858–1936)
"Because"

Pianist/composer, she was born near Boulogne-sur-Mer, France. She studied at the Paris Conservatoire under Renaud Maury at age fifteen. She composed many popular songs sung by Nellie Melba, Maurel and Pol Henri Plancon. In 1896, she toured the US as an accompanist for Emma Calve. She married W. L. Rhodes and settled in London. With words by Victor Hugo, she composed the music for "Sans Toi", which became very popular. With words by Fred E. Weatherly, she wrote the song cycle "Elle et lui" (1895); with words by H. L. Harris—"Three Green Bonnets" (1901); and with words by Edward Teschemacher—"Because" (1902), "The Dawn" (1902), and "I Know a Lovely Garden" (1903). She died at London on January 7th.

HARDIN, LILLIAN (1898–1971)
"When You Hear Two Knocks, Just Start Playing"

Pianist/vocalist/composer, she was born in Memphis, Tennessee. After attending Fisk University where she studied music, she worked at Jones' Music Store on South State Street in Chicago where she demonstrated sheet music. About 1919 she tried out as pianist for trumpeter "Sugar Johnny" Smiths' New Orleans Creole Jazz Band, and as she sat down to play, she asked for the sheet music and was told they didn't have any music and futhermore never used any. After she asked what key the first number would be in, the leader didn't know what she was talking about, and just said: "When you hear two knocks, just start playing." So when Lil heard the two knocks she hit the piano so loud they all turned around and looked at her. Within a second she knew what they were playing, so was hired on the spot. She worked part-time with King Oliver (1921–24) and led her own bands. On February 5, 1924, she married Louis Armstrong, who joined her band in 1925. She recorded with the Louis Armstrong Hot Five and Hot Seven (1925–27). After she separated from Armstrong in 1931, she led an all-girl orchestra in the early 1930s, then an all-male orchestra (1935–36). During the 1940s–60s she was mostly a soloist. In 1971 she was playing the "St. Louis Blues" at a Memorial for Louis Armstrong at the Civic Center Plaza in Chicago when she collapsed and died of a heart attack.

HARKNESS, REBEKAH (1915–)
Journey to Love

Composer, she was born on April 17th in St. Louis, Missouri, and was educated at a finishing school. She studied music with Nadia Boulanger in

Paris. She married B. H. Dean and established the ballet workshop the Rebekah Harkness Foundation at Watch Hill, Rhode Island, and the Harkness House in New York City. Her works include "Safari", "Gift of the Magi", "Barcelona Suite", "Music with a Heartbeat", and *Journey to Love* (ballet).

HARRIS, BELLE (1926–)
"You Taught Me Love"
Composer/songwriter, she was born on August 13th in Cincinnati, Ohio, and educated at Rollins College (BA) and the University of Pennsylvania. She wrote "You Taught Me Love" and other songs. ASCAP.

HARRIS, EMMYLOU (1947–)
The Ballad of Sally Rose
Musician/singer/songwriter, she was born April 2nd in Birmingham, Alabama. Her father was a Marine who spent 16 months in a Korean prisoner of war camp. She was raised in Alexandria, Virginia, and had a 4.0 grade point average in high school. She studied drama at the University of North Carolina but left to pursue the guitar. In 1970 she was singing in Greenwich Village nightclubs in New York City, where she met and married songwriter Tom Slocum. They had a daughter, Hallie, but split shortly thereafter. While singing at the Cellar Door in Washington, DC, she met and fell in love with Gram Parsons, and ex-Byrd country/rock musician who had just left the Flying Burrito Brothers. Emmylou cut two albums, *GP* and *Grievous Angel*. But in 1973 Parsons took an overdose of heroin and died at age twenty-six.

Emmylou fled to Los Angeles, where she met Warner Brothers record producer Brian Ahern, who cut her first successful LP, *Pieces of Sky* (1975) with the single "If I Could Only Win Your Love", which hit the Billboard country music chart. Ahern sponsored Emmylou's Hot Band. They were married in 1975 and they had a daughter, Meghann, born in 1978.

Her second LP *Elite Hotel* (1976) was No. 1 on three charts and won her a Grammy. The Hot Band had more hits with *Luxury Liner* (1977) and *Quarter Moon on a Ten Cent Town* (1978). Her *Roses in the Snow* won the Country Music Association award for the best album. In 1983 Harris split with Ahern, and in 1985 she married British-born producer/songwriter Paul Kennerley, who produced her songwriting project *The Ballad of Sally Rose* (1985). It had taken Emmylou six years to complete the lyrics, with the help of Kennerley and others at the end of the project. She sang with Johnny Cash and Willie Nelson on the album *The Other Side of Nashville* (1984). Her other albums and CDs were *Angel Band, Blue Kentucky Girl, Bluebird, Brand New Dance, Cimarron, Duets, Light of the Stable, Profile I: The Best of Emmylou Harris, Profile/Best of Emmylou Harris, Thirteen,* and *White Shoes*.

Emmylou won the TNN Humanitarian award (1992), she served as Grand Marshal for the 40th annual Christmas Parade in Nashville (1992), and appeared on CBS-TV special "Women of Country" in January 1993. Her album/CD *Emmylou Harris and the Nashville Ramblers at the Ryman* was rated A by *Entertainment Weekly* 2/7/92 and was a Grammy winner.

HARRISON, ANNE FORTESCUE (1851–1944)
"In the Gloaming"
Pianist/composer, she was born in England and married Lord Arthur Hill. With Meta Orred, she wrote, "In the Gloaming, Oh My Darling". She also composed piano pieces and two operas.

HATFIELD, JULIANA
"Simplicity Is Beautiful"
Guitarist/singer/songwriter. Her albums are *Hey Babe, Only Everything, Become What You Are*. Her song "Dumb Fun" was composed by stringing together her random thoughts on her bass guitar, her "Fleur de Lys" is sung in French, her "Universal Heart-Beat" combines touchy electric-piano notes with rock-guitar riffs.

HATTON, ALMA W. (1917–)
"Our Wedding Prayer"
Composer/songwriter, she was born on April 3rd in Waterford, New York, and educated at the Troy School of Art. With George Geiger she wrote songs, "Our wedding prayer", "Violino", etc. ASCAP.

HATTON, ANN JULIA KEMBLE (ca. 1757–d. after 1795)
Tammany, or the Indian Chief
She was born in England, and was the younger sister of the great English actress Mrs. Sarah Kemble Siddons (1755–1831). Ann's first husband was named Curtis. She was a large woman with a squint and called herself "Anne Siddons", much to the annoyance of her famous sister. She read lectures at Dr. Graham's Temple of Health in London and attempted to poison herself in Westminster Abbey to attract public attention. She came to New York City in 1793 and wrote the libretto for the opera *Tammany, or the Indian Chief*, with music by James Hewitt. The opera was produced in New York City on March 3, 1794. This was the first opera composed by an American. She also wrote the lyrics for *The Patriot— While Europe Strives with Mad Career* about 1795.

HAVERGAL, FRANCES RIDLEY (1836–1879)
Tune—HERMAS—"Golden Harps Are Sounding"
Composer and hymnist, the youngest child of William Henry Havergal,

she was born at Astley, Worcestershire, England, on December 14, 1836 and never married. In 1852–53, she studied in Dusseldorf, Germany. In 1880 she published *Life Chords, Coming to the King* (1886) and other books. In 1878 she moved from her home in Leamington to Oystermouth, Glamorganshire, Wales. She wrote many popular hymns, such as

Take my life, and let it be
Consecrated, Lord to Thee,
Truehearted, wholehearted, faithful and loyal,
King of our lives, by Thy grace we will be.

She once wrote to a friend. "It does seem wonderful that God should so use and bless my hymns, and yet it really does seem as if the seal of his own blessing were set upon them, for so many testimonies have reached me. Writing is *praying* for me." She died at Caswell Bay near Swansea, Wales on June 3, 1879. Her hymns appear in the *Broadman* (1977); *Christian Science* (1937); *Episcopal* (1940); *Lutheran* (1941); *Methodist* (1966); *Presbyterian* (1955) hymnals; and the *Pilgrim Hymnal* (1958).

HAYS, DORIS ENRNESTINE (1941–)
Southern Voices for Orchestra
Composer and pianist, she was born on August 6th in Memphis, Tennessee. After studying at the University of Chattanooga (BM 1963), piano and harpsichord at the Munich Hochschule fur Music (1963–66), composition and electronic music at the University of Wisconsin (MM 1968), composition and electronic music at the University of Iowa (1969), in 1971 she won first prize in the International Competition for Interpreters of New Music at Rotterdam. She has received many awards since. She has composed chamber music, instrumental and vocal music, electronic and mixed-media. The work mentioned above was commissioned for the 50th anniversary of the Chattanooga Symphony Orchestra in 1981.

HEARN, NAIDA O'HARA (1931–)
Tune—"Hearn"
Composer/pianist, she was born on December 28th in Palmerston North, New Zealand, and was graduated from Palmerston North Technical High School. She married and taught piano and musical theory. She served as a church pianist and composed several gospel choruses. Her tune "Jesus, Name Above All Names" appeared in *The Hymnal for Worship & Celebration* (Baptist 1986).

HELVERING, SANDI PATTI (1956–)
Tune—"Name of the Lord"
Composer/vocalist, she was born on July 12th in Oklahoma City, Oklahoma, the daughter of gospel singers Carolyn and Ron Patty. She was

educated at Anderson University in Indiana (BA in music 1979). For ten consecutive years she won awards as the best female vocalist from the Gospel Music Association. She is divorced from her manager and is the mother of four children. She wrote the tune "Name of the Lord" with the hymn by Gloria Gaither and Phil McHugh—"In the name of the Lord", which appeared in *The Hymnal for Worship & Celebration* (Baptist 1986).

HEMMENT, MARGUERITE E. (1908–)
   "Measures to Health"
Composer/songwriter, she was born on April 19th in Carlyle, Illinois, and was educated at Washington University and the University of Wisconsin. She wrote "Measures to Health" and other songs.

HENDERSON, GWEN (1908–)
   "Be My Lovin' Baby"
Composer/songwriter, she was born on July 11th in Toronto, Ontario, Canada, and received a high school education. With Al Trace and Perry Hettel, she wrote a number of songs, "Be My Lovin' Baby", "I Guess It Must Be Love", and "Let Me Be Your Honey, Honey".

HERITTE, LOUISE VIARDOT (1841–1918)
   "Das Bacchusfest"
Contralto/composer, she was born on December 14th in Paris, the daughger of singer/composer Pauline Garcia Viardot and Louis Viardot. She taught at the Conservatory in St. Petersburg, Russia, Hoch's Conservatory at Frankfort au Main and in Berlin. She married the French consul-general Heritte in 1862. Mrs. Heritte composed the comic opera *Lindoro,* performed at Weimar in 1879, the cantata "Das Bacchusfest" at Stockholm, Sweden, in 1880, and numerous songs. She died in Heidelberg on January 17th.

HERRING, ANNE (1945–)
   Tune—"Easter Song"
Composer/singer, she was born on September 22nd in Grafton, North Dakota. She is a singer/writer and recording artist for the folk/pop group called "Second Chapter of Acts". She married recording producer Buck Herring. She composed the tune "Easter Song", which appeared in *The Hymnal for Worship & Celebration* (Baptist 1986).

HERSH, EVELYN S. (1911–)
   "Have Faith"
Composer/songwriter, she was born on December 25th in Brooklyn, New York, and was educated at college. She wrote "Have Faith" and other songs. ASCAP.

HERSHEY, JUNE (1909–)
"Deep in the Heart of Texas"
Lyricist, she was born in Los Angeles. With music by her husband, Don Swander, she wrote the words for the above song in 1941 — "The stars at night are big and bright — Deep in the Heart of Texas".

HERZOG, FRIEDA L. (1932–)
"Acapulco"
Songwriter born February 7th in Tucson, Arizona, and educated at McBride's College, Trinity University, St. Mary's University. She also studied music privately and performed for the US Military Forces in Europe and Japan. With Jim Thomas she wrote a number of songs, "Acapulco", "My Dancing Doll", "Life of Love", "Sugar Lump", "Where Were You When the Button Popped?", and "You Are Mine."

HIER, ETHEL GLENN (1889–1971)
Asolo Bells
Composer, pianist, and teacher, she was born on June 25th in Cincinnati, Ohio. After graduating from the Cincinnati Conservatory in 1908, she taught piano lessons. Later she studied composition with Kelley at the Conservatory, then in 1912 with Hugo Kaun in Germany. After moving to New York City, she taught and also studied composition with Goerschius and later with Bloch at the Institute of Musical Art. Her orchestra work *Asolo Bells* was played at the Festival of American Music at Eastman Conservatory in Rochester, New York, in 1939 and later by the Cincinnati Symphony Orchestra. She composed chamber music, orchestral works, and songs.

HIGGINBOTHAM, IRENE (1918–Dec'd.)
Boogie Woogie Land
Composer/pianist, she was born on June 11th in Worcester, Massachusetts, and studied music with Kemper Harold and Frederic Hall. With Dan Fisher she wrote a number of songs, "Blue Violets", "Hello Suzanne", "Harlem Song", "Good Morning, Heartache", "That Did It Marie", "No Good Man", "A Knock on the Door", "This Will Make You Laugh", "No Sale", and the album *Boogie Woogie Land*. ASCAP.

HILER, CHARLOTTE ALLENE (1910–1958)
"The Kansas Waltz"
Composer born on January 9th in Junction City, Kansas. With Maria Grever, Teddy Powell, and Dave Ringle, she wrote a number of songs, such as "Billy Breeze Come Play With Me", "Funny Ole Romantic Me", "Have No Doubt in your Heart", "The Kansas Waltz", "Love One", and "Twinkle Toes". She died on June 3rd in Ho-ho-kus, New Jersey. ASCAP.

HILL, DEDETTE LEE (1900–1950)
"There's a Little Box of Pine on the 7:29"
Songwriter born on November 2nd in Lynchburg, Virginia, she married Billy Hill and wrote the lyrics for a number of songs with him and Johnny Marks. They include "Address Unknown", "Put On an Old Pair of Shoes", "Old Folks", "I Can't Find Anything to Suit My Mood", "There's Someone Else in My Place Now", and "We Speak of You Often". She died on June 5th in Hollywood, California. ASCAP.

HILL, MABEL WOOD (1891–1954)
The Jolly Beggars
Composer, she was born in Brooklyn, New York. She studied under Rothwell and Rubner (1917), and the first recital of her songs was given in 1918. She helped found the Brooklyn Music School Settlement and the Hudson River Music School. Her ballet pantomime, *Pinocchio,* was on tour throughout the US (1936–37). *The Jolly Beggars* was presented at the Banff Festival in Canada. She died in Stamford, Connecticut.

HILL, MAY (1888–Dec'd.)
"Everbody Loves a Big Brass Band"
Composer/organist/singer/songwriter, she was born on August 11th in Cleveland, Ohio, and was educated on scholarships to the Chicago Musical College and Columbia School of Music. She was a pianist in film theaters, with publishing companies, and on radio. With Roger Graham, Walter Hirsch, and Marvin Lee, she wrote a number of songs, "Dear Old Girl", "Everybody Loves a Big Brass Band", "I Believe in You", "Take Me Back to Dreamland", and "You'll Want Me Back Someday".

HILL, MILDRED J. (1859–1916)
"Happy Birthday to You"
Organist/concert pianist/arranger, she was born in Louisville, Kentucky. With words by her sister, Patty Smith Hill, she composed the music for "Good Morning to All" (1893), which later became "Happy Birthday to You". Actually the song appeared as "Happy Greetings to All" in *The Anniversary and Sunday School Music Book No. 2,* issued by Horace Waters in 1858 (per ad in the *New York Times* of October 6, 1858). After the Hill sisters changed the wording to "Happy Birthday to You", it became the most widely sung song in the history of the US. With a population of some 250 million people, it means the song is sung on an average of 684,931 times every day during the year—that is—every year.

HILLER, PHYLLIS (1927–)
"I Don't Want to Walk Alone"
Composer/songwriter she was born on August 5th in Petaluma, California, and was educated at San Francisco State College (BA) and the Uni-

versity of California (AA). She wrote a number of musical commercials and the songs "Lucky High Heels" and "I Don't Want to Walk Alone".

HODAS, DOROTHY GERTRUDE (1912–)
"Love of my Life"
Composer/pianist born on February 23rd at Perth Amboy, New Jersey, and educated at Newark State Teachers College. She wrote "Love of My Life" and "When the Boys Come Home Again". ASCAP.

HODGES, FAUSTINA HASSE (1823–1895)
"Dreams"
Organist and composer, she was born on August 7th in Malmesbury, England, the daughter of organist/composer Edward Hodges. With her father, she emigrated to Canada in 1838, then to New York City. In 1839 he served as organist of St. John's Chapel, then as organist at the new Trinity Church. She served as organist of churches in Brooklyn, New York, then became professor of organ, piano, and singing at the Troy Female Seminary in Troy, New York. Later she was an organist at churches in Philadelphia. Ms. Hodges composed piano pieces, hymn tunes, and songs. "Dreams" and "Rose Bush" were popular. She died on February 4th in Philadelphia.

HOFF, VIVIAN BEAUMONT (1911–)
"I Look to My Lord"
Composer/pianist/songwriter, she was born on December 17th in Shelby, Indiana, and educated at Butler University and Jordan College of Music. She studied with Bomar Cramer, William Pelz, and Thelma Todd. She wrote "My Father in Heaven", "I Look to My Lord", and "Keep the Star Spangled Banner waving." ASCAP.

HOKANSON, MARGRETHE (1893–1975)
Choral—*O Praise Him*
Composer, arranger, conductor, organist, and pianist, she was born in Duluth, Minnesota, on December 19, 1983, and was educated at the American Conservatory in Chicago, at the Margaret Morrison School with Joseph Lhevinne, and studied privately. She was dean of the Organ Department at St. Olaf College in Northfield, Minnesota, director of the Northland Choral Group, she founded the Nordic Choral Ensemble (1939–43), and was associate professor of music at Allegheny College in Meadville, Pennsylvania (1944–54). She died on April 24, 1975.

HOLDEN, ANNE STRATTON (1887–)
"Dusk Comes Floating By"
Composer born on April 17th in Cleburne, Texas, Holden was educated at the University of Texas and Damrosch Conservatory. She studied with

Howard Brockway and Etta Wilson. She wrote the songs, "Ah Love, How Soon?" "Boats of Mine", "Parting at Morning", "Plantation Ditty", "May Magic", "The sun at Last", and "Wash Day".

HOLDEN, LIBBY (1923–)
"The USS Constellation"
Composer/singer/songwriter, she was born on November 19th in Scranton, Pennsylvania, and was educated at the Engineering School of Pratt Institute and New York Technical Institute in engineering. Her instrumentals and songs include "All I Do Is Try", "I Guess I'm Good for Nothing But the Blues", "Don't Ever Say You're Gonna Leave Me", "Lonely Woman", "Sax-Man", and "The USS Constellation."

HOLIDAY, BILLIE (1915–1959)
"Fine and mellow"
Singer/songwriter, she was born Eleanor Fagan Gough in Baltimore, Maryland. She was the stepdaughter of banjoist/guitarist Clarence Holiday, who played in Fletcher Henderson's Band. She sang in clubs on Fifty-second Street in New York City during the 1930s, with Count Basie's band, Artie Shaw, Benny Carter, Paul Whiteman, and others. For a time her accompanist was Eddie Heywood, Jr. She became known as "Lady Day". She married trumpeter Joe Guy. She was arrested twice on narcotics charges.

With Arthur Herzog, Jr., Billie wrote "Don't Explain" and "God Bless the Child"; with Jeanne Burns she wrote "Who Needs You?"; alone she wrote "I Love My Man. I'm a Liar If I Say I Don't" and "Fine and Mellow—My Man Don't Love Me, Treats Me Oh So Mean." As of 1994 her videos available were *The Many Faces of Lady Day* and *Sound of Jazz*. A postage stamp was issued in her honor in 1994.

HOLMES, AUGUSTA (1847–1903)
Psalm—*In exita*
A composer, born Mary Anne Holmes of Irish parentage in Paris, France, on December 16, 1847, she studied harmony and counterpoint with H. Lambert, organist of the cathedral at Versailles, and later with César Franck (in 1875). *In exita* was performed by the Société Philharmonique (1873) and her "Hymme â la paix" at Florence in May 1890. She also wrote two or three symphonies and operas. She died in Paris on January 28, 1903.

HOLST, IMOGEN CLARE (1907–)
"Blow the Wind Southerly"
Pianist/composer/teacher, she was born on April 12th in Richmond, Surrey, England. She wrote "Southerly Winds—Blow the Wind Southerly" and other songs.

HOOVEN, MARILYN (1924–)
"Any Way the Wind Blows"
Composer/singer/songwriter born on October 17th in Aurora, Illinios,
and educated in public and private schools, she sang with the Ted Weems
orchestra (1934–44) and also on the "Steve Allen Show". She married
composer/trumpeter Joseph D. Hooven, and he wrote songs with her,
also Wm. D. "By" Dunham and Inez James, "Any Way the Wind
Blows", "Baby, Baby, Wait for Me", "Jesse James", "Lucky Duck",
"La-boulaya", "Oh, What a Beautiful Dream", "It'll Be a Merry Christmas." ASCAP.

HOPEKIRK, HELEN (1856–1945)
"A Norland Eve"
Composer, pianist, and teacher, she was born on May 20th in Edinburgh,
Scotland. After attending Leipzig Conservatory (1876–78), she made
her debut with the Leipzig Gewandhaus Orchestra on November 28,
1878. After giving concerts in Europe and Great Britain, she married music critic and landscape painter William A. Wilson on August 2, 1882.
After her debut with the Boston Symphony Orchestra on December 7,
1883, with her husband as her manager, she began a four-year concert
tour of the US. She then studied piano with Leschetizky (1887–89) and
composition in Paris (1892–94). After accepting a teaching position in
1897 at the New England Conservatory in Boston, she also taught privately. Hopekirk composed songs, chamber and instrumental pieces, and
piano pieces. She died on November 19th in Cambridge, Massachusetts.

HORNABROOK, MARY WISEMAN (1850–1930)
Tune—"Even Me" (2)
Composer, she studied under Walter Macfarren, and was the sister of the
Rev. F. L. Wiseman. She was the wife of the Rev. John Hornabrook. Her
hymn tune appeared in the *New People's Hymnary* (1922) and in the
British *Methodist Hymn-Book* (1935).

HORTON, ELIZABETH (1902–)
Adult Education Piano Method
Composer/pianist/singer/songwriter, she was born on March 10th in
Philadelphia, Pennsylvania, and was educated at the University of Cali-
fornia at Los Angeles. She wrote the song, "I'm Proud to Be an American"
and an *Adult Education Piano Method* in two volumes. ASCAP.

HOSEY, ATHENA (1929–)
"Saga of Tom Dooley"
Composer/songwriter, she was born on July 27th in New York, and was
educated at Barnard College (BA). She was a pianist in nightclubs in

New York City (1945–52). With Hal Gordon and Guy Wood she wrote a number of songs, such as "Highway of Love", "The Glide", "Lonely Road", "Making Time", "Saturday Dance", "Scene of the Crime", "Someone Else's Boy", "Saga of Tom Dooley", and "Tribute to the pioneers." ASCAP.

HOWE, JULIA WARD (1819–1910)

"Mine eyes have seen the glory of the coming of the Lord. . . Glory! Glory! Hallelujah!"

She was born in New York City on May 27, 1819, and married Dr. Samuel Gridley Howe in 1843, and then moved to Boston. Upon visiting the troops at Bailey's Cross Roads, near Fairfax Court House, Virginia, on November 20, 1861, and hearing the soldiers sing "John Brown's Body," she returned to her hotel in Washington, DC and that evening wrote her inspiring words, and called her hymn "The Battle Hymn of the Republic." A Unitarian, she died at Middletown, Rhode Island, on October 17, 1910. Her hymn was published in the *American Service* (1968); *Baptist* (1973); *Broadman* (1977); *Family of God* (1976); *Joyfully Sing* (1968); *Methodist* (1966); *Songs of Praise* (1931); and *The Pilgrim Hymnal* (1958); together with 46 recordings listed in *Phonolog Reports* (1978), Los Angeles, California.

HOWE, MARY (1882–1964)

Le jongleur de Notre Dame

Composer and pianist, she was born on April 4th in Richmond, Virginia. She studied piano with Burmeister in Germany, with Boulanger in Paris, with Hutcheson, Randolph, and composition with Strube at the Peabody Conservatory, then toured from 1920–35 with pianist Anita Hull. She was one of the founders of the Association of American Women Composers. Her ballet mentioned above was composed in 1959. She wrote over 20 orchestral works, chamber, vocal, and piano music. She died on September 14th in Washington, DC.

HOWE, MAUDE JOHNSON (1887–Dec'd.)

"Watch Your Step"

Composer, she was born on April 9th in Bartow, Florida, and was educated at Southern College. She married composer/conductor Edward S. Chennette (1895–1963) and collaborated with him writing songs, the National Safety song "Watch Your Step", "Flag of Liberty", "My Valentine", "Wanting You", and "Your Shrine". ASCAP.

HUEBNER, ILSE (1898–)

The Modern Pianist

Composer/pianist, she was born in Vienna, Austria, and educated at the Vienna Music Academy. She taught at the College of Music in Cincinnati, Ohio, founded and directed the Smokey Mountain Summer Music School. Her *The Modern Pianist* in three volumes was on music therapy; she also wrote *Musical One by One*.

HUNKINS, EUSEBIA SIMPSON (1902–)
Smokey Mountain
Composer, she was born on June 20th in Troy, Ohio, and studied with James Friskin, Rubin Goldmark, and Albert Stoessel on a foundation scholarship at Juilliard in New York City; she also studied with Darius Milhaud and Ernest Hutcheson; with Ernest Von Dohnanyi at Ohio University; at Tanglewood and Salzburg, Austria. Her works include the folk opera *Smokey Mountain;* the choral drama *Wondrous Love;* the one-act operas *Maniian, Mice in Council, Reluctant Hero, Young Lincoln,* a Knox College commission, *Young Lincoln II, Spirit Owl;* the octavios *Hey Betty Martin, Old Sister Phoebe, Shenandoah, What Wondrous Love, Forest Voices, Rosa, Shall I Marry?* and *Why*.

HUNTER, ALBERTA (1895–1984)
Down-hearted Blues
Composer and blues singer, she was born on April 1st in Memphis, Tennessee. She sang in nightclubs in Chicago and New York City in the 1920s, with Fletcher Henderson as her accompanist. After singing in Europe between 1927 and 1937, she returned to the US. She toured with the USO during World War II. In 1956 she retired as a singer and became a nurse. Then in 1977 she resumed her career and sang at The White House for President and Mrs. Carter in December 1978. She died on October 17, 1984, in New York City. Her blues composition mentioned above was written in 1922 and became popular. As of 1994 her available albums were *Amtrak Blues, London Sessions, The Silver Lining,* and *Young Alberta Hunter*.

HUNTER, NAN GREENE (1938–)
"Father, This Hour Has Been Our One Joy"
Hymnist born in Salt Lake City and educated at Brigham Young University, she married Richard A. Hunter and they have eight children. They live in San Jose, California. Her hymn appeared in the Mormon Hymnal (1985).

HUTCHINSON, ABBY (1829–1892)
"Kind Words Can Never Die"
Singer and composer, she was born on Augsut 29th in Milford, New Hampshire, one of 13 children of Mary Leavitt and Jesse Hutchinson. In 1842, Judson, John, Asa, and Abby Hutchinson toured the New England states as the Hutchinson Family Singers with great success and gave their

New York City debut in May 1843. The group sang before anti-slavery groups and temperance conventions. In 1844 they performed at The White House for President and Mrs. Tyler. In 1845–46 they toured Great Britain, and their concerts attracted thousands of people. Abby was married in 1849 and retired to compose songs. Her three brothers formed a trio, but failed to attract much attention; however, they did sing in 1862 in The White House for President and Mrs. Lincoln. Abby Hutchinson's song above was written in 1859 and a setting for Tennyson's *Ring out, Wild Bells* in 1891. Meanwhile she made several arrangements of southern black spirituals. Some of her family moved to Minnesota and founded the town of Hutchinson in 1855. Abby died on November 24th in New York City.

HUTTON, LAURA JOSEPHINE (1852–1888)
Tune—"Eternity"
A composer, the sister and fellow worker of the Rev. V. W. Hutton, Vicar of Sneinton, she was born at Spridlington, England, on July 17, 1852. When her brother retired, she went to live with him in Lincoln. She wrote tunes for Mrs. Alexander's *Hymns for Children* and also published a book of her own hymn tunes, *Twenty Hymns for Little Children* (1880). After her brother's death, she returned to Spridlington, where she died on June 17, 1888. Her hymn tune appeared in *Hymns Ancient and Modern* (1904).

HYDE, MADELINE (1907–)
"My Stubborn Heart"
Composer/songwriter, she was born on December 12th in Chicago, Illinois, and was educated at a girl's finishing school in Paris. She wrote "It's Happened Again", "Little Girl", "My Stubborn Heart", and "She Fell in the Fall of the Year". ASCAP.

HYMAN, PHYLLIS (1950–1995)
"It's Not About You"
R&B and jazz singer born on June 30, 1950. Her albums are *Living All Alone, Prime of My Life, Under Her Spell, I Don't Want to Change the World* (1991), and *I Refuse to Be Lonely* (issued in 1995 after her death), which included "It's Not About You, It's About Me", one of five songs on the album which she cowrote. After suffering the death of loved ones and disappointment, she committed suicide on her 45th birthday.

HYNDE, CHRISTINE E. "CHRISSIE" (1951–)
"Middle of the Road"
Born in Akron, Ohio, she was the lead singer/songwriter for The Pretenders with James Honeyman Scott and Pete Farndon, both of whom died in the 1980s. They were replaced by guitarist Adam Seymour and

bassist Andy Hobson. Her albums *Learning to Crawl* (1983) included "Middle of the Road", which she wrote; her other albums are *Get Close, Packed, Pretenders, Pretenders II, Singles, Last of the Independents* (1994). She has been a vegetarian since 1969 and thinks meat eaters are "retarded". Hynde has lived in England for the past 20 years.

-I-

IAN, JANIS (1951–)
"At Seventeen"
Singer and songwriter, born Janis Eddy Fink on April 7th, as a child she played the piano and guitar. At age fourteen she wrote "Society's Child" about a white girl and a black boy, which was No. 14 hit single in 1967. Her first album *Janis Ian* was successful but somewhat notorious and she retired from singing in 1971. She wrote the songs for her 1974 album *Stars*. Her 1975 album, still available in 1994, *Between the Lines* contained the song "At Seventeen", which became a platinum record and earned her a Grammy. In her 1993 album *Breaking the Silence*, she revealed she was a lesbian.

IANNELLI, THERESA ROSE (1936–)
"Secret Sorrow"
Composer/songwriter, born on August 4th in Philadelphia, Pennsylvania, and educated at Notre Dame Academy, she wrote songs such as "Secret Sorrow".

IRVINE, JESSIE SEYMOUR (1836–1887)
Tune—"Crimond"
Daughter of a Presbyterian minister in Dunottar, Aberdeenshire, Scotland, she was born there and later lived in manses at Peterhead and Crimond, Scotland, where she died, having named her hymn tune after the town. The tune was first used in the *Northern Psalter* (1872). Apparently she gave the tune to David Grant for harmonization. It appeared in the *Baptist Hymn Book* (London, 1966) and in *Hymns for the Living Church* (1974) with the hymn "The Lord's my shepherd, I shall not want."

IRWIN, LOIS (b. 1926)
"He'll make a way"
Pianist, singer, hymnist, and composer, she was born in Westmont, Illinois, on July 29, 1926. She was a gospel singer with her husband in evangelistic programs. Her hymn above is listed with five recordings in *Phonolog Reports* of Los Angeles, California, with four recordings for "It Was Jesus," three for "The Healer", and one for "There'll Be an Answer Bye and Bye" (1978).

IVANOFF, ROSE BRIGNOLE (1908–Dec'd.)
"Into the Lonely Night"
Composer/songwriter born on October 15th in Berlin, Germany, she studied music in Germany, Italy, and the United States. She wrote the songs "If My Love Has Eyes of Blue", "Into the Lonely Night", "Secret", and "Shadows". ASCAP.

IVEY, JEAN EICHELBERGER (1923–)
Sea-change
Composer, she was born on July 3rd in Washington, DC. After attending Trinity College (BA 1944), she earned her degrees in music at the Peabody Conservatory (MM in piano 1946) and the Eastman School (MM in composition 1956). She taught at the Peabody Conservatory in Baltimore and founded the electronic music studio there in 1969, which she directed. She toured Europe, Mexico, and the US as a pianist in the 1970s and received her doctorate at the University of Toronto (DMus in composition 1972). Ivey received grants from the NEA to compose *Sea-change,* performed by the Baltimore Symphony Orchestra in 1982 and was appointed coordinator of the composition department at Peabody in 1982. She has composed an opera, instrumental, orchestra, and vocal works.

-J-

JACKSON, JANET (1966–)
"That's the Way Love Goes"
Singer/songwriter, she was born on May 16th in Gary, Indiana, the sister of singer Michael Jackson. Her hit single "Control", in album *Rhythm Nation 1814,* sold over 2 million in 1989. She also had a platinum single "Miss You Much" (1989), a video *Rhythm Nation 1814,* with Luther Vandross on June 1990 Top singles for "The Best Things in Life Are Free", and an album *janet* (1993). With James Harris III and Terry Lewis, she wrote, "That's the Way Love Goes," which won a 1994 Grammy.

JACKSON, JILL (1913–)
"Let There Be Peace On Earth"
Composer/songwriter, she was born on August 25th in Independence, Missouri, and was educated at a junior college. She married composer/pianist Seymour "Sy" Miller and they wrote a number of songs: "Let There Be Peace on Earth . . . Let It Begin With Me", which was used in the crusade for Peace Program and in a USIA film for Japan; "I Like to Ride on My Bike", "Listen to the Wind", "My Very Good Friend, the Sandman", "Talk It Over with Your Heart", "Traffic Light Song", "High

Upon a Mountain", "Once Upon a Summertime", "Still Small Voice", "Ask Your Heart to Show the Way", "Keep in Touch with Your Heavenly Father", and "Lord Loves a Laughin' Man". ASCAP.

JACKSON, MAHALIA (1911–1972)
"Lord, Don't Move the Mountain"
Gospel/jazz singer/songwriter, she was born near New Orleans, Louisiana. After both her parents died, she went to Chicago at age fifteen. She sang on gospel tours throughout the Midwest. With Doris Akers she wrote "Lord, Don't Move the Mountain But Give Me Strength to Climb It." She recorded "God Gonna Separate the Wheat from the Tares" (1934); "Move On Up a Little Higher" (1954), her first hit record. Jackson sang at concerts at Carnegie Hall, New York City (1950–56); and at the inauguration of President Kennedy in January 1961; and at the march on Washington, DC in 1963. She sang "Precious Lord, Take My Hand" at Morehouse College, Atlanta, Georgia, following the funeral of the Reverend Dr. Martin Luther King, Jr. (1968). Jackson toured Europe (1971) and was hospitalized in Munich, Germany, for coronary heart disease. She died of heart disease at Evergreen Park, Illinois, in 1972. As of 1994 her available albums were *America's Favorite Hymns, Gospels, Spirituals, Hymns, Greatest Hits,* and *The Great Mahalia Jackson.*

JACKSON, MILLIE (1944–)
"If Loving You Is Wrong I Don't Want to Be Right"
Soul, country, pop, and rock singer and songwriter, she was born on July 15th in Thomson, Georgia. After moving to New Jersey in 1959, she sang in clubs in New York City in the 1960s–70s, and her single "Child of God" (1972) rated on the rhythm and blues chart and "Hurts So Good" on the pop charts. Her album *Caught Up* included soul, country, and rock music. Her song mentioned above, written in 1975, has been sung by many other performers. As of 1994 her albums *An Imitation of Love* and *Young Man, Older Woman* were available for purchase.

JACKSON, WANDA (1937–)
"Right or Wrong"
Country, pop, and gospel singer and songwriter, she was born on October 20th in Maud, Oklahoma. At age twelve she sang on a half-hour program on radio station KLPR in Oklahoma City, which became very popular. She recorded "You Can't Have My Love" with the Brazos Valley Boys in 1954, then toured with Hank Thompson and Elvis Presley from 1955–56. Jackson recorded her own song, mentioned above in 1961, and "Kicking Our Hearts Around" for Buck Owens. She toured Europe and Japan, married Wendell Goodman, who became her manager, and was honored at a country music festival in September 1992.

Her albums *Greatest Hits* and *Rocking in the Country* were available in 1994.

JAMES, CHERYL "SALT" (1963–)
Very Necessary
A rap singer/songwriter, she was born in Queens, New York City. While a senior in college, she met Sandi "Pepa" Denton in 1985. After graduation "Salt" worked at Sears in Queens. She heard of a job opening there and "Pepa" got the job. They formed the rap group Salt-N-Pepa and then asked De De "Spinderella" Roper to join the trio. Their hit "Push It" climbed to the top of the charts in 1987. Other hits were "Express Yourself " (1990); the single "Start Me Up" was in the film *Stay Tuned* (1992); "Black Magic", at Roseland in New York 1992, and recorded the album *Very Necessary* (1994). She has co-authored her songs with other writers.

JAMES, DOROTHY (1901–1982)
"Paola and Francesca"·
Composer and teacher, she was born on December 1st in Chicago, Illinois. She was a pupil of Adolf Weidig, Gruenberg, Hanson, Krenek and Healy Willan. She studied at the Chicago Musical College, received her master's degree at the American Conservatory of Music, and then taught at Eastern Michigan University at Ypsilanti (1927–68). Her opera mentioned above was composed in 1933. She wrote orchestral works and instrumental pieces and chorals: "Christmas Night" (1933), "The Little Jesus Came to Town" (1935), "Mary's Lullaby" (1937), "The Nativity Hymn" (1957), etc. She died on December 1st in St. Petersburg, Florida.

JAMES, ETTA (1938–)
"Roll With Me, Honey"
Blues/gospel/rock singer/songwriter, she wrote "Roll With Me, Honey" and other songs. Her albums are *At Last, Blues in the Night, Come a Little Closer, Gospel Soul of Etta James, Her Greatest Sides Volume I, R&B Dynamite, Rocks the House, Second Time Around, Seven Year Itch, Stickin' to My Guns,* and *Sweetest Peaches Part II.* Her album *The Right Time* won a 1993 Grammy.

JAMES, INEZ ELEANOR (1919–Dec'd.)
"Vaya con Dios"
Composer/songwriter, she was born on November 15th in New York, New York, and was educated at the Hollywood Conservatory. She wrote the film score for *Mr. Big;* songs for films *This Is the Life, Top Man, When Johnny Comes Marching Home.* Her collaborators include Buddy Pepper and Sidney Miller, film title songs "Pillow Talk", "Portrait in

Black"; songs "Come to Baby, Do", "I Can See It Your Way", "I'm Sorry But I'm Glad", "It's Christmas", "Now You've Gone and Hurt My Southern Pride", "Sing a Jingle", "That's the Way He Does It", "Walk It Off", etc. ASCAP.

JAMES, JEAN EILEEN (1934–)
"It's All Over Town"
Songwriter born on November 6th in Burlington, Wisconsin, with Sverre Elsmo she wrote "It's All Over Town".

JANES, ELSIE (BIERBOWER) (1889–1956)
"Love, your magic spell is everywhere"
Actress/songwriter born on March 16th in Columbus, Ohio, as a child she was known as "Little Elsie" in vaudeville. She appeared in Broadway musicals and made her London debut in 1914. She was the first American to entertain the troops in World War I. With Edmund Goulding, Jerome Kern, and others, she wrote a number of songs: "Any Time's the Time to Fall in Love", "From the Valley", "I'm True to the Navy Now", "Live and Love Today", "Molly-O-mine", "O Give Me Time for Tenderness", "Some Sort of Somebody", and "A Little Love". ASCAP.

JANIS, JOAN GARDNER (1926–Dec'd.)
"Learn to Rock"
Composer/songwriter born November 16th in Chicago and educated at Los Angeles Community College, she was an actress in films. With Adelaide Halpern, she wrote the songs, "Good Ship Rock 'n Roll", "Holly Time", "Learn' to Rock", "Spelling Rock 'n Roll", and "Toy Piano Boogie". She also wrote children's music books. ASCAP.

JANOTHA, NATALIA MARIE CECILIA (1856–1932)
Anthem—*Ave Maria*
Composer and pianist, born in Warsaw, Poland, on June 8, 1856, she was a pupil of Clara Schumann, Princess Czartoryska, Rudorff, F. Weber, and others. She played at the Prussian Court for William I, and later for Frederick III and for Kaiser Wilhelm II. She went to London and played for Queen Victoria, and later for Edward VII and for George V. She wrote her *Ave Maria* for Pope Leo XIII. She was known as the "Kaiser's pianist," and so was arrested in 1916 and deported. She settled at The Hague, in the Netherlands, where she died on June 9, 1932.

JARDON, DOROTHY (1889–)
"In the Land of Cherry Blossoms"
Composer/songwriter born June 1st in New York, and educated in public and parochial schools. She was a dramatic soprano with the Chicago

Opera Company and sang in Broadway musicals. During World War I, she entertained troops at Camp Upton and also sold Liberty Bonds. She married lyricist Edward Madden and with him and Joseph Daly, Arthur Lamb, and others wrote a number of songs, such as "In the Land of Cherry Blossoms", "Lotus Sam", "My Only One", "The World Can't Go 'Round Without You", "Violet", and "What Could Be Sweeter?".

JASMYN, JOAN (1888–1995)
"Under the Spell of Your Kiss"
Composer/songwriter born on July 26th in Hull, Iowa, she wrote "Angel Cake Lady and Gingerbread Man", "One More Kiss", "Rocky Mountain Rose", and "Under the Spell of Your Kiss". ASCAP. She died on July 3rd in New York City.

JAVITS, JOAN (1928–)
"Lovin' Spree"
Composer/songwriter born on August 17th in New York, and educated at Vassar College (BA), she wrote the stage scores for *Young Abe Lincoln, Quality Street, Hotel Passionato,* and songs with Mario Braggiotti, Philip Springer, and Victor Ziskin.

JEAN, ELSIE (1907–1953)
"Song of My Heart"
Composer/songwriter born on May 14th in New York City and educated at Columbia University and the National Conservatory on a scholarship. She won the Carl Schurz Society award. Jean conducted her own radio program for three years. She wrote "Come Love Me", "I Love You So", "On Hills of Freedom", and "Song of My Heart". ASCAP. She died on June 9th in New York City.

JENKINS, ELLA (1924–)
"Tah-boo"
Composer/singer/songwriter born on August 6th in St. Louis, Missouri and educated at San Francisco State College (BA), she served as a teenage program director for the YWCA in Chicago and toured US and Europe for the School Assembly Service (1962–63). She wrote "Tah-boo", "You'll Sing a Song and I'll Sing a Song", and other songs. ASCAP.

JESSYE, EVA (1895–Dec'd.)
The Chronicle of Job
Composer and choral conductor, she was born on January 20th in Coffeeville, Kansas. Sometime after studying at Western University, Kansas, and Langston University, Oklahoma, she moved to New York City,

where she studied under Goetschius and Will Marion Cook. After forming her own choral group, they toured and appeared on radio programs. She was choral director for Gershwin's *Porgy and Bess*. She composed the folk oratorio *Paradise Lost and Regained* (1934), the one mentioned above in 1936, and other works.

JETT, JOAN (1960–)
"Just As I Am"
Singer/songwriter, she was born on September 22nd in Philadelphia. Singer with the Blackbirds. After sitting through the 1992 Republican Convention in Houston, Texas, and hearing speech after speech filled with vitriol and animosity, Jett and songwriter Desmond Child wrote the words "I'm Only Flesh and Blood/Oh I Wish That You Could Love Me As I Am." They also wrote "Wonder" about the state of the world, and with Kathleen Hanna of Bikini Kill wrote "Spinster". Jett's albums are *Good Music, The Hit List, Notorious, Up Your Alley, Pure and Simple* (1994).

JOHNSON, LUCILLE (1907–Dec'd.)
"Little Switch Engine"
Singer/songwriter born on October 26th in Tukwila, Washington, and educated at the University of Washington and the Art Institute of Chicago. She had private singing lessons and sang in Broadway musicals and Billy Rose's Diamond Horseshoe club. During World War II she toured with the USO overseas. She married composer/conductor/pianist Ray Carter and wrote lyrics to his music, "All Right, Louie, Drop the Gun", "Cara, Cara, Bella, Bella", "The Cuckoo Who Lived in a Clock", "Little Mr. Big", "Merry-go-round", and "Sagebrush Serenade". ASCAP.

JOHNSTON, MARY (1925–)
"Somewhere in Hawaii"
Composer/songwriter born on February 7th in Oakland, California, she received a high school education but studied piano privately. With composer/songwriter Tony Todaro she wrote a number of songs—"Hula Cop Hop", "Keep Your Eyes on the Hands," "My Hawaiian Dream", "Somewhere in Hawaii", and "Ukulele Island". ASCAP.

JOHNSTON, PATRICIA (1922–1953)
"Ode to Victory"
A songwriter, she was born on October 24th in Kansas City, Missouri. With music by others she wrote the lyrics for "I'll Remember April", "Music and Rhythm", and "Ode to Victory". ASCAP. She died on November 24th in New York City.

JOLAS, BETSY (1926–)
Tales of a Summer Sea
Composer and teacher, she was born Elizabeth Illouz on August 5th in Paris, France. She attended the Lycee Français in Paris, came to America in 1940, and studied composition with Paul Beopple, piano with Helen Schnabel, and organ with Weinrich at Bennington College in Vermont (BA, 1946). She then returned to Paris and studied with Milhaud and Messiaen at the Conservatoire, where upon his request she taught at the Conservatoire from 1971–74, then was appointed to the faculty. Jolas has received many awards and has composed vocal and instrumental works. Her orchestral work mentioned above was composed for the Berkshire Music Center. In 1983 she was elected to the Institute of the American Academy of Arts and Letters.

JOLLEY, FLORENCE W. (b. 1917–)
Works: *Gloria in Excelcis*
Composer, arranger, and teacher, she was born at Kingsburg, California, on July 11, 1917, and was educated at Fresno State College (BA) in Fresno, California, and at the University of Southern California (MM) in Los Angeles. She was professor of music at Pierre Junior College in Los Angeles. She also composed an arrangement for *All People That on Earth Do Dwell*.

JONES, GRACE (1952–)
Living My Life
Singer/songwriter, she was born on May 19th in Spanishtown, Jamaica. After working as a model in Paris during the 1970s, she returned to America and sang in dance clubs in New York City. The 1982 album mentioned above contained many of her own songs. She is a soul/funk/reggae/rhythm and blues/rock singer. As of 1994 her available albums were *Warm Leatherette* (1980), *Island Life* (1985), *Nightclubbing, Portfolio,* and *Slave to Rhythm.*

JONES, RICKIE LEE (1954–)
"Easy Money"
Singer/songwriter/guitarist, she was born on November 8th in Chicago, Illinois. After living in Phoenix, Arizona, and Olympia, Washington, in 1973 she moved to Los Angeles where she sang in nightclubs. Her composition "Easy Money" was recorded by Lowell George in 1979 for his album *Thanks I'll Eat it Here.* Her rhythm and blues single "Chuck E's in Love" on her first album *Rickie Lee Jones* in 1979 hit the Top Five pop chart. As of 1994 her available albums were *Rickie Lee Jones* (1979), *Pirates* (1982), *Girl at Her Volcano* (1983), *The Magazine* (1984), *Flying Cowboys,* and *Pop Pop.*

JORDAN, DOROTHEA BLAND "DOLLY" (1762–1816)
"The Blue Bells of Scotland"
Actress/singer/composer, she was born near Waterford, England. She wrote "The Blue Bells of Scotland—Oh Where, Tell Me Where, Does Your Highland Laddie Dwell?" She is also referred to as Dora.

JORDAN, SASS (1967–)
"Breakaway"
Blues/rock singer/songwriter, she was born in England and raised in Montreal, Quebec, Canada. With her synthesizer player Bill Beaudoin, she co-wrote all 10 tunes on her album *Tell Somebody* (1990), and on her album *Racine* (1992).

JUDD, NAOMI (1946–)
"My Strongest Weakness"
Country guitarist/singer/songwriter, she was born on January 11th in Ashland, Kentucky. With daughter Wynonna Judd, she won a 1988 Grammy for "Give a Little Love", which was a track from her Greatest Hits. After Naomi became ill with chronic hepatitis and retired in 1991, Wynonna went solo. The Judds had many successful albums and CDs, *Christmas Time with the Judds, Collectors' Series, Greatest Hits, Greatest Hits II, Heartland, Judds Collection 1983–1990, Love Can Build a Bridge, River of Time, Rockin' With the Rhythm, The Judds: Wynonna & Naomi, Why Not Me?;* their videos are *Great Video Hits* and *Love Can Build a Bridge*. With Mike Reid, she wrote "My Strongest Weakness."

-K-

KABERRY, JEAN L. (1918–)
"Rise, Ye Saints and Temples Enter"
Hymnist born in Melbourne, Australia, she later lived in Perth, Western Australia. She was married and had four sons. Her hymn above and "Like Ten Thousand Legions Marching" and "So the Mighty Priesthood Gathered" appeared in the Mormon hymnal (1985).

KAHN, GRACE LeBOY (1891–Dec'd.)
"Lazy Day"
Composer/pianist born on September 22nd in Brooklyn, New York, she was educated in public schools. At age fifteen she was a pianist for a Chicago music publishing firm. She married songwriter Gus Kahn (1886–1941) and was the mother of composer/musician Dave Kahn and composer/pianist/songwriter Donald Kahn. With her husband, she wrote, "Everybody Rag with Me", "I Wish I Had a Girl", "Lazy Day",

"Evening", "Think of Me", "'Twas Only a Summer Night's Dream", and "You Gave Me Everything But Love". ASCAP.

KARLZEN, MARY (ca. 1973–)
"Yelling at Mary"
A rock & roll singer/songwriter, she sang as a teenager in an all-female rock act and produced two records on minor labels. With the help from members of Tom Petty's *Heartbreakers,* John Mellencamp's band, and Jackson Browne, she produced her album "Yelling at Mary," which was considered one of the best offerings in 1995 by an unknown singer/songwriter. The album deals with teenage passions and hardships between lovers who want to remain friends. Two classic rock stations pushed her album.

KARR, ELIZABETH R. (1925–)
"Paris This Spring"
Songwriter/publisher, born on September 23rd in New Haven, Connecticut, she was a partner with Realm Records, Rolls Music Company. With Joe Williams, she wrote the lyrics for "Look of Love", "Loverbug", "Ladybug", "Hide and Seek", "Paris This Spring", and "The Far Apple". ASCAP.

KELLOGG, KAY (1901–Dec'd.)
Rojo y Negro
Composer/pianist/songwriter born on September 9th in Los Angeles, California and educated at Mills College, she studied piano with Thilo Becker. She lived in India for a number of years. She composed piano pieces, *Miniature Portraits, Rojo y Negro, Sea Moods,* and the songs "Cradle Song", "Get Along, Little Pony", "Give Me a Ship and a Song", "Please Lord, Call me, Too", and "Song of the Sage".

KENT, CHARLOTTE (1907–Dec'd.)
"Overnight"
Composer/songwriter born February 12th in New York, New York, she received a BA and MA at college. With composer/pianist Louis Alter, she wrote a number of songs, including, "Nelly Pull Your Belly In It's for the USA", "Overnight", and "Stick to Your Dancing, Mabel". ASCAP.

KENT, SANDRA (1927–)
"Little Pink Toes"
Composer/singer/songwriter, she was born on May 1st in New York, New York, and educated at Brooklyn College. She was a singer with dance bands from 1945–52 and then a member of the Phoenix Theatre Repertoire Company. She wrote "I Never Had a Worry in the World", "I'm on a See-Saw of Love", "Li'l Ole You", "Little Pink Toes", "More Than Anything", "Oh, Mr. Romeo", and "Once I Loved You". ASCAP.

KERGER, ANN (1894–Dec'd.)
"Sunshine of Your Kiss"
Songwriter born on May 25th in Austria, she received a high school education. With music by Lelie Loth, she wrote the lyrics for "All of My Heart", "Little Children Come to Jesus", "Renita", "Sunshine of Your Kiss", and "You Took My Heart Away."

KERR, ANITA (1927–)
The Sea, The Earth, The Sky
Pianist/singer/composer, she was born in Memphis, Tennessee. She studied piano at age four and was a staff pianist on a Memphis radio station when she was only fourteen. She organized the Anita Kerr Singers in 1949, and they appeared on many shows, and later changed their name to the Anita Kerr Quartet. She composed the music for the albums *The Sea* (1966, with words by Rod McKuen), *The Earth* (1967, using a 70-piece orchestra), and *The Sky*. She also wrote the score for the film *Limbo* (1972). As of 1994 her albums and CDs available were *Music is Her Name, Round Midnight, Slightly Baroque*.

KERR, JEAN (1923–)
"Lazy moon"
Songwriter, she was born on July 10th in Scranton, Pennsylvania. She married Walter Kerr. With her husband, Joan Ford, and Leroy Anderson she wrote "Lazy Moon—Time to Get Up, You Good-for-Nothing Lazy Moon", "Be a Mess", "It'll Be All Right in a Hundred Years", "The Pussy Foot", and "This Had Better Be Love". She was also a well-known author, having written *Please Don't Eat the Daisies*. ASCAP.

KAHN, CHAKA (1953–)
The Woman I Am
Singer/songwriter, born Yvette Marie Stevens on March 23rd in Chicago, Illinois, she sang with the Rufus Group (1972–78) and then went solo. Her hits were "Through the Fire" (1985) and "I Feel for You"; with Ray Charles she won 1990 Grammy R&B for "I'll Be Good for You", "Love You All My Lifetime"; with Stevie Wonder on *Handel's Messiah: A Soulful Celebration* (1992). Her world tour was interrupted on September 27, 1992 when she underwent surgery for an appendectomy. *The Woman I Am* won a Grammy in 1993. As of 1994 her albums available were *C.K., I Feel for You, Life is a Dance, The Woman I Am*.

KILTZ, RITA (1895–Dec'd.)
Sing with Action
Composer/pianist/songwriter, she was born on May 18th in Milwaukee, Wisconsin. She was a concert soloist, piano teacher, director of the

Song Writers Guild, Inc. She wrote a book of 64 songs called *Sing with Action.*

KING, CAROLE (1942–)
"You Make Me Feel Like a Natural Woman"
Composer and singer, she was born Carole Klein on February 9th in Brooklyn, New York City. With her husband, lyricist Gerry Goffin, they wrote "Will You Still Love Me Tomorrow?" sung by the Shirelles 1961, which reached No. 1 on the charts, "Up on the Roof" (1962), sung by the Drifters, which reached No. 5. They wrote the song mentioned above for Aretha Franklin, "Go Away Little Girl" for Steve Lawrence, "Don't Bring Me Down" for the Animals, a rock group, etc. After her divorce from Goffin, King moved to Los Angeles and recorded her second album *Tapestry* (1971), which sold over 13 million copies and won four Grammy awards. She married bassist Charles Larkey. She wrote "Now and Forever", "A League of Their Own" and won a Grammy in 1993. As of 1994 her available albums were *Tapestry, City Streets, Fantasy,* and *Her Greatest Hits.*

KINGHAM, MILLICENT DOUGLAS (b. 1866)
Tune—"Benson"
Composer and organist, she served as organist for St. Andrew's in Hertford, England. Her tune was first published in leaflet form (Eton, 1894), and with the hymn "God is working his purpose out" in *Church Hymns* (1903), *Hymns Ancient & Modern* (1904; 1950). She also served as organist at St. Thomas' Hospital Chapel, London, a post that she relinquished in 1926. We have been unable to locate her date of death.

KINGSLEY, POLLY ARNOLD (1906–)
"Cinderella Polka"
Composer/songwriter born on December 9th in Lumberton, Mississippi, and educated at Wheeler College, she studied voice with J. Haupt and L. O'Rourke. With Alice Cornett and others, she wrote, "I Smells Trouble", "I'm Not Ashamed to Cry", "Plain Talkin' Man", "Rhythm in the Hills", "Slap 'er Down Agin, Paw", "Talkin' 'Bout Texas", and "Wind Song". ASCAP.

KINSCELLA, HAZEL GERTRUDE (1895–1960)
"Indian Sketches"
Composer born on April 27th in Nora Springs, Iowa, and educated at the University of Nebraska School of Music (BM, BFA, BA) Columbia University (MA); University of Washington (PhD), she studied music with Howard Brockway, Rossetter Gleason Cole, and Raphael Joseffy. Her

works are the string quartet "Indian Sketches"; cantata *A Child is Born;* choral settings for "My Days Have Been So Wondrous Free", "Folk Tune Trios", "Psalm 150", and "Our prayer". ASCAP. She died in Seattle, Washington, on July 15th.

KIRBY, LADY KIER
"Apple Juice Kissing"
A singer/songwriter, with her husband DJ Dmitry, she is a partner in the duo DEE-LITE. Her albums are *World Clique* (1990 gold), *Infinity Within,* and *Dewdrops in the Garden* (1994). Kirby and her husband wrote the songs for their albums, including, "Groove Is In the Heart", "Vote, Baby, Vote", "Party Happening People", "Apple Juice Kissing", and "Sampladelic".

KLEIN, LAURIE BRENDEMUCHI (1950–)
"I Love You, Lord"
Hymnist, she was born on November 29th in Watertown, Wisconsin, and educated at St. Olaf College (BA in Art with honors 1972) and at Whitworth College (1985–88 in Theater). With her husband Bill Klein, the two tour as storytelling musicians. Her hymn above appeared in the *Baptist Hymnal* (1986).

KLOPPER, CAROLYN HAMILSTON (1936–)
"Home Can Be a Heaven on Earth"
Hymnist/organist, she was born in Murray, Utah. While working at the Latter-day Saints Church Genealogical Society, she met her husband-to-be, composer W. Herbert Klopfer. They have four children. She wrote the above hymn and her husband composed the music for same, which appeared in the Mormon hymnal (1985).

KLOTZ, LEORA NYLEE (1928–)
"In Praise and Adoration"
Composer/conductor/singer born on October 17th in Canton, Ohio, she was educated at Mt. Union College (BM, BPSM) and Western Reserve University (MA). She wrote the hymns "In Praise and Admiration", "Sing Alleluia: Christ Is Born", "Sing We Now for Christ is King". ASCAP.

KNIGHT, BEATRICE (1925–)
"Give Me Jazz, Jazz, Jazz"
Guitarist/singer/songwriter, she was born on August 15th in Miami, Florida, and received a high school education. With Lemuel Davis, she wrote the lyrics for "Come Spring", "Give Me Jazz, Jazz, Jazz", and other songs. ASCAP.

KNOX, HELEN BOARDMAN (1870–1947)
"My Love of Londonderry"
Songwriter born on March 7th in South Lawrence, Massachusetts, and educated in public schools, she had private music study. In the late 1920s she was executive secretary of the American Academy of Arts and Sciences. She wrote the lyrics for "Hush, Ma Honey", "Carita", "Autumn", "Iljinsky Cradle Song", "The Silent Hour", "The Russian Nightingale", and "My Love of Londonderry". ASCAP. She died on November 10th in Blawenburg, New Jersey.

KOCH, MARIE (1912–)
"Where Is My Love?"
Composer/songwriter, she was born October 1st in New York. She wrote "The Christmas Tree", "Where Is My Love?", etc. ASCAP.

KOCH, MINNA (1845–1924)
Tune—"Minna"
A composer, she was German, and her tune was written to the original words of the hymn "Star Whose Light Shines O'er Me," which was translated from the German by Bishop Frank Houghton while attending a conference of the China Inland Mission in Germany in 1948. Her tune appeared in the English *Baptist Hymn Book* (London, 1962).

KOHLER, DONNA JEAN (1937–)
"Miss Teenage America"
Composer/songwriter born on March 2nd in Cleveland, Ohio, she received a high school education. She wrote "Hula Hoop Song", "Limbo Low", "Miss Teenage America", "Mr. John", "Sombrero", "So do I", and "Trapped Love". ASCAP.

KOLB, BARBARA (1939–)
Spring River Flowers Moon Night
Composer/clarinetist, she was born on February 10th in Hartford, Connecticut. After studying clarinet and composition with Franchetti at the Hartt School of Music, University of Hartford (BM, 1961; MM, 1964), she studied with Schuller and Foss at the Berkshire Music Center. During the early 1960s, she played the clarinet in the Hartford Symphony Orchestra. Kolb was the first American woman to receive the Rome Prize (1969–71) and numerous prizes after that. She has held teaching positions at Brooklyn College, CUNY, and Temple University. Her instrumental piece mentioned above, two pianoforte, percussion and tape (1974–75), orchestral, instrumental, and vocal works have established her reputation.

KRUGMAN, LIILIAN D. (1911–)
"Song Tales of the West Indies"
Pianist/songwriter born on December 4th in Brooklyn, New York, and educated at Brooklyn College, she studied piano. With Mort Fryberg and Dorothy Olsen she wrote the lyrics for "Calypso Songs for Children", "Ballad of Abe Lincoln", "Ducks on Parade", "Little Calypsos", "Pretty, Pretty", "Now We Are Six", and "Songs of Animals and Birds for Children". ASCAP.

KUMMER, CLARE RODMAN BEECHER (1888–1958)
"Lover of Mine"
Composer/songwriter born on January 9th in Brooklyn, New York City, and educated at Packer Institute, she had private music study. She wrote a number of plays and Broadway stage scores. With Jerome Kern, Sigmund Romberg, and others she wrote a number of songs—"Blushing June Roses", "Dearie," "Egypt", "Only With You", "Lover of Mine", "Other Eyes", "The Bluebird", "The Road to Yesterday", "Somebody's Eyes", "Thro' All the World", "Garden of Dreams", and "Sunset". ASCAP. She died on April 21st in Carmel, California.

-L-

LA BARBARA, JOAN (1947–)
The Solar Wind III
Composer/vocalist, she was born Joan Lotz on June 8th in Philadelphia, Pennsylvania. After studying voice with Helen Boatwright at Syracuse University, composition at New York University (BA, 1970), and voice again at the Berkshire Music Center, she took additional courses from Freschl at the Juilliard School in New York City. During the 1970s, she sang with both Reich's and Glass's ensembles and with the New Wilderness Board. She has received a number of grants and was composer-in-residence in West Berlin under the Deutscher Akademischer Austauschdienst. In 1981, she was appointed to teach singing and composition at the California Institute of the Arts. The chamber orchestral work mentioned above was composed in 1984. She has written numerous vocal works, amplified and with tape. She married composer Morton Subotnick. As of 1994 her albums available were *Singing Through John Cage* and *Sound Paintings*.

LACEY, MARY (1909–)
"Cha-cha polka"
Songwriter born on July 30th in Yorkshire, England, she received a high school education. She moved to Canada, then to California in 1947. She wrote TV dramatic shows and songs with Paul Werick, such as "Cha-cha Polka" and "Outer Space Santa."

LACKMAN, SUSAN CAROLE COHN (1948–)
Symphony No. 1

Composer born on July 1st in Tsingtao, China, and educated at Temple University (BMusEd-cum laude), American University (MA), and Rutgers University (PhD). She studied composition with Robert Moeus, Lloyd Ultan, and Rolv Yttrehus; piano with Natalie Hinderas; voice with Else Fink; further study with Lukas Foss, Milton Bobbitt, T. J. Anderson, Pierre Boulez, and Ned Rorem. Since 1981 she has been associate professor, music theory and composition at Rollins College, Winter Park, Florida. She composed the opera *Lisa Stratos;* for orchestra *Symphony No. 1 (Waltzes for Small Orchestra, Festive Overture;* chamber music *String Quartets Nos. 1&2, Woodwind Quintet, Dinner Music* (Brass Trio), *String Trio, Brass Quintet, Fanfares* (commissioned series); the piano solos *Rondo, Meditation, Three Characters, Fits, Sketch;* vocal music miscellaneous solo songs, and choral works; and the electronic music: *Four Love Songs,* Moog Synthesizer on tape.

LAFERTY, KAREN (1948–)
Tune—"Seek Ye First"

Guitarist/singer/songwriter, she was born on February 29th at Alamogordo, New Mexico. After obtaining the degree of bachelor of music education, she was an entertainer in restaurants and hotel lounges when in 1971 she attended a Bible study at her home church, the Calvary Chapel in Costa Mesa, California, where the subject was "Seek ye first the Kingdom of God" before pursuing your own career ideas. After she went home she started playing a melody on her guitar and recorded it on her cassette. She discovered an "Allelujah" chorus fit the song perfectly and composed "Seek ye First", which appeared in *The Hymnal for Worship & Celebration* (Baptist 1986), the *United Methodist Hymnal* (1989), and *The Presbyterian Hymnal* (1990).

Laferty spent the first four years in ministry with Maranatha Music where she recorded four albums. She also composed "Don't Build Your House on the Sandy Land", a children's song. In 1979 she moved to Amsterdam, The Netherlands, where she founded and became the director of Musicians For Missions International (A Ministry of Youth with a Mission). (Information from Wilma Siewers, Musicians for Missions, Kadijksplein 18, 1018 AC Amsterdam, The Netherlands)

LA FRENIERE, EMMA P. SCHNEIDER (1881–1961)
"Dog House Polka"

Composer/pianist/songwriter born on September 23rd in Brooklyn, New York, she was the daughter of musician Frederick Schneider and she studied with her father. She was educated at the Leipzig Conservatory. She was an accompanist to Emma Calve and Blanche Duffield and was also a concert pianist. With her son, songwriter Charles F. La Freniere and also Hugo Rubens, she wrote a number of songs, "Mia Venezia", "A Valley in Valparaiso", "Long After Midnight", "Blue Illusion", "Dancing 'Till Dawn", "Midnight Kiss", "Meet Me at the Football Game", "White Sands", "Strolling on the Boulevard", "Suitcase Susie", "My Margarita", and "The Tide has Turned at Last". ASCAP. She died on September 11th in Hempstead, New York.

LA GUERRE, ELIZABETH CLAUDE JACQUET DE (1659–1729)
Te Deum
Composer and harpsichordist, born in Paris, France, the daughter of a harpsichord maker, she made her debut playing at the French Court at age fifteen. Her Opera, *Céphale and Procis*, was the first opera by a woman composer performed at the Académie Royal de Musique (1694). She also composed three books of cantatas. She was married to Marin de la Guerre, organist of the Church of Saint Severin in Paris. Her *Te Deum*, for full choruses, was performed in 1721 in the Chapel of the Louvre for the Convalescence of His Majesty, Louis XV. She died in Paris on June 27, 1729.

LAINE, FLORA SPRAKER (1924–)
"How Many Times Must We Say Goodbye?"
Composer/songwriter born on January 20th in New York, New York, she received a high school education. She had various jobs and was in real estate. Her songs are the one above and "No More". ASCAP.

LANCING, CAROLE (1940–)
"Hey Mr. DJ"
Composer/singer/songwriter born on February 22nd in Indianapolis, Indiana and educated at high school, she recorded songs and wrote "Hey Mr. DJ". ASCAP.

LANDESMAN, FRANCES (1927–)
"Listen, Little Girl"
Songwriter born on October 21st in New York, New York. She wrote stage scores and songs for nightclub revues. With music by Tommy Wolf, Roy Kral, and Russell Freeman, she wrote the lyrics for "Ballad of the Sad Young Men", "Fun Life", "Listen, Little Girl", "Night People", "Spring Can Really Hang You Up the Most", "Season in the Sun", "It Isn't So Good, It Couldn't Be Better", "Laugh, I Thought I'd Die", "Say Cheese", "Tell Me Lies", "You Smell So Good", "The Heart that Broke Was Mine", "This Life We've Led", "I Love You Real", "Money Talks", "Nothing Like You", "Stoppin' the Clock", and "You're free". ASCAP.

LANDSBERG, PHYLLIS G. FAIRBANKS (1927–)
"The Green Beret"
Songwriter born on April 9th in Syracuse, New York, she was educated at Cornell University (BS). With Chester Gierlach, Kenneth Whitcomb, and Leonard Whitcup, she wrote the lyrics for "The Green Beret" (Citation from Special Warfare Center, Ft. Bragg, North Carolina); "The Loving Heart", "The Ain't Not Tree", "An Empty Glass", "The 'A' Team". ASCAP.

LANE, LAURA (1927–)
"Quicksand"
Singer/songwriter born on June 13th in Orange, New Jersey, she studied with Lillian Goodman; went to Sevilla Fort School of Dance; Group Theatre, New York City. She sang in nightclubs, led her own trio for five years, sang with Four Barons and with the Freddie Martin Orchestra. She wrote "Quicksand", "Old Salt Mine", and "Riding with the Lord."

LANG, JOSEPHINE CAROLINE (1815–1880)
"She has the gift of composing and singing songs in a manner I have never heard anything to match." (Mendelssohn)
Singer/composer, she was born on March 14th in Munich, Germany, the granddaughter of coloratura soprano Sabina Renk Hitzelberger and the daughter of soprano Regina Hitzelberger Land and court director of music Theobald Lang. She was a niece of pianist/contralto Catharina Elizabeth Hitzelberger, soprano Kunigunde Hitzelberger, and contralto Johanna Hitzelberger. She studied singing with her mother and musical theory with Mendelssohn (1830–31) during his visits to Munich. Lang married attorney Christian Reinhold Kostlin. She wrote numerous songs and published 30 opus numbers in several books. The quote above is from a letter of Mendelssohn dated October 6, 1831. She died at Tubingen on December 2nd.

LANG, MARGARET RUTHVEN (1867–1972)
"An Irish Love Song"
Composer, born on November 27th in Boston, Massachusetts. While studying piano and composition with her father pianist/organist/composer B. J. Johnson, at age twelve she composed her first piece. After studying violin with Louis Schmidt in Boston, with Dreschler and Abel in Munich in the late 1880s, and counterpoint and fugue with Gluth, she returned to Boston and studied orchestration with Chadwick and MacDowell. After her song "Ojala" was performed at a concert during the Paris Exposition of 1889, it was repeated at the opening of the Lincoln Concert Hall in Washington, DC in 1890 and established her reputation. Her song above was a favorite of Madame Schumann-Heink. Lang,

through her *Dramatic Overture op. 12,* performed by the Boston Symphony Orchestra under Arthur Nikisch conducting, was the first woman in the US to have a work played by a major orchestra. The Boston Symphony gave a concert in her honor on her 100th birthday.

LARAMORE, VIVIAN YEISER (1895–Dec'd.)
"My Florida"
Songwriter born on November 8th in St. Louis, Missouri, and educated at Columbia University, New York, she wrote a column for the Miami *Daily News* for 14 years and was poet laureate of Florida in 1931. She wrote the songs, "Autumn", "Beneath a Southern Sky", "Mango Moon", "My Florida", "Together and Alone", "When You Are Near", "Little River", "Not Enough", "White Jade", and "Wind Song".

LARSEN, LIBBY (1950–)
'Clair de lune' (Opera)
Composer, she was born on December 24th in Wilmington, Delaware. After studying composition with Argento, Fetler, and Stokes at the University of Minnesota (BA 1971), (MM 1975), and (PhD 1978), she composed her first opera *The Words upon the Windowpane* in 1978. She has written over three operas and a number of instrumental and vocal pieces. She received a fellowship from the National Opera Institute in 1980.

LAUFER, BEATRICE (1923–)
Concerto for Flute, Oboe, Trumpet, Strings
Composer born on April 27th in New York, and educated at Juilliard with Roger Sessions, Marion Bauer, and Vittorio Giannimi, her works include two symphonies; concerto (above); "Prelude and Prayer", "Ile" musical setting to an O'Neill play; choral "Song of the Fountain", "Spring Thunder", "Under the Pines", "He Who Knows Not", "Everyone Sang", and "Do You Fear the Wind". She also wrote a "Soldier's Prayer". ASCAP.

LAUPER, CYNTHIA "CINDI" (1953–)
"The Goonies 'R' Good Enough"
Singer/songwriter, she was born on June 20th in New York City. With Stephen Broughton Lunt and Arthur Stead, she wrote "The Goonies 'r' good enough—Here we are hanging on the strains of greed and blues" and with Rob Hyman, "Time after time—Lyin' in my bed I hear the clock tick and think of you". Her hit "She's So Unusual" broke the record for most Top Ten singles, and won a Grammy in 1984. She had a hit with "Girls Just Want to Have Fun", and had the albums *A Night to Remember, True Colors,* and the video *Live in Paris.* With electric magic she sang with Frank Sinatra his 1947 vocal "Santa Claus Is Coming to Town" on the Special Olympics benefit album *A Very Special Christmas* (1992).

LAZARUS, EMMA (1849–1894)
"The Banner of the Jew"
Poet/songwriter, she was born in New York City. She wrote "The New
Colossus" (1883) inscribed below the Statue of Liberty in New York
Harbor in 1903:
"Give me your tired, your poor,
Your huddled masses yearning to breathe free,
The wretched refuse of your teeming shore.
Send these, the homeless, tempest-tost to me,
I lift my lamp beside the golden door."
Her "Songs of a Semite" (1883) included "The Banner of the Jew",
which became a popular Zionist anthem.

LEAVITT, MARYLOU CUNNINGHAM (1928–)
"We Listen to a Prophet's Voice"
Hymnist born in Washington State and educated at the University of
Washington, she was raised as a Catholic, yet at age twenty-one she was
baptized as a Latter-day Saint. She was married and raised ten children
of her own and two stepchildren; she resides in Salt Lake City, Utah. She
writes poems and song lyrics. her hymn above was published in the Mormon hymnal (1985).

LE BARON, ALICE ANN (1953–)
Lamentation/Invocation
Composer, she was born on May 30th in Baton Rouge, Louisiana. After
graduating from the University of Alabama (BA, 1974), she studied harp
under Alice Chalifoux; then under Gyorgy Ligeti at the Hochschule fur
Musik in Cologne; the State University of New York at Stony Brook
(MA, 1978). On July 6, 1982, she married Edward Eadon. She studied
composition under Bulent Arel and Chou Wen-chung at Columbia University, New York (DMA, 1989). She has taught at the State University
at Stony Brook, University of Alabama, and courses in classical music
and jazz at Columbia University in New York (1984–85). She has received numerous prizes and scholarships. She has composed choral and
orchestral works, two operas, and chamber music. Her piece mentioned
above was written for baritone, clarinet, harp, cello, and was first performed in New York City on November 7, 1984.

LE BAU, BLANCHE (1905–)
"Sing and Play Piano Method"
Composer/pianist/singer/songwriter she was born on April 17th in Brook-
lyn, New York. She taught voice/piano/accordian, and ⸤ rformed for the
Armed Forces during World War II. Besides the piano method men-
tioned above, she wrote the song, "Santa's Music Box".

LEBENBOM, ELAINE F.
"Lullaby for a Newborn Baby—Too Soon Gone"
Composer, she wrote the above music performed by the Canticum
Novum Singers; it was directed by Harold Rosenbaum at the Mostly
Women Composers Festival at the Horace Mann Auditorium, Columbia
University. The work was commissioned by "Meet the Composer".

LEE, JULIA, (1902–1958)
(Popular songs)
Pianist/singer/composer, she was born in Boonesville, Missouri. She
played the piano in the band of her brother baritone saxist George E.
Jones at Lyric Hall in Kansas City in the 1920s. She left the band and
was a soloist at Milton's place in Kansas City (1934–48). After living in
Los Angeles, California, for two years (1948–50) she moved back to
Kansas City and worked at the Cuban Room, High Hall Bar, and other
clubs in Kansas City where she died.

LEE, KATIE (1919–)
"Hold Me Tight"
Composer/singer/songwriter born on October 23rd in Tucson, Arizona,
and educated at the University of Arizona (BFA). She sang folk songs;
was a singer on the "Gildersleeve Show", "Halls of Ivy", "Railroad
Hour" on TV from 1950–53; and has made many records. She wrote
songs "Baby, Did You Hear?", "Delia's Gone", "Hold Me Tight". Her
album is *Spicy Songs for Cool Knights*. ASCAP.

LEE, MARJORIE LEDERER (1921–)
"What Have You Done All Day?"
Songwriter born on June 28th on Long Island, New York, and educated
at Sarah Lawrence College (BAEd), she wrote books and songs, including the one mentioned above. ASCAP.

LEE, NORAH (1898–1941)
"Lying Lips"
Composer born on October 25th in Sutton, West Virginia, and educated
at the Peabody Institute, she wrote music for vaudeville and films, and
songs, "At the End of the Lane", "Foolish Wives", "I'll Get You Some
Day", "It's Too Late to Forget You", "Lying Lips", "Miss Mandy", "She
Knows It". ASCAP. She died on June 17th in Norfolk, Connecticut.

LEE, PEGGY (1920–)
"Mañana"
Singer/songwriter, she was born Norma Dolores Egstrom on May 26th
in Jamestown, North Dakota. After singing in a church choir and on a

Fargo, North Dakota, radio station at age sixteen, she toured with Will Osborne's band. Lee recorded "Elmer's Tune" for Benny Goodman, married guitarist Dave Barbour, and appeared in films. She wrote "Mañana" with her husband, left bands in 1944, toured on her own, and sang in New York City. "Is That All There Is?" won a Grammy in 1969. She toured Japan in 1975 and sang with Tony Bennett in 1982. Lee appeared in a wheelchair at a party for k. d. lang in New York City in 1992. She has written or co-written over 500 songs. As of 1994, her albums available were *All Time Greatest Hits, Capitol Collectors Series, Christmas Carousel, Close Enough for Love, Miss Peggy Lee Sings Blues, Peggy Lee Sings with Benny Goodman, The Best of Peggy Lee, There'll Be Another Spring.*

LEECH, LYDIA SHIVERS (1875–1962)
Tune—GIVING—"Bring ye all the tithes into the storehouse"
Composer, hymnist, and pianist, she was born in Mayville, New Jersey, on July 12, 1873, raised at Cape May Court House, New Jersey, and was educated at Columbia University in New York City and Temple University in Philadelphia, Pennsylvania. She was organist at the Bethany Methodist Church in Camden, New Jersey, and also traveled as a pianist, companist for singing evangelist services. She wrote about 500 gospel songs. "We Often Grow Weary, and Lonely, and Sad" and "This I Would Ask from Day to Day" were published in *Rodeheaver's Gospel Solos and Duets* No. 3 and "God's Way" had three recordings listed in *Phonolog Reports* (1978) of Los Angeles; there were two recordings for "Someday He'll Make It Plain." Her hymn above appeared in the *Baptist Hymnal* (1956) and her hymn "I Was a Sinner, But Now I'm Free. He Rescued Me," appeared in the *Baptist Hymnal* (1973). She died at Long Beach, California, on March 4, 1962.

LEEDS, CORINE (1909–)
"In a Million Years"
Composer/songwriter born on December 5th in New York City and educated in high school, she had private music study. She wrote the songs "In a Million Years", "Kissless Blues", and "Pray Today". ASCAP.

LEEDS, NANCY (1924–)
"I Stayed Awake All Night"
A songwriter, she was born on December 22nd in New York, New York, and educated at Pine Manor Junior College. With music by Gwen Lynd and Don McAfee, she wrote the lyrics for "At the Crossing", "Fish Swim in Paris", "Take Me Away from the Crowd", "What Have You Got to Show?", and "You're My Love". ASCAP.

LeFANU, NICOLA FRANCES (1947–)
The Story of Mary O'Neill
Composer, she was born on April 28th in Essex, England, the daughter of composer Dame Elizabeth Maconchy. She studied at St. Hilda's College, Oxford (BA, 1968, MA 1971); Royal College of Music, London; composition under Earl Kim and Seymour Shifrin on a Harkness Fellowship at Brandeis University, Waltham, Massachusetts (1973–74); senior lecturer (1977–79) at King's College, London, along with Australian composer David Lumsdaine, whom she married on March 16, 1979. They have one son. Along with husband composer in residence, New South Wales Conservatorium, Sydney (1979), she has been back at King's College since 1979. She has composed choral and instrumental works, chamber music, operas, etc. Her radiophonic opera for soprano with 16 solo voices (1986) was broadcast by the BBC on January 4, 1989.

LEGINSKA, ETHEL (1886–1970)
Gale
Composer/pianist/conductor, she was born Ethel Liggins on April 13th in Hull, Great Britain, and early in her career she changed her name to Leginska. As a child prodigy, she studied piano at the Hoch Conservatory in Frankfurt, with Theodor Leschetisky in Vienna and in Berlin. After making her debut in London at age 16, she toured Europe and became known as the "Paderewski of woman pianists". She came to the US in 1913 and became a favorite of the public. After studying composition with Bloch in 1918, she composed piano and chamber music, symphonic poems, and songs. In 1923 her interest turned to conducting, and after studying with Goossens and Heger, she directed major orchestras in Berlin, Munich, London, and Paris. After conducting the New York Symphony Orchestra on January 9, 1925, she conducted several other orchestras, including her one-act opera *Gale* with the Chicago City Opera in 1935. After moving to Los Angeles, California, in 1940, she taught piano until her death there on February 26, 1970.

LEHMANN, NINA MARY FREDERICA "LIZA" (1862–1918)
In a Persian Garden
Soprano/composer, she was born on July 11th in London, England, the daughter of songwriter Amelia Lehmann and painter Rudolf Lehmann. She studied singing with Alberto Randegger and Jenny Lind in London and composition with Raunkilde in Rome, Freudenberg in Wiesbaden, and Hamisch MacCunn in London. As a concert singer, she toured England from 1885–94 and then married painter/composer Herbert Bedford. Based on FitzGerald's *Rubayyat of Omar Khayyam* she composed the

music cycle of quatrains for four soloists and piano—*In a Persian garden*. She toured the US in 1910, and then served as first president of the Society of Women Musicians in London. She died in Pinner on September 19th.

LEIGH, CAROLYN (1926–1983)

"On the Other Side of the Tracks"

Songwriter, she was born on April 21st in the Bronx, New York. With Cy Coleman she wrote: "The Best Is Yet to Come", "A Doodlin' Song", "Firefly", "Give a Little Whistle", "Hey, Look Me Over", "I Walk a Little Faster", "It Amazes Me", "I've Got Your Number", "On Second Thought", "On the Other Side of the Tracks", "Pass Me By", "Playboy's Theme", "Real Live Girl", "The Rules of the Road", "Tall Hope", "When in Rome", "Witchcraft", "You Fascinate Me So", "You've Come Home".

With Johnny Richards she wrote "Young at Heart"; with Mark Charlap, "I Won't Grow Up", "I'm Flying" and "I've Gotta Crow"; with Sammy Fain, "My Son John"; and with Johnny Mercer and Hoagy Carmichael, "How Little We Know".

LEMMEL, HELEN HOWARTH (1863–1961)

"O Soul, Are you Weary and Troubled?"

A composer and hymnist, born in Wardle, England, on November 14, 1863, she was brought to Milwaukee, Wisconsin, when she was only nine years old and later lived in Madison, Wisconsin. She was a concert singer, hymnist, and composer, and wrote more than 400 hymns. For many years she traveled the Chautauqua Circuit as a member of a quartet, which she organized. In 1904 she moved to Seattle, Washington, where she joined the Ballard Baptist Church there. She died in Seattle on November 1, 1961, just two weeks short of her 98th birthday. Her hymn appeared in the *American Service* (1968); *Baptist* (1975); *Broadman* (1977); and *Family of God* (1976) hymnals, and *Hymns for the Living Church* (1974).

LENNOX, ANNIE (1954–)

"Walking on Broken Glass"

British singer/songwriter, she was born on December 25. She sang with The Eurthymics, which included guitarist David Stewart. Her hit singles were "Would I Lie to You?" (1985) and "Sweet Dreams Are Made of This". Her albums and CDs are *1984* (Soundtrack), *Be Yourself Tonight*, *Greatest Hits, Revenge, Savage, Sweet Dreams, Touch*, and *We Too Are One;* her videos are *Live, Greatest Hits Home Video, Sweet Dreams*, and *We Too Are One*. She wrote "Walking on Broken Glass" (1994).

LEON, TANIA (1943–)
Scourge of the Hyacinths
Composer/conductor born in Havana, Cuba. Her Chinese grandfather bought her a piano. Her other ancestors were African, French and Spanish. Her grandmother enrolled Tania in the Carlos Alfredo Peyrellade Conservatory and she gave her first piano recital at age five. Raised in a Havana ghetto, she had few friends. In 1967 she flew from Havana to Miami, then on to New York City. After she met Arthur Mitchell who started the Dance Theatre of Harlem, he hired Leon as a pianist. Shortly thereafter she became his music director. Leon founded an orchestra for the dance company. She collaborated on the ballet *Tones* with Mitchell, then *Dougla* with Geoffrey Holder and *Spiritual Suite* with Marian Anderson. With composers Julius Eastman and Talib Rasul Hakim she founded the Brooklyn Philharmonic's Community Concert Series.

Leon composed the music and wrote the libretto for the opera *Scourge of Hyacinths* based on the radio play by Wole Soyinka, the Nigerian Nobel prize winner. In May 1994 Tania Leon conducted her first opera in Munich, with Soyinka in attendance. She won the BMW Music Theatre Prize. In February 1995 Leon flew to South Africa and conducted the National Symphony in Johannesburg.

LEONARD, ANITA (1922–)
"A Sunday Kind of Love"
Composer born on August 26th in New York, New York, and educated at New York University (BS), she studied with Otto Cesana, Bruno Eisner, Modena Lane, Wallingford Riegger, and Herman Wasserman. She wrote the scores for four ballets, variety shows, and songs—"The Bee Song", "Chitterlin-switch", "A Sunday Kind of Love", and "William Didn't Tell". ASCAP.

LEONARDA, ISABELLA (c. 1620–c. 1700)
Masses and Motets.
Composer of church music, she was born at Novara, Italy, and entered the Convent of St. Ursula there and later became abbess of the convent. She composed several masses, motets, and other pieces of church music. Her last composition was published at Bologna, Italy, in 1700.

LEVITT, ESTELLE (1941–)
"In the Name of Love"
Composer/songwriter, she was born on December 18th in Brooklyn, New York, and educated at Hunter College. With Tommy Goodman, Camille Monte, and Lee Pockriss, she wrote a number of songs, including, "In the Name of Love", "I Can't Grow Peaches on a Cherry Tree". ASCAP.

LEWIS, JANET (1899–)
The Wife of Martin Guerre
Librettist, she was born on August 17th in Chicago, Illinois, and educated at Lewis Institute, Chicago (AA) and the University of Chicago (PhD.) on a Guggenheim scholarship. She taught short story writing at the University of Missouri and at Denver University. She also wrote novels. She wrote the libretto for William Bergsma's opera *The Wife of Martin Guerre*. She married Yvor Winters. ASCAP.

LIEBLING, ESTELLE (1884–1970)
Carnival of Venice (arrangement)
Composer/arranger/singer, she was born on April 21st in New York, New York, and educated at Hunter College; Stern Conservatory in Berlin; and she studied with Nicklass Kempner and Matilde Marchesi. She made her debut as Lucia in *Lucia Di Lammermoor* at the Dresden Opera House. She was a soloist with the John Philip Sousa Band on a world tour; and a soloist with the New York Philharmonic, Boston Symphony, Detroit Symphony, Philadelphia Orchestra, Leipzig Gewandhaus Orchestra. She taught music—her pupils included Galli-Curci, Maria Jeritza, Jessica Dragonette, Gertrude Lawrence, and Adele Astaire. She wrote arrangements for a number of waltzes. ASCAP.

LILI'UOKALANI KAMAKA'EHA PAKI, QUEEN (1838–1917)
"Aloha 'oe"
Composer/choir director/organist/pianist, she was born on September 2nd in Honolulu, Hawaii, of a musical family. At age four, she began her musical training at the Chief's Children School and composed her first published song "Nani Na Pua" in 1869. Among her other songs were "Ku'u pua i paoakalani", "Ho'oheno Song" and "Aloha 'oe" composed in 1878. While a princess, she wrote "He mele lahui Hawaii", which became the Hawaiian national anthem and was played at official functions for the next 20 years. In 1891 she succeeded her brother King Kalakua to the throne. A Committee of Safety headed by Sanford B. Dole seized control of the kingdom on January 17, 1893, and arrested Queen Lili'uokalani. She was sentenced to life in prison, but was kept guarded in Iolani Palace. The provisional government created the Republic of Hawaii on July 4, 1894, with Sanford B. Dole as the first president. He released the queen in September 1895. She appealed to President Grover Cleveland, but he did nothing for her. Finally President William McKinley, who proclaimed the doctrine of "eminent domain", called for annexation, Congress agreed, and the US Territory of Hawaii was created as of July 6, 1898. The queen protested to President McKinley, to no avail, but he was assassinated on September 6, 1901, and died eight days later. The queen became embittered by the treatment she received from the Americans and died on November 11, 1917 in Honolulu.

LILLENAS, BERTHA MAE WILSON (1889–1945)
"Jesus took my burden."
"Jesus is always there."
Hymnist and composer, she was born in Hanson, Kentucky, on March 1, 1889, and was ordained a minister in the Church of the Nazarene in 1912. She married Haldor Lillenas, an evangelist preacher, and they traveled for ten years (1914–24). In 1924 he founded the Lillenas Music Company in Indianapolis, Indiana, which was purchased by the Nazarene Publishing Company in 1930. Her hymn, "When the clouds are hanging low," was included in *The Hymnbook* (Presbyterian, 1955). Her hymns above appear in *Phonolog Reports* of Los Angeles, California. She died at Tuscumbia, Missouri on March 13, 1945.

LILLIE, JESSIE (1890–Dec'd.)
"Way Out West in Wyoming"
Composer/songwriter born on June 4th in Elk Point, South Dakota and educated at South Dakota State University and private music study. With Ray Magee she wrote a number of songs: "Is it wrong?", "Just a prairie song at Twilight", "There's something 'bout the prairie", "Way out west in Wyoming", "When the cowboys gather home", "Song of a pioneer", "Seven reasons". ASCAP.

LINDEMAN, EDITH (1898–)
"Little Things Mean a Lot"
Songwriter born on March 21st in Pittsburgh, Pennsylvania, she was educated at Barnard College. Drama, film, radio commentator, she was also on staff of Richmond, Virginia's *Times-Dispatch* from 1933–64. With Carl Stutz, she wrote the lyrics for "Cling to Me", "I Know", "The Kissing Tree", and "Red-headed Stranger". She wrote the words for the *Jamestown Festival Suite*. ASCAP.

LINN, GERTRUDE (1905–)
"Yesterday, Today and Tomorrow"
Composer/pianist/songwriter born on January 16th in Chicago, Illinois, she was educated at the Chicago Musical College. She was a staff pianist for NBC and on radio. With Walter Hirsch and others, she wrote, "I Want to Go Round on a Merry-go-round", "My Jean", "Yesterday, Today and Tomorrow".

LIPSCOMB, HELEN (1921–)
Quintet for Clarinet, Strings
Composer/pianist born on April 20th in Georgetown, Kentucky, she was educated at the University of Kentucky (BA, MA); Indiana University; and studied with Nadia Boulanger in Paris. Her works include *Quintet for Clarinet, Strings*.

LISTON, MELBA DORETTA (1925–)
"All Deliberate Speed"
Trombonist/composer/arranger, she was born in Kansas City, Missouri. She was a trombonist and arranger for Billie Holiday, Dizzy Gillespie, Count Basie, Quincy Jones, and others in the 1940s–50s; and an arranger for Charlie Mingus, Duke Ellington, Tony Bennett, and others in the 1960s. She lived in Jamaica for five and a half years, then returned to New York City in 1980, whereupon she formed a septet at the third Salute to Women in Jazz at Lincoln Center in June. She composed the music and wrote "Melba's Blues", "Just Waiting", and "All Deliberate Speed".

LITKEI, ANDREA FODOR (1932–)
"The John Fitzgerald Kennedy March"
Singer/songwriter, she was born on April 26th in New York, New York. She was a soloist with the Metropolitan Opera and with Sadler Wells Ballet, wrote songs for films. With music by Ervin Litkei, she wrote the words for "I Waited By the Chapel Door", "On Madchen Oh Madchen", "Cleopatra", "Tonight I'm Not Just Pretending", "The John Fitzgerald Kennedy March", and "The Lyndon Baines Johnson March". ASCAP.

LIVINGSTON, HELEN (1900–)
"Kaddish"
Composer born on March 26th in New York, New York, she was educated at a business college, With Yosh Aeri and Helene Wach, she wrote *Kaddish.*

LOCKWOOD, ANNEA FERGUSON (1939–)
"Delta Run"
Composer, she was born on July 29th at Christchurch, New Zealand. After studying at Canterbury University in New Zealand (BMus 1961), she studied composition at the Ferienkurs fur Neu Musik at Darmstadt (1961–62), piano and composition at the Royal College of Music in London (1963), in Cologne, and at the Electronic Music Center at Bilthoven, The Netherlands (1963–64). After 1972 she taught at Hunter College, CUNY, and performed and gave lectures in Europe and New Zealand. After 1982 she taught at Vassar College. Her compositions include vocal and electronic and mixed media works. Her "Delta Run" (1981) was composed for the New Music America Festival and performed in Chicago in 1982.

LOCKWOOD, CHARLOTTE MATHEWSON (1903–1961)
Tune—"Rock of Ages"
Organist and composer, she was born at Granby, Connecticut, but was raised in Reidsville, North Carolina. She was graduated from the School

of Sacred Music at Union Theological Seminary in New York City
(Master SM) and studied with Widor in Paris and with Ramin at Leipzig,
Germany. She was organist at the Crescent Avenue Presbyterian Church
in Plainfield, New Jersey, when she wrote her tune based on an old He-
brew melody for the hymn "Men and children everywhere" written by
the Rev. John J. Moment, minister of her church. The hymn with her tune
appeared in *The Baptist Hymnal* (1973). "Charlotte Lockwood Garden
was killed in a very tragic automobile accident on May 19, 1961." (Information from Kathleen M. Upton, director of music, Crescent Avenue
Presbyterian Church, Plainfield, New Jersey.)

LOHOEFER, EVELYN (1921–)
    "Conversation Piece"
Composer/pianist born on December 28th in Clinton, North Carolina,
she was educated at Women's College, University of North Carolina
(BS), Bennington College; Juilliard School of Music; she studied with
Giannini, Horst, Norman Lloyd, and Stokowski. She was an accompanist on the USO dance tour of Europe in 1944. Her works: "Sometime-
Anytime", "Conversation Piece", the album *Come and See the Pepper-
mint Tree*, theater and ballet scores *Shakers, Pony Tails, Madeleine and
the Bad Hat, Modern Fantasy*. ASCAP.

LOPES, LISA "LEFT EYE"
    "Ain't 2 Proud 2 Beg"
Funky singer/songwriter, she is a member of the trio TLC, which stands
for their nicknames, Tionne "T-Boz" Watkins, Lisa "Left Eye" Lopes, and
Rozanda "Chilli" Thomas. Their debut album *Oooooooohhh . . . on the TLC
Trip* (1992) sold 3 million copies. On Top Ten Singles were "BabyBaby-
Baby" and "What About Your Friends?" They were on the "Tonight
Show" with Jay Leno, "Showtime at the Apollo", on the "Oprah Winfrey"
show, and "Dick Clark's New Year's Rockin' Eve" on ABC-TV (1992).
With Dallas Austin, Lisa Lopes wrote the 1993 Grammy Winner "Ain't 2
Proud to Beg". Their CD *Crazy Sexy Cool* (1994) included "Creep", a
funky jazzy dance number, "Waterfalls" about inner-city despair and "Red
Light Special", a saucy love song by Kenneth "Babyface" Edmonds. In
1994, Lopez was charged with burning down her boyfriend's house.

LORENZ, ELLEN JANE (1907–)
    Tune—"The Lamb"
Choirmaster/composer/arranger, she was born on May 3rd in Dayton,
Ohio. She married James B. Porter. Lorenz composed chamber music, organ, orchestral and choral works, and an opera. Her tune "The Lamb—O
the lamb, the loving lamb" was adapted from a 19th-century camp meeting song and appeared in *The United Methodist Hymnal* (1989). ASCAP.

LOUDOVA, IVANA (1941–)
Variations on a Stamic Theme
Composer, she was born on March 8th in Chlumee nad Cidlinou (now the Czech Republic). After studying piano with her mother, she studied composition under Miroslav Kabelac at the Prague Conservatory (1958–61) and under Emil Hlobil at the Prague Academy of Arts & Music (1961–66), where she was the first woman student of composition at the academy. She also received a French scholarship. On August 16, 1973, she married Milos Hasse and they have one son. She has won numerous prizes in composition. She has written symphonies, choral and orchestral works, chamber music, and a ballet *Rhapsody in Black* (1966) first performed in Prague in 1967. Her string quartet mentioned above (1989) was performed at Prague in 1990.

LOVE, COURTNEY
"Live Through This"
A singer/songwriter, Love is the lead singer for the rock band Hole. She married Kurt Cobain (1967–1994), the lead singer of Nirvana. Love's first album was *Pretty on the Inside* (1991), followed by *Live Through This* (1994). Known as the Dragon Queen, her first album spit bile, shrieking a paint-peeling "F--- yooooou" on "I think that I would die", one of eleven songs Love co-wrote, during her custody battle for baby Frances Bean after a *Vanity Fair* article said she used heroin while pregnant. Love uses venom and sarcasm in her punk music verses. While in Rome, Italy, her husband suffered from an overdose of heroin and was hospitalized. After their return to Seattle, Washington, Cobain shot himself and died on April 8, 1994.

LOVETT, COLLEEN (1936–)
"Sidewalks of Paree"
Composer/singer/songwriter she was born on November 3rd in Monroe, Louisiana, and educated at North Texas State University. She wrote "Out for the Day", "Sidewalks of Paree", etc.

LOWE, RUTH (1914–Dec'd.)
"I'll Never Smile Again"
Composer/pianist/songwriter, Lowe was born on August 12th in Toronto, Ontario, Canada, and educated in public schools. She was a pianist on Canadian Broadcasting Company radio and also with the Ina Ray Hutton orchestra. She wrote "A Short, Short Story", "A Touch of Love", "I'll Never Smile Again", "Ode to an Alligator", "Put Your Dreams Away", "Take Your Sins to the River", "A Touch of Love", "Won't Somebody Please Write a Song?", and "Too Beautiful to Last". ASCAP.

LUPBERGER, PAULINE (1931–Dec'd.)
"Chimes of Love"
Composer/songwriter, she was born on January 15th in St. James, Missouri, and received a high school education. She wrote "Hidden Gold," "Chimes of Love", "Hidden Violins", "Violins, Roses and Rainbows", and "Whistlin' Red Bird's Love Call". ASCAP.

LUSSI, MARIE (1892–Dec'd.)
"De Massus and de Missus"
Songwriter born on October 4th in Santa Clara Valley, California, and educated at Cathedral College and Hunter College in New York City, she lived in Ontario, Canada, for many years. With David Guion, she wrote the lyrics for "Greatest Miracle of All", "Love Is Lord of All", "Li'l Black Rose", "Life and Love", "In Galam", "Resurrection", and "Compensation".

LYNN, JUDY (1936–)
"The Calm Before the Storm"
Singer/songwriter, she was born in Boise, Idaho. At age sixteen she was crowned "Queen of the Snake River Stampede" in Nampa, Idaho. She was Miss Idaho (1955) and a runner-up for Miss America. She married promoter John Kelly. Lynn wrote "Antique in My Closet", "The Calm Before the Storm", "Honey Stuff", and "My Father's Voice".

LYNN, LORETTA (1935–)
"Coal Miner's Daughter"
Country singer/songwriter/guitarist, she was born Loretta Webb in Butcher Hollow, near Van Lear, Kentucky, on April 14th, the daughter of a coal miner. She lived in Wabash, Indiana, married Oliver V. Lynn when she was only thirteen years old and they lived in Bellingham, Washington. She formed her own band for nightclub spots, toured the US, Canada, and Europe during the 1960s. As a lyricist she wrote "Don't Come Home A-drinkin" (1966), "Fist City" (1968), "Coal Miner's Daughter" (1970), and "Your Looking at Country" (1971). She recorded a number of songs with Conway Twitty. As of 1994 her available albums were *20 Greatest Hits, Coalminer's Daughter, Country Music Hall of Fame, Don't Come Home A Drinkin, Drinkin' You, Greatest Hits, Greatest Hits Vol. II, Hymns,* and *I Remember Patsy.*

LYNN, TAMIYA
Tamiya Lynn
Singer/songwriter from New Orleans, she sang with the Rolling Stones, the Neville Brothers, and Dr. John. Her album is *Tamiya Lynn* (1992).

-M-

MACHADO, LENA (1907–Dec'd.)
"Kaulana O Hilo Hanakahi"
Composer/singer/songwriter born on October 16th in Honolulu, Hawaii, and educated at the Sacred Heart Convent. She sang in nightclubs, entertained troops during World War II, and sang with the Royal Hawaiian Band. She wrote the songs "Kaooha Mai", "Ei Nei", "Hawaii Aloha", "None Hula", "Pua Mamane", and "Kuu Wa Liilii." ASCAP.

MACKEN, JANE VIRGINIA (1912–)
"Tired of Being Lonely"
Composer/songwriter born on January 14th in St. Louis, Missouri, and educated at St. Mary-of-the-Woods and Ursuline Academy, she also had private music study. She wrote songs and the anthem "The Cross on the Hill".

MACONCHY, DAME ELIZABETH (1907–)
Puck Fair
Composer, she was born March 19th in Broxbourne, Hertfordshire, England, and was raised in Ireland. After studying composition under Charles Wood and Ralph Vaughan Williams, counterpoint under C. H. Kitson, and piano under Arthur Alexander at the Royal College of Music in London (1923–27), she studied under Karel Jirak in Prague, Czechoslovakia (1929–30). In 1930 she married William LeFanu and they had two daughters. Her daughter Nicola Le Fanu is also a composer. She has won numerous awards. In 1977 she became president of the Society for Promotion of New Music. Her works include symphonies, choral and orchestral works, opera, chamber music, etc. Her ballet suite *Puck Fair* (1940) was broadcast by the British Broadcasting Corporation in 1944, *Two Dances from Puck Fair* on the BBC Wales (1950). Almost all of her works have been performed, broadcast, or recorded.

MADONNA (1958–)
"Take a Bow"
Singer/songwriter, she was born Madonna Louise Ciccone on August 16 in Bay City, Michigan. Her albums *Like a Prayer* (1989) and *I'm Breathless* sold over 2 million copies; another of her albums is *Vogue;* she is also known for her platinum video *Justify My Love* (1990), *Erotica* (1992), her hit singles "Like a Virgin", "Material Girl", "This Used to Be My Playground" (1992); her book of pictures, *Sex* (1992). Her film *Body of Evidence* was released in January 1993. With "Take a Bow" in February 1995, she has had 11 No. 1 hits with her co-writer Kenneth "Babyface" Edmonds. Her 20th album *Bedtime Stories* (which included "Take a Bow") produced the No. 3 "Secret" in November 1994.

MAGEAU, MARY JANE MAGDALEN (1934–)
Indian Summer
Composer, she was born on September 4th in Milwaukee, Wisconsin. After studying under Leon Stein at DePaul University, Chicago (BMus, 1963) and composition under Leslie Bassett and Ross Lee Finney and continuo harpsichord with Ellwood Derr at the University of Michigan at Ann Arbor (MMus, 1969), she was Composer Fellowship Programme at the Berkshire Music Centre at Tanglewood, Massachusetts (1970). On December 26, 1974, she married Kenneth Luton White, and they have two sons. She has resided in Sydney, New South Wales, Australia, since 1974. She has composed vocal and orchestral works, chamber music, etc. Her Indian Summer for youth orchestra (1976) was written to celebrate the American Bicentennial and first performed on October 24, 1977 in Brisbane, Australia.

MALEY, FLORENCE TURNER (1871–1962)
"The Fields of O'Bally Clare"
Composer/singer born on August 23rd in Jersey City, New Jersey, and educated at the University of Geneva, Switzerland, she studied music with Joseffy, Gustave Becker, Alberta Lawrence, Jaques Bouhy, Joseph Barnaby, Me. Marchesia, and Cora D. Roucourt. She was a soprano soloist with the Brick Presbyterian Church in New York City, New York Symphony, Cincinnati Orchestra, etc. She wrote the songs "In a Little Town Nearby", "In a Garden Wild", "Lass O'mine", "Light at Evening Time", "Long and Long Ago", and "Song of Sunshine". ASCAP. She died on January 3rd in Point Pleasant, New Jersey.

MAMLOCK, URSULA (1928–)
When Summer Sang
Composer/teacher she was born on February 1st in Berlin, Germany. After studying piano and composition in Berlin, the family moved to Ecuador for a year, then to New York City in 1941, where she studied with Szell at the Mannes College (1942–46), and with Giannini at the Manhattan School of Music (BM and MM 1958). She taught at New York University (1967–76), then at the Manhattan School since 1976. She is known for her chamber music and piano pieces, string quartets and woodwind quintets. Her piece mentioned above was selected to represent the USA at the 1984 International Rostrum of Composers.

MANA ZUCCA (1885–1981)
"I Love Life"
Composer/pianist, she was born Augusta Zuckermann on December 25th in New York City, but changed her name to Mana Zucca while in her teens. She studied the piano with Alexander Lambert and played an

arrangement of Liszt's 14th Hungarian Rhapsody with Frank Damrosch in 1902 in the concert series for young people at Carnegie Hall. She toured Europe and gave concerts with the Spanish violinist Juan Manon in the late 1900s. The Cincinnati Symphony Orchestra performed her *Novelette* in 1917 and the New York Philharmonic her *Fugato humoresque* that year, as did the Cincinnati SO. Mana Zucca gave the first performance of her *Piano Concerto* with the Los Angeles Symphony on August 20, 1919. Many of her songs were written with Yiddish texts. Her song "I Love Life" (1923) was sung by Lawrence Tibbett, Nelson Eddy, and John Charles Thomas. She died on March 9, 1981 in Miami, Florida.

MANCHESTER, MELISSA (1951–)
"Come in from the rain"
Singer/songwriter, she was born on February 15th in New York, New York. She was a backup singer for Bette Midler. With Carole Bayer Sager, she wrote "Midnight Blue", "Come In From the Rain", and with Kenny Loggins wrote "Whenever I Call You 'Friend'". Manchester toured the US in 1992. In 1994 her albums and CDs available were *Greatest Hits* and *Tribute*. Her video is *Music of Melissa Manchester*.

MANION, MARY E. (1907–Dec'd.)
"Shadow in Love"
Composer/songwriter born on February 16th in Philadelphia, Pennsylvania, she wrote songs. ASCAP.

MANN, MARY ANN MORTON (1826–1897)
"Sweet Is the Peace the Gospel Brings"
A hymnist born in England, she came to America in 1856 and married George Mann. Her hymn above appeared in the Mormon hymnal (1985).

MANNING, KATHLEEN LOCKHART (1890–1951)
"In the Luxembourg Gardens"
Composer/singer, she was born on October 24th in Hollywood, California. After she studied composition with Moritz Moszkowski in Paris in 1908, she toured England and Europe until the outbreak of World War I. Her song circle *Sketches of Paris,* which included the song, "In the Luxembourg Gardens", was so popular she arranged it for women's choir. Most of her songs were written in the early 1920s, including, "Water Lily", "Japanese Ghost Songs", "Sketches of London", and in the 1930s "Chinese Impressions", "Vignettes", and "Sketches of New York". She died on March 20th at Los Angeles, California.

MARCH, MYRNA FOX (1935–)
"Crying Up a Storm"
Composer/singer/songwriter born on November 19th in Los Angeles, California, she received a high school education. She sang in nightclubs and wrote songs including, "Why?". ASCAP.

MARCUS, BUNITA (1952–)
The Rugmaker
Composer, she was born on May 5th in Madison, Wisconsin. After studying composition under Franz Loschnigg (1968–73); and music theory at the University of Wisconsin at Madison (BM 1976), she studied under Morton Feldman at the State University of New York at Buffalo (PhD, 1981). She has taught at the State College at Buffalo, Lincoln Center Institute in New York City, Columbia University, Brooklyn College, and has been an independent composer since 1986. She has composed instrumental and choral works, chamber music, etc. *The Rugmaker,* a string quartet, was first performed at Middleburg in The Netherlands (1986). It is considered one of the finest string quartets of the 20th century.

MARGOLIS, KITTY
"Firm Roots"
Jazz scatter/swinger/songwriter, her album is *Anthropology;* she wrote the lyrics for "Firm Roots"; "Live at the Jazz Workshop"; with saxist Joe Henderson on "Evolution" (1994–see also Oleta Adams).

MARINSKI, SOPHIE (1917–)
"Tu Sei Cosi Amabile"
Composer/songwriter born October 3rd in Toledo, Ohio, she received a high school education. With George Cardini and Sonny Skylar, she wrote some songs: "With These Rings" and "Tu Sei Cosi Amabile".

MARSHALL, JANE MANTON (b. 1924–)
Tune — "Northaven"
Composer, she was born in Dallas, Texas, on December 5, 1924, and educated at Southern Methodist University (BM, 1945; MM, 1968) in Dallas, Texas. She married Elbert Marshall, an engineer with Texas Instruments. An active member of the Northaven Methodist Church, she served as choir director and organist there (1957–60). She taught music at Southern Methodist University (1969–74), then at Perkins School of Theology. She has composed numerous anthems, three collections of children's choir music, and has contributed to church music journals. In 1974 the Southern Baptist Church Music Conference awarded her a certificate for

distinguished service to church music. Her tune above appeared in the *Baptist Hymnal* (1975).

MARSTARS, ANN (1918–)
"This Town of New York"
Songwriter born on March 1st in Boston, Massachusetts, she was educated at the Child Walker School of Art. With Bill Snyder, she wrote the lyrics for "Be Sure to Tell Him", "My Pony Macaroni", "Teresa Smiles", etc. ASCAP.

MARTH, HELEN JUN (1903–)
Sing O Ye Heavens
Composer/pianist born on May 24th in Alton, Illinois, and educated at high school, she received private music study. She was a pianist accompanist on the Chautauqua circuit; worked in Little Theatre for 30 years; and composed the anthem "You Taught Me How to Pray" and the cantatas *The Triumph of Christ* and *Sing O Ye Heavens*. ASCAP.

MARTIN, ROBERTA (1907–1969)
"God Is Still on the Throne"
Gospel singer/pianist/composer, she was born on February 12th in Helena, Arkansas. When she was a teenager the family moved to Chicago and Roberta became the pianist of the Ebenezer Baptist Church where Thomas A. Dorsey was the pastor. In 1933 with composer Theodore R. Frye she organized the Martin-Frye Quartet with herself as pianist. Within two years the group became known as the Roberta Martin Singers. Martin wrote about 100 gospel songs, including, "Try Jesus, He Satisfies" (1943), the one mentioned above in 1959, "Let It Be" (1962), and "Just Jesus and Me" (1966). She died in Chicago on January 18th. As of 1994 the album of the Roberta Martin Singers available was *Stars of the Gospel Highway*.

MARTIN, RUTH KELLEY (1914–)
'The Magic Flute' (translation)
Translator/songwriter born on April 14th in Jersey City, New Jersey, and educated at Smith College (BA); Columbia University; and University of Munich, Salzburg Mozarteum, she married conductor Thomas Martin and they wrote English translations of works by Mozart, Verdi, Puccini, Rossini, Bizet, and Johann Strauss. ASCAP.

MARTINEZ, MARIANNE (1744–1812)
Oratorio—*Santa Elena at Calvario*
Composer of Spanish descent, she was born in Vienna, Austria, on May 4, 1744, the daughter of the master of ceremonies to the Papal nuncio

there. Young Haydn, while poor and unknown, occupied a garret in their house and gave her lessons on the harpsichord. The Italian poet and librettist, Pietro Metasyasio, also lived in the same house and was her private tutor. She also composed a *Psalm* to an Italian translation by Metastasio, for four to eight voices, a Mass, arias, cantatas, and various sacred music. She died in Vienna on December 13, 1812.

MARTINEZ, ODALINE de la (1949–)
Sister Aimee
Composer/conductor she was born on October 31st in Matanzas, Cuba. At age twelve she was brought to the states and became a US citizen in 1971. She was graduated from Tulane University (BFA, 1972), then studied composition with Paul Paterson at the Royal Academy of Music in London and with Brindle at the University of Surrey (MM, 1977). Since 1975 she has been conductor of the chamber ensemble Lontano. She has composed a number of vocal and instrumental works. Her opera *Sister Aimee* is based on the life of Aimee Semple McPherson, an American evangelist preacher and was composed between 1978–83. She has resided in London for the past 20 years.

MARTONE, PRUDENCE (1933–)
"All Roads Lead Me to Rome"
Songwriter born on October 1st in Brooklyn, New York, the daughter of composer/conductor/violinist Don Martone, she wrote the lyrics for the above song and "My Last Night in Venice", etc.

MASCIA, MADELINE T. (1928–Dec'd.)
"Maddonina di Loreto"
Composer/songwriter born on January 28th in Port Chester, New York, she was educated at the College of New Rochelle, New York. She wrote the above song and "Ciao for Now", etc. ASCAP.

MASSON, ELIZABETH (1806–1865)
Composer and singer, born in Scotland, she was the pupil of Mrs. Henry Smart and later of Guiditta Pasta in Italy. She wrote the music for several hymns by Adelaide Ann Procter (1825–1864). She founded the Royal Society of Female Musicians in London in 1839, and died in London on January 9, 1865.

MATTIS, LILLIAN (1925–)
"We've Got a World that Swings"
Songwriter born on December 6th in New York, New York, Mattis was educated at Hunter College in New York City. With Louis Brown and Neal Hefti, she wrote the lyrics for a number of songs, including, the

song above, "A Now and Later Love", "I Must Know", and "How to Murder Your Wife" (film title song). ASCAP.

MATUSZCZAK, BERNADETTA (1933–)
Julia i Romeo
Composer, she was born on March 10th in Torun, Poland. She studied piano under Trena Kurpisz-Stefanowa and music theory under Z. Sitowski at the State Music College in Poznan, then composition under T. Szeligowski and T. Sikorski at the State Music College in Warsaw (graduated 1964). She also studied composition under Nadia Boulanger in Paris (1968). She has been awarded a number of prizes. She has composed choral and orchestral works, operas, chamber music, etc. Her chamber opera after Shakespeare *Julia i Romeo* (1967) was first produced at Wiesbaden in 1972, then throughout Germany.

MAXWELL, HELEN PURCELL (1901–)
"Wheels a-Rolling"
Composer born on December 20th in Vincennes, Indiana, and educated at De Pauw University School of Music (BM), she married author/ lyricist Philip Maxwell and they wrote "Wheels a-Rolling" (Chicago Railroad Fair Pageant theme song), "Autumn Ballet", "Campus Days", "Give Us a Campus", "I'm a Little Christmas Tree", "Let's Sing to Victory", "All My Love, Dear", "Toast to Music", and "Hawaiian Holiday".

MAYER, NATALIE (1925–)
The Charling Series
Composer/pianist/singer/songwriter born on May 17th in New York, New York, and educated at the Leonardi School in Switzerland, she had private music study. Her works are *The Charling Series* (children's musicals), and the songs "Build a House of God", "Do-it-together", "Kiss and Remember", "Sing-Along", "Song-stories", and "We'll Meet Again".

MAYES, CAROL (1924–)
"We Give This Child to You"
Hymnist/pianist/singer, she was born on February 19th in Loma Linda, California, and received a high school education. She studied music and journalism. She wrote the hymn above, which appeared in the *Baptist Hymnal* (1986).

McALLISTER, LOUISE (1913–1960)
Tune—"Bourbon"
An old folk-hymn melody, the tune was harmonized by McAllister. Composer and arranger, the daughter of the professor of English Bible

at the Louisville Presbyterian Theological Seminary in Louisville, Kentucky, she was born there. In 1925 the family moved to Richmond, Virginia, where her father became a professor at the Union Theological Seminary. After graduating from the Collegiate School in Richmond, she attended Mary Baldwin College in Staunton, Virginia, but was unable to continue her studies after she injured her hands. She then studied privately with Mrs. Crosby Adams and John Powell. Her tune with the hymn "'Twas on that dark and doleful night" appeared in *The Pilgrim Hymnal* (1958). Her tune, "Aylesbury", harmonized from a melody in the *Hesperian Harp* (1848), together with the hymn, "O Love of God Most Full," appeared in the Presbyterian *Hymnbook* (1955).

MC CARTHY, CHARLOTTE (1918–)
"I Don't Want to Be Hurt Anymore"
Composer/songwriter born on September 12th in Tangier, Indiana, and educated at the Colorado Women's College, she wrote songs. ASCAP.

MC CARTNEY, LINDA EASTMAN
"Live and Let Die"
Songwriter, she was born on September 24th in New York City. She married Paul McCartney of the Beatles. With music by her husband, she wrote the words for "Live and Let Die—When you were young and your heart was an open book" and "My Love—And when I go away I know my heart can stay with my love". ASCAP.

MC CAW, MAXINE GAMBS (1919–)
Music—"Church Is People"
Composer and concert pianist, she was born in Des Moines, Iowa, on November 14, 1919. "Regarding Maxine Gambs McCaw, she is the wife of Dr. John E. McCaw, who is retiring from his professorship at Drake University, Des Moines, next month. I am John's second mother, making Maxine my daughter-in-law. She was born in Des Moines and has lived most of her life here. She is an accomplished concert pianist, and currently teaching music in her home. She, too, feels honored to be included in your forthcoming book. Accept our best wishes for success in this enterprise." (Letter dated April 20, 1982 from Mrs. Mabel N. McCaw, Des Moines, Iowa.) With words by Mabel McCaw, her tune appeared in the hymnal *Joyfully Sing* (1968).

MC CLEARY, FIONA (1900–)
Trois Melodies
Composer/pianist born on January 29th in Sanderstead, Surrey, England and educated in private schools in England, France, and Italy, she studied music with Harriet Cohen, Myra Hess, Arnold Bax, Tobias Matthay, and

Vaughan Williams. She also studied at the Royal Academy of Music, Matthay Piano School. She came to the US in 1928 and toured the nation as a concert pianist. She became a US citizen in 1932. Her instrumentals are *Trois Melodies, Melody* (cello), and *Whispering Waltz* (piano).

MC CLOUD, SUSAN EVANS (1945–)
"As Zion's Youth in Latter Days"
A hymnist born in Ogden, Utah, and educated at Brigham Young University, she married James W. McCloud and they have six children. She has written fiction, poetry, childrens' books, etc. Her hymn above and "Lord, I Would Follow Thee" appeared in the Mormon hymnal (1985).

MC CLUSKY, ANGELA
"Philadelphia Story"
Scottish folk/rock singer/songwriter, she came to America and formed a quartet in Los Angeles. She wrote most of the songs on her album *Wild Colonials* (1994), including "Philadelphia Story". While violinist Paul Cantelon was playing a bluegrass version of a love scene from Bizet's *Carmen,* McClusky broke in with a rocking chorus about a middle-aged crisis victim "who forgot the need to kiss."

MC COLLIN, FRANCES (1892–1960)
Anthem—*The Lord is Kind*
Composer and conductor, she was born in Philadelphia, Pennsylvania, on October 24, 1892, and educated at the Institute for the Blind, and at Bryn Mawr College, Bryn Mawr, Pennsylvania, as well as studying music privately. She was chorus conductor at the Burd School in Philadelphia (1922–33), and at Swarthmore College in Swarthmore, Pennsylvania (1923–24). Her anthem above won the Clemson award; *O Sing unto the Lord* won the Philadelphia Manuscript Society award; *Then Shall the Religious Shine* won the Mendelssohn Club prize; *Come Hither Ye Faithful* won the Dayton Westminster Choir prize. She died in Philadelphia, Pennsylvania, on February 26, 1960.

MC COMB, JEANNE (1913–)
"Hail the United World"
Dancer/songwriter, she was born on December 17th in Detroit, Michigan, and received a high school education and studied dancing. With the dancing team of Jeanne and Gloria, she appeared in nightclubs and toured the US. With Shelly Bond and Willard Robison, she wrote the lyrics for a number of songs, including, "Hail the United World", which became the official theme song of the United Nations.

MC CONOCHIE, BARBARA A. (1940–)
  Tune—"Peace"
Composer/organist/pianist/hymnist, she was born in Ogden, Utah. At age five she studied piano at the McCune School of Music and Art, and later graduated from the University of Utah. She married Douglas A. McConochie, they have nine children, and live in Oakland, California. She has composed several choral works and wrote the words for the above and "Keep the Commandments", which appeared in the Mormon hymnal (1985).

MC GIBNEY, RUTH T. (1896–)
  Childhood Memories
A songwriter, she was born on February 10th in Chicago, Illinois, and educated in college. With Rica Moore she wrote the lyrics for her albums *Childhood Memories* and *Zoo Songs*.

MC GILL, JOSEPHINE (1877–1919)
  "Duna, When I Was a Little Child"
Composer/arranger of folk songs, she was born on October 20th in Louisville, Kentucky. Although she had no formal training as a composer, she spent the summer of 1914 searching the origin of Scottish and English folksongs and transcribing them, which she published in *Folk-songs of the Kentucky Mountains* in 1917. The book has been reprinted three times. She wrote the above song in 1914, also "O Sleep", and "Less than Clouds". She died at Louisville on February 24th.

MC GLINN, ANN J. (1922–)
  "Song of Love"
Composer/songwriter born on July 27th in St. Paul, Minnesota, she was educated at Pine Manor College and Bryn Mawr College. She wrote the songs "I Love for You to Tell Me", "Song of Love".

MC LEAN, PRISCILLA ANNE TAYLOR (1942–)
  "Elan' A Dance to All Things Rising From the Earth
Composer/flutist/pianist/producer, she was born on May 27th in Fitchburg, Massachusetts. After attending the State College at Fitchburg (BEd, 1963), the University of Lowell (BME, 1965), and Indiana University (MM, 1969), she taught at Indiana University at Kokomo (1973–76). After marrying composer/pianist Barton McLean, the two performed as the McLean Mix presenting their own music. Her chamber piece mentioned above was composed in the early 1980s. She has composed other chamber music, choruses, orchestral work, and tape music.

MC MASTER, CLARA ELIZABETH WATKINS (1904–)
Tune—"Autumn"
Composer/singer/hymnist born at Beaver Dam, Box Elder County,
Utah, the eleventh child in a musical family. She married J. Stuart Mc-
Master and they have four children. She sang in the Tabernacle Choir
for 23 years. She composed the music for the above and also wrote the
words "Teach me to walk in the light", which is in the Mormon hymnal
(1985).

MC MULLEN, DOROTHY (1926–)
"The Game of Broken Hearts"
Singer/songwriter born on June 9th in Florida, New York, and educated
in high school. She was a singer in vaudeville and nightclubs. She married composer/conductor Edwin D. McMullen. With her husband she
wrote the lyrics for "Four Season Sweetheart", "Moon Song", and "The
Game of Broken Hearts". ASCAP.

MC PARTLAND, MARION TURNER (1920–)
"There'll Be Other Times"
Jazz pianist/composer, she was born on March 20th in Slough, Buck-
inghamshire, England. She dropped out of the Guildhall School of Mu-
sic in London to join a piano vaudeville act. She toured with the USO
during World War II, and while in Belgium in 1944, she met cornetist
Jimmy McPartland. The next year, they were married and returned to the
states in 1946. She formed her own trio, which played at the Embers
Club in New York City, and at the Hickory House in the 1950s–60s. Her
compositions include the song mentioned above recorded by Sarah
Vaughan, "In the Days of Our Love", "So Many Things", "Ambiance",
"With You on My Mind", and "Twilight World" played on the "Tonight
Show". As of 1994, her albums and CDs available were *Concert in Ar-
gentina,* 'From this Moment on', 'Live at Maybeck Hall Vol. 9', *Personal Choice, Plays Billy Strayhorn, Plays Benny Carter, Portrait of
Marian McPartland, Willow Creek and Ballads.* Her husband died in
1991.

MC PHAIL, LENORA CARPENTER (1907–)
"New Orleans Town"
Cellist/songwriter born on March 16th in Duluth, Minnesota, and educated at Northwestern University School of Music, she had private cello
study. She was the cellist with the Duluth Symphony and the Evanston
Symphony. With composer/conductor/pianist, Lindsay McPhail, she
wrote the lyrics for "Down in Charleston", "I Want a Dog for Christmas", and "Wanna know somethin'", etc.

MC VIE, CHRISTINE
"Don't stop"
A singer/songwriter, she sang with drummer/singer Mic Fleetwood. The band's album *Rumors* was the second best seller of 1977. With Robbie Patton she wrote "Hold me—Can you understand me?"; with Jim Recor, "Love in store—All I know is the way I feel whenever you're around"; she wrote "Songbird—For you, there'll be no more again", "You make lovin' fun—Sweet, wonderful you, you make me happy with the things you do"; "Don't stop—If you wake up and don't want to smile, don't stop thinking about tomorrow", which was the theme song of presidential candidate Bill Clinton at the Democratic National Convention in New York City in 1992. Fleetwood Mac band played at an inaugural ball for President Clinton in January 1993.

MEDLEY, CYNTHIA CONWELL (1929–)
"The Everglades"
Composer/songwriter born on June 23rd in Frankfort, Kentucky, she was educated at Mary Washington College, University of Virginia (BA) and had private piano study. With Michael Cordia and Marion Chaplin, she wrote a number of songs, including, "Patiently Waiting", "Sea Power", "To You from Me". ASCAP.

MELLING, ELLEN KNOWLES (1820–1905)
Tune—"Jacques"
Composer born in Lancashire, England, baptized as a Latter-day Saint by Heber C. Kimball and confirmed by Orson Hyde. In 1855 she sailed for America with her husband John Melling and while on the difficult trek to Salt Lake City, Utah, she gave birth to a daughter. She wrote the above tune to a hymn by John Jacques—"Oh say, What Is Truth?", which first appeared in the *Latter-day Saints' Psalmody* in 1889 and again in the Mormon hymnal of 1985.

MENDELSSOHN-BARTHOLDY, FANNY CACILLE (1805–1847)
Lieder ohne Worte
Pianist/composer, she was born on November 14th in Hamburg, Germany, the sister of Felix Mendelssohn. In 1811 the family fled to Berlin to escape Napoleonic oppression in Hamburg. She studied piano with Ludwig Berger and composition with Karl Zelter. The family went to Paris in 1816. Fanny was an accomplished pianist at age thirteen. In 1829 she married painter Wilhelm Hensel. In the 1840s she led Sunday morning concerts at the Elternhaus in Berlin. Mendelssohn composed choral and piano works. She died on May 14th during a rehearsal for a Sunday concert.

MENDOZA, LYDIA (1916–)

"Una historia de la musica de la frontera"

Singer/guitarist/songwriter, she was born on May 31st in Houston, Texas. During the late 1920s she sang with El Cuarteto Carra Blanca, the family ensemble, and in 1928 recorded 10 sides for Okeh Records. Between 1930–34, the family performed at the Plaza del Zacate in San Antonio. Between 1934–40, Mendoza made about 200 recordings for Bluebird Records and performed as a soloist. Her songs are recorded on *Texas-Mexican Border Music* issued by Folklyric Records.

MEREDITH, JOLEEN G. (1935–)

Tune—"Grant"

Composer/pianist born in American Fork, Utah, where her grandfather, William Grant settled and was a musician there, she has composed a number of piano pieces, choral works, etc. Her tune above was written to words by Emma Lou Thayne—"Where can I turn for peace?" in the Mormon hymnal (1985).

MERO, YOLANDO (1887–Dec'd.)

Capriccio Ungharese

Pianist/composer, she was born on August 30th in Budapest, Hungary. After studying at the Conservatory in Budapest, she made her debut as a solo pianist with the Dresden Philharmonic in 1907. She toured Europe, Central and South America, and the states, residing here for a number of years. She married Hermann Irion, a member of the firm of Steinway & Sons. She composed *Capriccio Ungharese* for piano and orchestra.

MERRILL, AMY (1889–Dec'd.)

"You Thrill Me in the Moonlight"

Composer/pianist/songwriter born on October 22nd in Raffadoli, Italy, she was educated at Damrosch Institute of Musical Art and also had private music study. She was a pianist accompanist to various singers and violinists. With Ralph Genger and Ralph Stein, she wrote a number of songs, including, "Baby, It's a Sin to Lie", "Rock a Rolla the Old Pianola", and "Share Your Dreams with Me."

MERRILL, BLANCHE (1895–Dec'd.)

"I'm from Chicago"

Songwriter born on July 23rd in Philadelphia, Pennsylvania, she was educated at Teacher Training School. She wrote songs for Belle Baker, Fanny Brice, Nora Bayes, and Eva Tanguay. With Leo Edwards and others, she wrote "Becky Is Back at the Ballet", "Bye and Bye", "I'm an Indian", "Just Around the Corner from Broadway", "Poor Little Cinderella", and "Trailing Along in a Trailer". ASCAP.

MEYER, LUCY RIDER (1849–1922)
Tune—*Northfield Benediction*
A composer born in New Haven, near Middlebury, Vermont, on September 9, 1849, she was educated in public schools and while still in her teens she taught in the high school at Brandon, Vermont, and in a school for freedmen at Greensboro, North Carolina. She entered the Junior class at Oberlin College in Ohio (1869). After becoming engaged to a young man studying to become a medical missionary, she decided to follow his career and enrolled in the Women's Medical School in Philadelphia. But her fiancé died, and she abandoned that career. She served as principal of the Troy (Methodist) Conference Academy in Poultney, Vermont, and as professor of chemistry at McKendree College in Illinois, and taught at Northfield Seminary. In 1885 she married Josiah S. Meyer, a Methodist Episcopal minister of the Rock River Conference, and they opened the Chicago Training School for City, Home and Foreign Missions, where she served as principal (1885–1917). She died in Chicago, Illinois, on March 16, 1922. Her musical setting for "The Lord bless thee and keep thee" appeared in the *Methodist Hymnal* (1935).

MEYERS, CLAUDIA D. (1915–)
"On that Day You Came Along"
Songwriter born on March 2nd in Leeds, Alabama, she was educated in public schools. She wrote "No One Else Can Make Me Blue" and "On that Day You Came Along."

MICHAEL, ELAINE (1930–)
"Make Believe Island of Dreams"
Composer/songwriter born on January 9th in New York, New York, and educated at Long Island University and Brooklyn College. With Hal Gordon and Bill Schulman, she wrote the songs, "Drink to a Fool", "Don't Say Goodbye", "Little Boy", "They're Playing Our Song", and also the album *Moonlight Magic*. ASCAP.

MIEIR, AUDREY MAE WAGNER (1916–)
"His Name is Wonderful"
The daughter of Marie Elizabeth Dorsey and Dow C. Wagner, she was born at Leechburg, Pennsylvania, on May 12, 1916, and educated at L.I.F.E. Bible College. In 1936 she was married to Charles B. Mieir and in 1937 she was ordained a minister in the International Church of Foursquare Gospel. She has played gospel songs on the piano on radio and made personal appearances (1937–45); she was director and organizer of various choirs (1946–58), director of the Mieir Choir Clinic, and vice-president of Mieir Music Foundation, Inc., Hollywood, California, since 1960. She wrote "The Desert Shall Bloom Like a Rose" and other

beautiful songs while suffering with cancer. A member of the Bethel Chapel, Assembly of God Church in San Jose, California, she was active as of April 1982. Her hymn appeared in the *Baptist* (1975); *Family of God* (1976); and *Broadman* (1977) hymnals.

MILLER, ANNE LANGDON (1908–)
    Tune—"Vermont"
Composer and violinist, she was born at New York City on January 6, 1908, and educated there at the Institute of Musical Art and the David Mannes School of Music. After several years as first violinist in the Vermont State Symphony Orchestra, in 1948 she entered the Community of Poor Clares. Her tune appeared in *The Hymnal* of the Protestant Episcopal Church (1940).

MILLER, LILLIAN ANNE (1916–)
    "I Will Call Upon God"
Composer, hymnist, pianist, and teacher, she was born at North Haddonfield, New Jersey, on May 31, 1916, and was educated at the Sternberg School of Music, Rutgers University in New Brunswick, New Jersey, and she studied privately. She taught at the North Haddonfield branch of the Sternberg School and was a pianist-accompanist for the Philadelphia Light Opera Company. She had her own trio with the Cosmopolitan Opera Company and was a teacher in Newark, New Jersey. She also wrote "Blessed Land of Mine," "O Lord Behold the Earth," "Exult in Glory," etc.

MILLS, PAULINE MICHAEL (1898–)
    Tune—"Worthy"
Composer/songwriter, she was born on October 13th in Portland, Indiana, was graduated from L.I.F.E. Bible College and ordained. She was married, had six children, and wrote some 300 love songs and songs with Biblical settings. As of 1992 she was living in a retirement/nursing home. Her tune "Worthy-Thou art worthy" appeared in *The Hymnal for Worship & Celebration* (Baptist 1986).

MINEO, ANTOINETTE (1926–)
    Rhapsody 21
Composer/pianist born on November 26th in Tacoma, Washington, she studied privately. She married Attilio Mineo and they founded Mineo Music, Inc. She composed *Music Out of Century 21* and *Rhapsody 21* for the Seattle World's Fair. ASCAP.

MINKOFF, FRANCES (1915–)
    "The Honey Wind Blows"
Songwriter born on February 5th in Brooklyn, New York, she was educated at Brooklyn College (BA). With Fred Hellerman she wrote

the lyrics for "The Biggest Ride (since Paul Revere)", "Along About Now", "Healing River", "Come Away Melinda", and "Sailor man". ASCAP.

MITCHELL, JONI (1943–)
"Both Sides Now"

Singer/guitarist/songwriter she was born Roberta Joan Anderson on November 1st in what is now Macleod, Alberta. She was raised in Saskatoon, Canada, where she took piano lessons and learned to play the ukulele and guitar. After studying at the Alberta College of Art in Calgary for one year, she sang folk songs in Calgary, then Toronto in the 1960s. She married singer Chuck Mitchell and they moved to Detroit, but soon separated. She wrote "The Circle Game" recorded by Tom Rush and "Both Sides Now" recorded by Judy Collins. Her own recording of "Both Sides Now" won a Grammy folk performance award for 1970. Crosby, Stills, Nash, and Young recorded her "Woodstock", which was a hit. She moved to the Los Angeles suburbs and wrote the lyrics for jazz bassist Charlie Mingus's music and completed the album *Mingus* after his death. In 1994 her albums available were *Blue, Chalk Mark in a Rain Storm, Clouds, Court & Spark, Dog Eat Dog, Don Juan's Reckless Daughter, For the Roses, Hejira, Hissing of Summer Lawns, Joni Mitchell, Ladies of the Canyon, Miles of Aisles, Mingus, Night Ride Home, Shadows and Light, Wild Things Run Fast.*

MOFFATT, KATY
Hearts Gone Wild

Falsetto singer/songwriter, she resides in California. Her albums are *Child Bride* and *Hearts Gone Wild* (1995), the latter of which included "Junkyard Heart" ("I'll never sell her for parts") and "Ruin This Romance", a switcheroo song about the joys and comforts of a relationship that can't be broken or messed up.

MONK, MEREDITH (1943–)
Quarry

Composer/singer, she was born on November 20th in Lima, Peru, while her mother, the pop singer known as Audrey Marsh, was on tour. She was raised in New York and Connecticut and was educated in performing arts at Sarah Lawrence College in Bronxville, New York. From an early age she was interested in the theater, and her composition *Juice* was given its debut at the Guggenheim in New York City in 1969. She founded the Meredith Monk Vocal Ensemble, consisting of three men and three women in 1978 and the group has performed in the US and Europe. Her opera *Quarry* with 38 solo voices, two harmoniums, and 2 record tapes was written in 1976. She has composed solo vocals, vocal ensembles, and various theater pieces.

MONTANA, PATSY (1914–)
"I've Found My Cowboy Sweetheart"
Singer/songwriter, she was born Rubye Blevins on October 30th in Hot Springs, Arkansas. She attended the University of Western Louisiana, then became lead singer for the Prairie Ramblers in 1934. She married Paul Rose. She wrote "I'm a Little Cowboy Girl", "The Buckaroo", "Me and My Cowboy Sweetheart", "The Moon Hangs Low", "I've Found My Cowboy Sweetheart", "My Baby's Lullaby", "Cowboy Rhythm", and "My Poncho Pony". She was honored at a country music concert in September 1992. ASCAP.

MONTGOMERY, EDYTHE (1908–)
"Jazztime beat"
A songwriter, she was born on March 23rd in New Bedford, Massachusetts, and educated in public school. She wrote "Champagne Polka", "Chickadee Polka", "Cute Little Ice Cube", "Hug and Kiss Me", "Rocks in the Head", "You Teaser You", etc.

MOODY, MAY WHITTLE (1870–1963)
Tune—"Whittle"
Composer and daughter of evangelist Daniel W. Whittle (1840–1891), she was named "Mary" but chose "May" and at age fifteen attended the Girl's School in Northfield, Massachusetts, which was founded by evangelist Dwight L. Moody. Later she attended Oberlin College (1888–89) in Oberlin, Ohio, and the Royal Academy of Music in London, England (1890–91). She sang gospel songs in the evangelistic campaigns of Moody and Whittle. On August 29, 1894, she married William R. Moody, son of the famous evangelist, and they had six children, two of whom died in infancy. They lived at Northfield where Will Moody headed the Northfield Schools and also the Mount Hermon Conference center, which had been founded by his father. With Charles M. Alexander, she was co-editor of *Northfield Hymnal No. 3*. Her tune appeared in *Sacred Songs No. 1* edited by Ira D. Sankey, James McGranahan, and George C. Stebbins (1896) and with the hymn, "Dying with Jesus" in *Hymns for the Living Church* (1974). She died in Northfield on August 20, 1963.

MOORE, DOROTHY RUDD (1940–)
Frederick Douglass
Composer, she was born on June 4th in New Castle, Delaware. After studying composition with Mark Fax at Howard University, Washington, DC (BMus 1963), and with Nadia Boulanger at the American Conservatory at Fontainebleau in France, she studied with Chou Wen-chung in New York City (1965). She then taught piano and theory at the Harlem School of the Arts, and music history and appreciation at New York Uni-

versity and Bronx Community College. She was also one of the founders of the Society of Black Composers. She married cellist Kermit Moore. Her opera *Frederick Douglass,* was written from 1979–85. Mrs. Moore has written a number of songs, piano pieces, and orchestral works.

MOORE, ELIZABETH EVELYN (1891–Dec'd.)
"Moonlight in Old Granada"
Songwriter born on June 22nd in Poughkeepsie, New York, and educated at the Quincy School, she also had private study. She was a newspaper columnist and with her daughter Sylvia Dee, Noble Cain, Robert Flagler, Geoffrey O'Hara, Gustave Klemm, and Huntington Woodman, she wrote the lyrics for "He Could Only Sing a C", "In the Night", "Let There Be a Song", "Let All My Life Be Music," "How Sweet the Bells of Christmas", "Music of Life", "Maripo", "Where Heaven Is", "My Rosary of Roses", "O Sing Again", and "White Swans". ASCAP.

MOORE, MARY LOUISE CARR (1873–1957)
Narcissa, or The Cost of Empire
Composer/teacher, she was born on August 6th in Memphis, Tennessee. She studied composition with J. H. Pratt and singing with H. B. Passmore and had a song published at age sixteen. Her first operetta *The Oracle* was performed on March 19, 1894 in San Francisco, and she sang the leading role. She moved to Seattle, Washington, in 1901, taught and composed there, having given up her singing. She conducted her opera mentioned above, which was performed on April 22, 1912 in Seattle. She moved back to San Francisco in 1915 and conducted her opera there in 1945. Moore wrote two more operas, songs, choral works, and piano pieces. She died on January 9th in Inglewood, California.

MOORE, MILTONA (1902–)
In a Russian Village
Composer/pianist born on February 7th in Joliet, Illinois, she was educated at Chicago College of Music (MM) and The Principia. She studied with Maurice DePackh, Leopold Godoswky, and Charles Wakefield Cadman. She was a piano soloist with the Chicago Symphony. With Kate Hammond, she composed the following piano pieces: *Gremlins, In a Russian Village, Island Fantasy, Little Ballerina,* and *On Venetian Waters.* ASCAP.

MOORE, RICA OWEN (1929–)
"My Monkey and Me"
Composer/conductor/pianist/singer she was born on January 3rd in Lake Forest, Illinois, and studied music with Leon Benditsky, Guy Maier, Lee Pattison, and Margaret Wilson. She was a piano soloist with the Waukegan

(Illinois) Philharmonic and the Chicago Symphony; she was director of an a capella singing group; wrote "I Can Do Anything" and other songs; and the albums *Zoo Songs* and *Childrens' Songs for Adults*. She married King-man Moore.

MOORE, UNDINE SMITH (1905–Dec'd.)
Scenes from the Life of a Martyr
Composer/teacher, she was born on August 25th at Jarratt, Virginia. After studying piano and organ with Alice M. Grass at Fisk University, Nashville (BA, BMus), at the Juilliard School, she received her professional diploma at Columbia University Teachers College (MA). She taught in public schools in Goldsboro, North Carolina, then at Virginia State College, Petersburg (1927–1972). She was a co-founder and co-director of the Black Music Center (1969–72) when she retired. The oratorio above was composed in 1982. She wrote a number of choral and instrumental works.

MORGAN, DORINDA (1909–Dec'd.)
"Moonlight on the Hudson"
Composer/songwriter born on November 25th in Cincinnati, Ohio, she was educated at the Cincinnati Academy of Art. With Bill Anson, Al Piantadosi, and Mike Riley, she wrote a number of songs, including, "Bluer than the Blues", "Confidential", "Cypress", "C'est Fini", "Anne Frank", "Fantasy", "Little Women", "Man Upstairs", "A Flag Is Born", "Lolita", and "Moonlight on the Hudson". ASCAP.

MORGAN, JESSICA E. (1929–)
"I'm Through With You"
Composer/songwriter she was born on May 25th in Cheswold, Delaware, and educated at Springfield High School; she studied piano with her mother. With Robert Duke Morgan, she wrote the above song. ASCAP.

MORGAN, MC KAYLA K. (1927–)
"The Ballad of the One-eyed Jacks"
Composer/songwriter born on June 29th at Westfield, New Jersey, she received a high school education. She wrote the above song. ASCAP.

MORRIS, LELIA NAYLOR (1862–1929)
"Jesus is coming to earth again."
Tunes—"Second Coming", "McConnesville", and "Morris"
A composer and hymnist, born in Pennsville, Morgan County, Ohio, on April 15, 1862, she moved with her family to Malta, Ohio, just across the Muskingum River from McConnelsville in 1866 when her father returned from the Civil War. After her father died, with her mother and sister, the three women opened a millinery shop in McConnelsville. She

was a member of the Methodist Protestant Church, but after her marriage in 1881 to Charles H. Morris, she joined the Methodist Episcopal Church with her husband. She attended various Methodist camp meetings—Old Camp Sychar in Mt. Vernon, Ohio, Sebring Camp at Sebring, Ohio, and Mountain Lake Park, Maryland. She also wrote the music for her hymns, and when her eyesight failed in 1913, her son erected a large blackboard, 28 feet long, with music staff lines on it, so she could continue her hymn writing. She died in Auburn, Ohio, on July 23, 1929. Her hymns appeared in *Baptist* (1975); *Broadman* (1977); and *Family of God* (1976) hymnals.

MORISSETTE, ALANIS
"You Oughta Know"
Singer/songwriter. Her album *Jagged Little Pill* (1995) contains her songs "Not the Doctor" where she can't stand her dependent, smothering lover and "You Oughta Know" where she confronts a man who dropped her for an older woman.

MORSE, ANNA JUSTINA (1893–1979)
Tunes—"Consecration" and "Kemper"
Composer and organist, she was born at Haverhill, Massachusetts, on July 29, 1893, and was educated at Wellesley College (BA, 1919), Wellesley, Massachusetts, with graduate study at Yale University, New Haven, Connecticut, and at Northwestern University, Evanston, Illinois. She taught in high schools in Washington, DC and in New Haven, Connecticut, where she was assistant organist at Christ Church until 1925. Later she was in charge of the junior school at Kemper Hall in Kenosha, Wisconsin (1925–38) and from 1938 director of studies and choir director. Her two hymn tunes mentioned above appeared in *The Hymnal* (1940) of the Protestant Episcopal Church. She died on December 15, 1979.

MORSE, THEODORA "DOLLY" (1890–1953)
"Siboney"
Lyricist, she was born in Brooklyn, New York. She married the popular composer Theodore F. Morse and used the pen names "Dorothy Terris" and "D. A. Estrom" for her writings. With music by her husband, she wrote "Hail, Hail the Gang's All Here" (1917) based on *The Pirates of Penzance,* with music by Julian Robledo, "Three O'clock in the Morning" (1919), and with music by Ernesto Lecuona, "Siboney". Her husband died in 1924 and she died in 1953 in White Plains, New York.

MULDAUR, MARIA (1943–)
"Midnight at the Oasis"
Blues/rock/jazz/folk/gospel/country singer/songwriter, she wrote the hit song "Midnight at the Oasis" (1973; on CD 1995). She has two

other albums with Geoff Muldaur: *Pottery Pie* and *Louisiana Love Call* (1993).

MURDAUGH, ELLA LEE (1910–)
   "Song of Love"
A composer/songwriter, she was born on July 3rd in Lexington County, South Carolina, and educated at Southern College, and Merchants and Bankers School in New York City. She wrote songs.

MURPHY, ANNE S. (1877–1942)
   Tune—"Constantly Abiding"
   "There's a peace in my heart"
Composer and hymnist, she was born at Sebring, Ohio, and was the wife of Will L. Murphy, who at one time had a successful pottery business, but then the depression years came, her husband died, and she lost all her money. Penniless, she went to live with a sister in Burbank, California. She was a singer, musician, composer, evangelist, and had written many hymns, both the words and music. Despite her problems and heartaches, she came through her bad times with an inner peace reflected in her hymns. She died at Burbank on March 30, 1942. Her hymn appeared in *Hymns for the Living Church* (1974). (Information received from the Public Library, Burbank, California.)

MURPHY, ESTELLE PRINDLE (1918–)
   "A Man Named Jack"
Composer/songwriter born on August 26th in Brooklyn, New York, she was educated at Euclid Academy and Columbia University. She wrote the songs "The President's Lady", "A Man Named Jack", "Contrast", "Doorway to a Dream", "Margaret Rose", "Margie Now", "Pony Tail", "To Hearts".

MUSGRAVE, THEA (1928–)
   A Christmas Carol
Composer/conductor, she was born on May 27th in Barnton, Midlothian, Scotland. After graduating from the University of Edinburgh (BMus, 1958), she studied with Nadia Boulanger at the Paris Conservatory. After she came to the US in 1959, she studied with Aaron Copland, then served as a lecturer at London University until 1965. After marrying American violinist Peter Mark in 1971, they resided in Santa Barbara, California, but she made many trips to London. She wrote the operas *Mary, Queen of Scots* (1975–77), *A Christmas Carol* (1978–79), *Harriet, the Woman Called Moses* (1982–84), (the Story of Harriet Tubman), and other works. She conducted her Concerto for Orchestra with the Philadelphia Orchestra (1976), then conducted works in other cities: New York, London, San Francisco, etc.

-N-

MYLES, HEATHER
"Until I Couldn't Have You"

Singer/songwriter lives in Southern California. Her albums are *Just Like Old Times* (1992) and *Untamed* (1995) with eight songs she wrote or cowrote including "It Ain't Over", "Indigo Moon", "Gone Too Long" (guitar-driven rocker travelin' down the highway) and "Until I Couldn''t Have You" (a romantic tale of remorse).

NAIRNE, CAROLINA OLIPHANT, BARONESS (1766–1845)
"The Land o' the Leal"

Composer, hymnist, and songwriter, daughter of Laurence Oliphant, she was born at Gask, Perthshire, Scotland, on August 16, 1766 and was a Jacobite (devoted to Royal House of Stuart). She married a Jacobite, Major William Nairne in 1806, who became the 5th Baron Nairne in 1824. Using the pen name "Mrs. Bogan of Bogan," her poems were published in *The Scottish Minstrel* (1821–24). She is known for her songs "Charlie is My Darling," "The Hundred Pipers," "The Laird O' Cockpen," etc. She died on October 26, 1845, and her collected poems were published in *Lays from Strathearn* (1846) and more recently in *Masterpieces of Religious Verse* (Harper, 1948) and *The World's Greatest Religious Poetry* (Macmillan, 1934). In Scotland a laverock is a lark, and she wrote:

Sweet's the laverock's note and lang,
Lilting wildly up the glen!
But aye to me he sings ae sang,
Will ye no' come back again?

NASH, IDA MAE (1926–)
"Youthtown, USA"

Composer/songwriter born on February 19th in Beards Fork, West Virginia, and educated at college (BD), she wrote songs.

NDEGÉ-OCELLO, ME'SHELL (1970–)
Plantation Lullabies

Bassist/rapper/singer/songwriter, she was born Michelle Johnson in Berlin, Germany, the daughter of a soldier stationed there. After moving from station to station, the family finally settled in Washington, DC, where her saxist dad interested her in jazz. She studied music at Howard University and played in go-go bands. After she became a righteous Five Percenter (Muslim), she changed her name. While she was rejected by several recording companies, her big chance came when Madonna signed her to her Maverick label. On her debut album *Plantation Lullabies* she wrote all the songs and played all the instruments rapping and singing about inner-city black life melding hip-hop with jazz funk. Her songs include "If That's Your Boyfriend (He Wasn't Last Night)" and in "Soul on Ice" she assails black men who date white women, "Excuse me, does your white woman go better with your Brooks Brothers suit?". She has a five-year-old son, Askia.

NEMOY, PRISCILLA (1919–)
"The Christmas Toy"
Composer/pianist born on December 12th in Chicago, Illinois, she was educated at a junior city college. She was a member of a piano duo and has written songs.

NEUFVILLE, RENEE see JEAN NORRIS

NEVIN, ALICE (1837–1925)
Tunes—"Resurrection," "Cecil," and "Elsie"
Composer and organist, the daughter of Martha Jenkins and Dr. John Williamson Nevin, she was born at Allegheny (now Pittsburgh), Pennsylvania, on August 1, 1837, where her father occupied the chair of biblical literature at Western Theological Seminary (1828–40). She was raised in Mercersburg, Pennsylvania, where her father was a professor at the Reformed Church Theological Seminary (1840–51), when he became a professor at Franklin and Marshall College, Lancaster, Pennsylvania, until his death in 1892 at age eighty-six. Unfortunately, while an infant, she was dropped by a nurse and the rest of her life she walked with a limp. For many years she was organist and choir director at Franklin and Marshall College and also at the First Reformed Church in Lancaster, Pennsylvania. In 1879 she published *Hymns and Carols for Church and Sunday School,* which included her tunes "Resurrection," "Cecil," "Elsie," and two unnamed tunes and three arrangements, "Williamson," "Coblentz," and "Cornish Melody." She also published her Poems (1922). She was active in founding St. Luke's Reformed Church. She died in Lancaster on November 19, 1925. Her tunes "Resurrection" and "Williamson" appeared in the Evangelical and Reformed Church *Hymnal* (1941).

NEWELL, CHARLENE A. (1938–).
Tune—"Key"
Newell is a composer born in Price, Utah, and educated at the College of Eastern Utah and Brigham Young University (BA) where she studied piano, organ, and voice. She also went to BYU in Hawaii and the New England Conservatory of Music in Boston. She has composed a number of songs. Her tune above was put to words by Jan Underwood Pinborough—"A key was turned in Latter Days" in the Mormon hymnal (1985). She married Robert Newell and they have twelve children.

NEWELL, LAURA E. PIXLEY (1854–1916)
"Across the years"
Composer, hymnist, poet, and songwriter, the daughter of Ann Laura Osborne and Edward A. Pixley, she was born in New Marlborough, near Great Barrington, Massachusetts, on February 5, 1854. When she was only four years old, her mother died, and she was adopted by an aunt, Mrs. Hiram Mabie, who took her to a farm near Wamego, Kansas. On August 30, 1871, she married Lauren Newell at Zeandale, Kansas. He entered the Civil War as a Sergeant in May 1862, served with the 2nd Regiment, Company F, Kansas State Volunteer Cavalry, and was discharged as a 1st Lieutenant on April 30, 1865. He was a carpenter and builder, and they resided near Manhattan, Kansas. She was active in the Sunday School of the Congregational Church. Her first poem was published when she was only fourteen, and she wrote many songs. She wrote the hymn above for which she also composed the music. Newell and her husband had four sons and two daughters. "A City Awaits Us" was included in the *Evangelical Lutheran* and *Presbyterian* (1955) hymnals. She died in Manhattan, Kansas, on October 13, 1916. (Information from Cheryl Collins and Jean C. Dallas of the Riley County Historical Society & Museum, Manhattan, Kansas)

NEWTON-JOHN, OLIVIA (1947–)
"Take a Chance"
Singer/songwriter, she was born on September 26th in Cambridge, England but grew up in Australia. With a song composed by Peter Allen, "I Honestly Love You" she won a 1974 Grammy. She acted with John Travolta in the film *Grease* (1978). Her top song was "Physical" (1981). With David Foster and Steven Lukather she wrote "Take a Chance—Could It Be We're the Perfect Pair?". She had to postpone her 1992 tour after having been diagnosed with breast cancer. As of 1994 her albums and CDs available were *Come on Over, Greatest Hits, Warm and Tender,* and *Back to Basics* (1992), and she had the videos *At the Universal Ampitheatre, Physical,* and *Soul Kiss.*

NICHOL, CLARISSA B. (1895–Dec'd.)
Sing and Play
Composer/arranger/songwriter, she was born on August 16th in Homestead, Pennsylvania. Her album *Sing and Play* was a collection of American patriotic songs.

NICHOLS, ALBERTA (1898–1957)
"Gay Paree"
Composer born on December 3rd in Lincoln, Illinois, she was educated at the Louisville Conservatory with Alfred Calzin and George Copeland.

She wrote the Broadway stage scores *Gay Paree* and *Angela*; songs for *Blackbirds of 1933, Luckee Girl,* and *Rhapsody in Black.* She married Mann Holiner and wrote a number of songs with him: "A Love Like Ours", "I Just Couldn't Take It, Baby", "Sing a Little Tune", "There Never Was a Town Like Paris", "Until the Real Thing Comes Along", "What's Keeping My Prince Charming", and "You Can't Stop Me from Loving You." ASCAP. She died on February 4th in Hollywood, California.

NIGHTINGALE, MAE WHEELER (1898–Dec'd.)
Queen of the Sawdust
Composer born on December 30th in Blencoe, Iowa, she was educated at the University of California at Los Angeles, the University of Southern California, and Fresno State College. She taught in California schools and conducted choruses. Her works include *Choral Concert Series, Troubadour Series* (2 volumes), *Nightingale Choral Series, American Heritage Songs, Folk and Fun Songs, Young Singers' Choir Book;* and the operettas *Ride 'Em Cowboy* and *Queen of the Sawdust.* ASCAP.

NOBLITT, KATHERYN MC CALL (1909–)
'March of the Americans'
Composer/musician/songwriter born on February 10th in Marion, North Carolina, and educated at Greensboro College, (BM, summa cum laude), her instrumentals are *March of the Americans, Twinkling Keys,* and *Waltz Mood.* ASCAP.

NORDEN, ELFRIDA (1916–)
"Love Is Waiting in Hawaii"
A songwriter, she was born on November 5th in Englewood, New Jersey, and educated at the University des Annales in Paris; Beerbohm Tree Academy in London; and Alviene School of Dramatic Arts in New York City. With Marcel Frank, John Klein, Hugo Rubens, and Kenneth Walton, she wrote the lyrics for a number of songs: "Carmelita", "Good-for-nothin' Lover", "Forever Means Always", "Joy Is Born in the Heart", Let There Be Light, O Lord", "Hush, My Love", "Our God", "Sing to the World", and "Starlight Lullaby".

NORRIS, JEAN (1970–)
"Hey Mr. D. J."
Singer/pianist/songwriter, she met her teammate Renee Neufville in 1988 while the two were first-year students at Temple University in Philadelphia, Pennsylvania. Norris concentrated on jazz vocals while Neufville pursued English literature, and the two wrote some 40 songs. They called their duo Zhane and did some background vocals for Rapper DJ Jazzy Jeff and his production company Touch of Jazz. After Kay Gee produced their

record "Hey Mr. D. J.—Hey D. J. keep playing that song all night/On and on and on", it was a top 10 R&B hit and was followed by "Groove Thang". Their debut album in 1994 *Pronounced Jah-Nay* hit the top 10 R&B chart and the top 40 of Billboard's 200 album chart.

NUGENT, MAUDE (1874–1958)
"Sweet Rosie O'Grady"
Singer/actress/composer, she was born on January 12th in Brooklyn, New York. She sang in vaudeville and introduced her song "Sweet Rosie O'Grady" at The Abbey, Johnny Reilly's place on Eighth Avenue, New York, in 1896. It was a tremendous success. Nugent married lyricist William Jerome. She wrote many more songs, often both the lyrics as well as the music—"Mamie Reilly" (1897), "There's No Other Girl Like My Girl", "My Pretty Little China Maid", etc. In 1902 she left the stage to raise a family, but in the 1940s she appeared in "Gay Nineties" shows and on TV in the early 1950s. She died on June 3rd in New York City.

NYRO, LAURA (1947–)
"New York Tendaberry"
Singer/composer, she was born on October 18th in New York City. She has written a number of songs for noted artists such as Barbra Streisand and most are pop/r&b/jazz oriented. As of 1994 her available albums were *Eli & the 13th Confession* (1968), *New York Tendaberry* (1969), *Christmas and Beads of Sweat,* and *Smile.*

-O-

O'CONNOR, SINEAD (1966–)
The Lion and the Cobra
Singer/songwriter, she was born on December 8th in Dublin, Ireland. Her father, a barrister, and her mother, a seamstress, separated when Sinead was only nine years old. Often she raised £100 a day pretending to collect money for a charity but instead gave the money to her mother. After many escapades at shoplifting, at age fourteen she was arrested for stealing shoes and sent to a hospice for the dying; it was infested with rats and filled with vomiting old women. After her release at age sixteen she strummed the guitar and sang on the streets and in pubs for a living. In 1986, she became pregnant by drummer John Reynolds, age thirty.

Her first LP *The Lion and the Cobra* (1987), a mix of reggae, rock, and Celtic folk sounds was written and produced by herself. Five weeks after *Lion* was finished in July 1987, she gave birth to a son, Jake. Sinead is bald, and claims it makes her feel womanly because she feels natural. By 1988 the *Lion* had sold 600,000 copies.

In 1990 she won the Grammy Alternate Music award for *I Do Not Want What I Haven't Got,* which sold 2 million albums. Her videos are *The Value of Ignorance* and *Year of the Horse.* While on NBC's "Saturday Night Live" on October 3, 1992, she said: "Fight the real enemy" and tore apart an 8-by-12-inch photo of Pope John Paul II. Later she explained the Vatican had "used marriage, divorce, and birth control and abortion to control us through our children and fear."

Universal Mother album (1994) includes many of her songs.

O'DEA, ANNE CALDWELL (1867–1936)
"A Night in Spain"
Singer/actress/lyricist, she was born in Boston. She sang with the Juvenile Opera Company, New York City. She wrote the libretto for *Take the Air* and with music by Vincent M. Youmans wrote the lyrics for "I Know That You Know" (1926) and with music by Jean Schwartz, "A Night in Spain" (1927).

O'FLYNN, CAROL COMER (1944–)
"The Angelus"
Composer/songwriter born on August 21st in New York, New York, the daughter of composer Honoria and songwriter Charles O'Flynn, she was educated at Manhattanville College in New York City. With lyrics by her father, she wrote "God's Rain", "Happy Nothing to You", and "Who Threw the Confetti in Angelo's Spaghetti?". ASCAP.

O'FLYNN, HONORIA (1909–)
"Dancing at the Crossroads"
A composer/songwriter, she was born Noreen Mack on September 1st in Galway, Ireland, and educated in the national schools of Ireland. She was the wife of songwriter/publisher Charles O'Flynn and mother of Carol O'Flynn. Honoria wrote "Dancing at the Crossroads" and "I'll Give Up the Late, Late Show for You".

OGILVIE, RUTH SIMMONS (1920–)
"Chickadee Valley"
Composer/singer/songwriter born on April 5th in Boston, Massachusetts, she was educated at college preparatory school. With her twin sister, Ruby Simmons, she was one of the "Moonmaids" with the Vaughn Monroe orchestra. She wrote "Bacia Ba Lu", "Chickadee Valley", "Echoing Mailbox", and "It's All Over But the Crying."

OLIVER, MADRA EMOGENE (1905–)
"Whispering Wisconsin"
A composer/pianist/singer/songwriter, she was born on October 28th in Three Rivers, Michigan, and educated at University of Michigan (BSM);

Claremont College; Oberlin College and Conservatory. She composed *Danza Giocosa, Danza Graziosa, 2 Portraits for the Pianoforte,* an album *7 Songs for Youth;* and other instrumentals and songs.

OLIVEROS, PAULINE (1932–)
Bonn Feier
Composer/musician, she was born on May 30th in Houston, Texas. After studying composition at the University of Houston and San Francisco State College (BA, 1957), she studied privately with Robert Erickson. She served as co-director and then director of the Mills Tape Music Center (1961–67), then taught at the University of California at San Diego (1967–81). She received a commission from the city of Bonn, Germany, in 1977 for *Bonn Feier,* a theater piece with actors, dances, and pianists. She has composed a number of theater pieces, vocal and chamber work. As of 1994, her albums available were *Deep Listening* and *Roots of the Moment.*

O'NEALE, MARGIE (1923–)
"The Diggie Song"
Songwriter born on November 25th in Stanberry, Missouri, O'Neale received a high school education. She wrote "Calypso Joe", "Mucho Gusto", "Sin in Satin", "So Near Yet So Far," "Strong Man", and "Water Can't Quench the Fire of Love". ASCAP.

O'NEILL, SELENA (1899–)
Irish Rhapsody for Orchestra
Composer born on March 20th in Chicago, Illinois, she composed the above piece and other works.

ONO, YOKO (1933–)
'Season of Glass'
Pop/rock singer and songwriter, she was born on February 18th in Tokyo, Japan, of a wealthy banking family who wanted her to have a good education. So in 1953 they sent her to Sarah Lawrence College in New York. After her graduation she painted pictures. While exhibiting her work in London in 1966, she met John Lennon of the Beatles. They were married and recorded an album *Unfinished Business no. 1: Two Virgins* in 1968. After their divorce they recorded *Live Peace in Toronto* and remarried in 1969. Their *Double Fantasy* won a Grammy in 1981 and they wrote "Happy Christmas (War is Over)". Albums *Onobox* and *Walking on Thin Ice* include her chilling vocals and Lennon's stunning guitar. These two albums were available in 1994. John Lennon was shot and killed on December 8, 1980 in New York City.

Ono produced *New York Rock* (1994), a play with a music that she had composed over the past 25 years.

ORE, CECILLE (1954–)
Praesens subitus
A composer, she was born on July 19th in Oslo, Norway. After studying composition and sonology under Lasse Thoresen and Olav Anton Thommessen at Norges Musikhochschule in Oslo, she took postgraduate courses in piano under Liv Glaser, Jens Harald Bratlie, and Elizabeth Klein. She also studied electroacoustic composition at the Institute of Sonology at Utrecht in The Netherlands and composition under Ton de Leeuw at the Sweelinck Conservatorium at Amsterdam. She was won several prizes and composed choral and orchestral works, chamber music, etc. Her string quartet *Praesens subitus* was first performed in Oslo in 1989.

ORME, DAPHNE (1889–Dec'd.)
"Old-fashioned Christmas"
Composer/songwriter born on October 21st in Avoca, Iowa, & the Academy of Art, she studied music with her father. With Jennie Brockway and Roy Jackson, she wrote a number of songs, including "Spinning in My Heart". ASCAP.

ORNISH, NATALIE (1926–)
Songs for Suburban Children
Composer/songwriter born on February 15th in Galveston, Texas, Ornish was educated at Sam Houston State Teachers College (BA) and Northwestern University (MS). She wrote the stage score for *Just Twelve,* and the album *Songs for Suburban Children.* ASCAP.

ORTLUND, ELIZABETH ANNE SWEET (b. 1923)
"The Vision of a Dying World Is Vast Before Our Eyes"
Composer, hymnist, and organist, the daughter of Brigadier General Joseph B. Sweet, she was born in Wichita, Kansas, on December 3, 1923, and was educated at the University of Redlands, California. She was married to Raymond C. Ortlund, pastor of the Lake Avenue Congregational Church in Pasadena, California. She held the A.A.G.O. certificate from the American Guild of Organists and served as organist for the "Old Fashioned Revival Hour" radio broadcasts, and also with the successor broadcasts, "The Joyful Sound." She has written 25 hymn text and tunes, about 100 anthems, sacred and secular solos, and various instrumental works. Her hymn appeared in *Hymns for the Living Church* (1974).

OSLIN, K.T. (1941–)
"80's Ladies"
Country singer/songwriter, born in Crossit, Arkansas. She was the first female songwriter to win the Country Music Association's prestigious

Song of the Year award in 1987 for her "80's Ladies" anthem. She once worked as a Broadway chorus girl, won the 1988 Grammy for Country Vocalist for the "Hold Me" track from *This Woman*. Her albums included *80's Ladies, Love in a Small Town, This Woman*. She sang "Tumbling Tumbleweeds" with Roy Rogers on the album *Tribute to Roy Rogers* in 1992. She is a three-time Grammy winner but recently has spent more time gardening than singing. On August 28, 1995 she was admitted to St. Thomas Hospital in Nashville, Tennessee with a major blockage of her coronary arteries. The next day she underwent coronary artery bypass surgery.

OSSER, EDNA (1919–)
"Ah Yes, There's Good Blues Tonight"
A composer/songwriter, she was born on April 26th in New York, and was educated at Brooklyn College. She married composer/conductor Glenn Osser. With her husband and Marjorie Goetschius, she wrote a number of songs: "Can I Canoe You Up the River?", "Carol", "Heavenly", "I Dream of You", "I'll Always Be With You", "Roseanne", "The Last Time I Saw You", "There You Go", "You're Different", "Young Man with the Blues". ASCAP.

OTTO, INGA (1936–)
"China Surf"
Composer/songwriter, she was born on March 1st in Leipzig, Germany. She wrote "China Surf", "Follow Me", and "Rubino". ASCAP.

OWENS, BONNIE (1933–)
"The Legend of Bonnie and Clyde"
Singer/songwriter, she was born in Blanchard, Oklahoma. She sang on station KTYL in Mesa, Arizona, with her husband, Buck Owens. After their divorce she sang in Bakersfield, California, and then married Merle Haggard. With Merle she wrote "The Legend of Bonnie and Clyde". Their songs appeared on the LP record *Just Between the Two of Us* (1965). Her other records were *Hi-Fi to Cry By, Lead Me On, Philadelphia Lawyer,* and *That Little Boy of Mine.*

OWENS, CAROL SUE (1931–)
Tune—"Freely, Freely"
Composer, hymnist, and teacher, she was born on October 30th in El Reno, Oklahoma, and attended San Jose State College, San Jose, California, and the Cathedral School of the Bible, Oakland, California. Carol and her husband James are active composing church musicals, writing hymns, and teaching songwriting. Her tune above, with her words "God forgave my sin in Jesus' name" (based on Matthew 10:8, 28:18) written

in 1972, appeared in *The Hymnal for Worship and Celebration* (Baptist 1986) and in *The United Methodist Hymnal* (1989).

OWENS-COLLINS, JAMIE (1955–)
   Tune—"The Battle"
A composer, she was born on September 25th in Castro Valley, California, the daughter of composers/songwriters Carol Sue and Jimmy Owens. She is a traveling gospel evangelist, and has been to Canada, Europe, and New Zealand. She now lives in Newbury Park, California, with her husband, where they operate the Fairhill Music Company. Her tune—"The Battle-The Battle belongs to the Lord"—appeared in *The Hymnal for Worship & Celebration* (Baptist 1986).

-P-

PALLOTTA, LORRAINE (1934–)
   "I Think of You"
Composer/songwriter born on March 8th in Chicago, Illinois, and educated in high school, she wrote songs. ASCAP.

PARADIES, MARIA THERESIA von (1759–1824)
   Adriadne und Bacchus
Pianist/organist/composer, she was born on May 15th in Vienna, Austria, the daughter of Joseph Anton von Paradies. Although blind from early childhood, she studied piano with Richter of the Netherlands and with Kozeluk, singing with Salieri and Righini and composition with Freberth and Vogler. Her father was an imperial councillor, and his daughter Maria became the goddaughter of Empress Maria Theresa of Austria. The empress gave the young musician an allowance of 200 florins annually. After playing for the court in Paris in 1784, she played before the royal family in London. She played in Brussels and various courts in Germany. Paradies composed *Ariadne und Bacchus,* performed at Luxemburg before Emperor Leopold (1791), *Der Schul-candidat* at the Leopoldstadt Theatre (1792), *Deutsches Monument,* a mourning cantata on the anniversary of the death of King Louis XVI of France (1794), and *Rinaldo und Alcina,* a magic opera at Prague (1797). She also composed sonates and songs. She died on February 1st in Vienna.

PARENTE, SISTER ELIZABETH (b. 1918)
   Works—*Mass in Honor of Our Lady of Victory*
Composer, choir conductor, and pianist, she was born in Cambridge, New York, on March 20, 1918, and was educated at Georgian Court College, Lakewood, New Jersey (MB, 1938), New York University, and

Catholic University of America in Washington, DC (MM, 1962). She was music department head of Villa Victoria Academy in Trenton, New Jersey (1938–66), and Principal (1967–73); Music Department head at Bethlehem University in Bethlehem, Israel (1973–79). Her *Mass* (above) was published by G. Shirmer (New York, 1959). She also wrote an *Ave Maria* (vocal) for the centenary of Our Lady of Lourdes (1958) and more than 10 piano pieces. She performed at Town Hall (1943) and Carnegie Hall (1959–63) in New York City, at the NEMC Convention in Atlantic City, New Jersey (1959); N.J. Performing Arts Festival in Princeton (1963–64); N.J. State Symphony at South Orange (1972), and numerous other concert performances. (Letter from Sister Elizabeth from Our Lady of Mercy Convent, where she was residing in March 1982, Park Ridge, New Jersey)

PARIS, TWILA (1958–)
    Tune—"We Will Glorify"
Composer/songwriter, she was born on December 28th in Springdale, Arkansas, one of four children of pastor Oren and Inez Paris of the Missions Network Center of Youth With a Mission in Elm Springs, Arkansas. In 1985, she married Jack Wright, and they live in Fayetteville, Arkansas. She has produced almost a dozen albums in the past 12 years. She composed the tune—"We Will Glorify", which appeared in *The Hymnal for Worship & Celebration* (Baptist 1986).

PARKER, ALICE STUART (b. 1925)
    Tune—"Hawley"
Composer, conductor, and teacher, she was born in Boston, Massachusetts, on December 16, 1925, and was educated at Smith College (BA, 1947), Northampton, Massachusetts, and at the Julliard School (MS, 1949), in New York City. On August 20, 1954, she married Thomas Pyle, and they had two sons and three daughters. She was an arranger for the Robert Shaw Chorale (1948–67), taught privately in New York from 1951, was conductor at the Mennonite Church Center in Laurelville, Pennsylvania (1961–70), and a lecturer at Meadowbrook, Michigan (1967), Blossom Festival School (1964–71). She composed various choral works and carols. The tune above is a choral setting for "A Hymn for Confirmation" (text by Fred Kaan) in the *Hymn Concerto Series,* published by The Hymn Society of America (1982).

PARKER, DOROTHY (1893–1967)
    Candide
An author/songwriter born on August 22nd in West End, New Jersey, she was educated at the Blessed Sacrament Convent in New York City. She wrote short stories, verse, and book reviews for the *New Yorker*

magazine. With Leonard Bernstein, Jack King, and Ralph Ranger, she wrote lyrics for the songs "How Am I To Know?", "I Wished on the Moon", "Gavotte", and the score for the Broadway musical *Candide*. ASCAP.

PARSHALLE, EVE (1900–)
"Kingdom of the Sun"
Songwriter born on December 24th in New York, and she received a high school education. With Carter Writer she wrote the lyrics for the songs "Nuns at Evening", "The Girl I'll Remember".

PARTON, DOLLY REBECCA (1946–)
"Coat of Many Colors"
Country singer/guitarist/songwriter, she was born on January 19th in Locust Ridge, Tennessee. Her grandfather was a minister, and as a child she sang in his church. Later she moved to Nashville and sang on the Porter Wagoner TV show from 1967–74. She wrote "Dumb Blonde" (1967), "Something Fishy", "Coat of Many Colors" (1971), which was based on her childhood, and many other songs including "9 to 5", which was also a film in which she appeared. As of 1994 her available albums were *Best of Dolly Parton, Best of Dolly Parton vol. 3, Eagle When She Flies, Greatest Hits, Here You Come Again, Home for Christmas, Rainbow, The Best There Is, The World of Dolly Parton vol. 1, The World of Dolly Parton vol. 2*, and *White Limozeen*.

PATTERSON, CORDELLA M. (b. 1907)
"The first Christmas"
A hymnist and songwriter, she was born in St. Mary's, Kansas, on November 17, 1907 and had a high school education. She also wrote the words for "St. Philomena, the Beloved."

PATTERSON, JOY F. (b. 1931)
"Isaiah the prophet has written of old"
Composer and hymnist, she was born in Lansing, Michigan, on October 11, 1931 and was educated at the University of Wisconsin (BA; MA) and was a Fulbright scholar at the University of Strasbourg, France. She was married to C. Duane Patterson, an attorney, and they had one son and two daughters. Despite the lack of formal musical training, she began composing music in 1970 with the assistance of Sterling L. Anderson, minister of music at the First Presbyterian Church of Wausau, where she is an active member, and now has six sacred choral works in print. The above hymn was published in the booklet, *New Hymns for Children*, as one of seven winning hymns, by the Choristers Guild and The Hymn Society of America (1982).

PATTERSON, WILEY (b. 1910)
"The Baby Jesus Stirred in Sleep"
Composer, hymnist, and choral director, she was born in Chatham, Virginia, on July 20, 1910 and was educated at Chatham Hall, Hollins College in Hollins, Virginia, and at the Cincinnati Conservatory in Ohio. She taught music and drama at the Low-Heywood School in Stamford, Connecticut, and was director of the junior choir at the First Congregational Church in Darien, Connecticut. She married Maurice J. Reis.

PATTON, ABIGAIL JEMIMA "ABBY" HUTCHINSON (1829–1892)
"Kind Words Can Never Die"
Composer, contralto, and hymnist, daughter of Mary Leavitt and Jesse Hutchinson, one of 16 children, she was born in Milford, New Hampshire, on August 29, 1829 and was educated at Hancock Academy and later at Edes Seminary in Plymouth, Massachusetts. At age ten she made her first public appearance as a singer at a concert given in the Baptist church in Milford. Thirteen of the sixteen children in her family survived to adulthood, and all were singers, but the quartet of Abby, Asa, John, and Judson became famous in the 1840s. They toured New England (1841–43) and made their first visit to New York City in May 1843. Their concerts were given in the old Broadway Tabernacle, and they took the city by storm. The Hutchinson Family Singers toured England and Scotland (1846) and were the guests of Charles Dickens, Harriet Martineau, John Bright, the Honorable Mrs. Norton, and others. On February 28, 1849 she married Ludlow Patton, a stock broker in New York City. The Hutchinsons were abolitionists, temperance leaders, and advocates of women's suffrage. They sang in the Republican campaigns of 1856 and 1860. They sang at The White House for President John Tyler and later in the Green Room of The White House for President Lincoln (1862). She composed the music for Alfred Tennyson's "Ring Out Wild Bells" and other songs. She founded the first kindergarten in America in Orange, New Jersey. Her hymn appeared in Schaff's *Christ in Song* (1869). Abby died in New York City on November 24, 1892.

PAUL, DORIS A. (b. 1903)
Works—*Remember Now Thy Creator*
Composer, conductor, hymnist, and teacher, she was born in Upland, Indiana, on August 16, 1903 and educated at Taylor University (BA; BMusEd) in Upland; at Northwestern University; University of Michigan, (MM); and with Fred Waring at the Fred Waring Workshop. She taught in public schools, at Taylor University, and at Iowa State Teachers College in Ames, Iowa; she also conducted the Lansing Matinee Musicale Chorus in Lansing, Michigan. Her works include *Thou Art My Lamp; We Give Thee Thanks;* and with Esther Fuller, *A Book of*

Responses (38 introits and responses). As of March 1982 she was enjoying her retirement.

PAYMER, ADA (1896–Dec'd.)
"In a Spanish Tavern"
Composer/songwriter born on July 14th in Lithuania and educated at the New York College of Music with Jacques Danielson and Frederick Schlieder, she composed the following songs and instrumentals: "In An English Village", "The Happy Bugler", "Sunshine and Shadow", "Colonial Tea Party", "Hiking song", "Treasure Hunt", and "Tiptoes".

PAYNE, MAGGI (1945–)
"A Winter's Tale"
Composer/flutist, she was born on December 23rd in Temple, Texas. After studying flute and composition at Northwestern University (BM, 1968), she studied at Yale University and the University of Illinois (MM in flute, 1970). She studied electronic music and sound recording at Mills College (MFA, 1972), then worked there as a recoding engineer (1972–81). She has performed as a flutist in the US and Europe. She has composed mostly electronic music, some with slides. Her piece mentioned above was written in 1975.

PEARCE, ALMEDA JONES (1893–1986)
Tune — "Pearce"
Composer/singer she was born on January 4th in Carlyle, Pennsylvania, and sang soprano with her three sisters in her church and at nearby Dickinson College. After attending the Walter Damrosch School of Music in New York City, she returned to Carlyle and married baritone/evangelist preacher Rowan Pearce. They had three children who sang with them on a Camden, New Jersey, radio station on Sunday mornings from 1932 until the 1960s. She composed the tune "Pearce- When he shall come", which appeared in *The Hymnal of Worship & Celebration* (Baptist 1986).

PEARL-MANN, DORA (PERELMAN) (1905–)
Piano Concerto
Composer/conductor/pianist born on January 4th in St. Petersburg, Russia, she was educated at the St. Petersburg Academy; State Academy, Vienna; Mozarteum Academy on a scholarship; Juilliard in New York City and Curtis Institute in Philadelphia; Teachers College, Columbia University; she studied with Felix Blemenfeld and Egon Petri. She became a US citizen in 1933; had her debut as conductor at the State Academy orchestra in Vienna (1935); and her debut as pianist in Tel Aviv. She was a concert pianist for the Metropolitan Opera in New York City and the Ballet Theatre Company. Her works are *Tone Poem* for piano and orchestra; *Pi-*

ano Concerto (American Composers award); *Night Violet's Dream* (piano); *Nightingale and the Rose* (ballet); and *Vision Victorieuse*.

PEEBLES, ANN
"I Can't Stand the Rain"
Singer/songwriter from Memphis, Tennessee, she married pianist Donald Bryant, who co-wrote her song, "I Can't Stand the Rain 'Gainst My Window" (1973). "Girlfriend" was on the 1988 Top Ten Black Singles list. Her albums are *Always, Peebles, Giving You the Benefit* (1992), and with guitarist Thomas Bingham on *Full Time Love* (1992).

PERKINS, EMILY SWAN (1866–1941)
Tune—"Laufer"
Composer and hymnist, she was born in Chicago, Illinois, on October 19, 1866 and later resided at Riverdale-on-Hudson, New York. She initiated the idea of a society devoted to hymns, and was one of the five organizers of The Hymn Society of America (1922) and became its recording secretary. She was a member of the Presbyterian Church in the US. Four of her hymns, with 54 of her hymn tunes, were published in *Stonehurst Hymn Tunes* (1921). Her hymn "Thou Art, O God, the God of Might" appeared in the *Presbyterian Hymnal* (1933) and her tune above in the *Methodist Hymnal* (1935).

PERRONE, VALENTINA (1906–)
"Sleep Precious Babe"
Songwriter born on February 14th in the Bronx, New York City, she was educated at the College of Mount St. Vincent and Fordham University (MA). With Virginia De Neergaard, she wrote lyrics for songs.

PERRY, JANICE KNAPP (1938–)
Tune—"Saunders"
A composer, she was born in Ogden, Utah, and educated at Brigham Young University where she studied music. She married Douglas C. Perry, and they have five children and of their own and several foster children. They live in Provo, Utah. She has composed four cantatas, two full-length musicals, including, *It's a Miracle,* twelve albums and songbooks. Her tune above was written to a hymn by Emily H. Woodmansee—"As Sisters of Zion" in the Mormon hymnal (1985).

PERRY, JULIA AMANDA (1924–1979)
Soul Symphony
Composer, she was born on March 25th in Lexington, Kentucky. After studying at Westminster Choir College (MMus, 1948) and the Juilliard School, she studied in Europe with Nadia Boulanger and com-

position with Luigi Dallapiccola and others and won the Boulanger Grand Prix. She Has written operas, orchestral, and vocal works. Her *Soul Symphony* was written in 1972, her *Quinary Quixotic Songs* in 1976.

PETERSON, BETTY J. (1918–)
"Sailing on a Moonbeam"
Composer/songwriter born on June 15th in Spurgeon, Missouri, and educated at a business college, she had private music study. She married Louis Blasco and became a partner in his music publishing business, and later president of Happiness Music. She wrote "Crying My Heart Out for You", "I Want It in Black and White," "I'm Coming Back", "My Happiness", "The Meaning of a Lonely Heart", That's the Place for Me", and "You Can't Go Wrong". ASCAP.

PETKERE, BERNICE (1906–)
"Dancing Butterfly"
Composer/songwriter born on August 11th in Chicago, Illinois, she was educated at the Henshaw Conservatory on a scholarship at age twelve. She was a pianist for publishing firms, then a publisher herself in 1960. With Joe Young, she wrote the songs "Close Your Eyes", "Lullaby of the Leaves", "The Lady I Love", "Oh Moon", "It's All So New to Me", "Starlight", "Stay Out of My Dreams", "Lonesome Melody", "That's You Sweetheart", and "Tell the Truth". ASCAP.

PETTIT, MILDRED T. (1895–1977)
Tune—"Light Divine"
Tune—"Child of God"
Composer born in Salt Lake City, Utah, and she was educated at the Latter-day Saints College there. She married Dr. William A. Pettit. Mildred collaborated with Matilda Watts Cahoon on programs and songs for the young people of the church. After moving to Philadelphia in 1934, she continued her musical studies at the ZeckwerHahn Institute; she also had private study with Frank W. Asper, Alexander Schreiner, and others. In 1935 the family moved to southern California. She composed the above tunes for the words "The Light Divine" and "I Am a Child of God" in the Mormon Hymnal (1985).

PETTY, VIOLET ANN (1928–Dec'd.)
"Someone, Someone"
Composer born on September 17th in Clovis, New Mexico, and educated at the University of New Mexico, she studied piano and organ and wrote songs. ASCAP.

PHAIR, LIZ (1966–)
"Alice Springs"
Rocker/guitarist/singer/songwriter, she was born in Chicago, the daughter of a doctor. She graduated from Oberlin College in Ohio. Her debut album *Exile in Guyville* (1993) dealt angrily and profanely with sexual desires, whereas on her CD *Whip Smart* (1994) she appeared much happier in her sexual relationships. Her songs included were "Supernova", "May Queen", and "Shame", singing about her joys and fears. She wrote the tune for "Don't Have Time" on the *Higher Learning* soundtrack.

PHILLIPS KATHERINE (1912–)
"Sweethearts of Aggie Land"
Songwriter born on March 22nd in Brenham, Texas, and educated at high school, she had private music study and studied voice with Mrs. John Graham. With Cliff Friend, she wrote the lyrics for "Gonna Build a Big Fence Around Texas" and other songs. ASCAP.

PHILLIPS, LIZ (1951–)
"Windspun for Minneapolis"
Composer, she was born Elizabeth Phillips on June 13th in Jersey City, New Jersey. At Bennington College in Vermont, she studied both art and music (BA, 1973). With her art she made sculptures using light, and later incorporated sound. Her "Windspun" used electronic circuitry positioned for the environment, the speed and direction effect of the hollow shaft of a windmill on nearby people, gathered by an electronic sensor and transformed into sound by a synthesizer. Her compositions include *TV Dinner* (1971), *Electric Spaghetti* (1972), *Broken/Unbroken Terra Cotta* (1975), *Cityflow* (1977), *Metrosonic Province* (1978), *Sunspots* (1979), *Windspun for Minneapolis* (1980), *Come About* (1981), *Windspin* (1981), *Multiple Perspectives* (1982), and *Sound Syzygy* (1982).

PICON, MOLLY (1898–)
"That's How You Go with Me"
Actress/songwriter, she was born on February 28th in New York City. She toured in vaudeville, acted in the Yiddish Theatre in New York City for some 10 years, appeared in London and Broadway shows and on radio, TV, and in films. She wrote the words for "That's How You Go with Me." ASCAP.

PIGOTT, JEAN SOPHIA (1845–1882)
"Jesus, I am resting, resting In the joy of what Thou art."
Composer and hymnist, born in Ireland in 1845, she attended an evangelistic Keswick Convention in Brighton, England, in July 1875, after

which she was afflicted with invalidism. Despite her illness, she wrote the above hymn of hope and confidence. She discarded all her medicines, relying on God for help in her prayers. Two of her brothers went to China as missionaries, one of them to a martyr's grave. She was not only a hymnist, but also a composer of music and an artist. Her hymns appeared in the *Keswick Hymn Book; Hymns for the Family of God* (1976); the *Presbyterian Hymnal* (1933); and *Hymns for the Living Church* (1974).

PINBOROUGH, JAN UNDERWOOD (1954–)
"A Key Was Turned in Latter Days"
Hymnist born in Midland, Texas, and educated at Brigham Young University (BA and MA), she married Thomas Vince Pinborough and they have one daughter. She was written articles for a number of church publications. Her hymn above appeared in the Mormon hymnal (1985).

PINKARD, EDNA BELLE (1892–Dec'd.)
"Make Those Naughty Eyes Behave"
Composer/songwriter born on March 19th in Ottumwa, Iowa, she was educated at Juilliard in New York City and had private study. She wrote, "Does My Sweetie Do?", "I'll Always Remember Livin' High", "Sugar Granny", "You're in Wrong with the Right Baby", and "When Loves Come Along". ASCAP.

POLK, MARY JANE (1916–)
"I Told a Lie"
Composer/songwriter born on August 19th in New York City and educated at the University of Pennsylvania Dental School (DDS), she wrote "I Told a Lie" and other songs. ASCAP.

POLL, RUTH (1899–1955)
"It Was So Good While It Lasted"
Songwriter born on June 10th in New York, New York, she wrote the songs "I'd Love to Make Love to You", "I'm a Military Man", "I'm Wearing a New Shade of Blues", "If Yesterday Could Only Be Tomorrow", "These Things Money Can't Buy", and "Weary Little Fellow". ASCAP.

POPPLEWELL, MARY (1920–)
"It's a Crying Shame"
Composer/songwriter, she was born on October 15th in Italy, Texas, and was educated at a business college. She wrote "How Softly a Heart Breaks" and "It's a Crying Shame". ASCAP.

PORTER, ETHEL K. FLENTYE (1901–)
   Tune—"Christ Ist Erstanden"
Pianist/composer, she was born in Wilmette, Illinois. While attending
Northwestern University (AB, 1923), she met her future husband, Dr.
Porter. While at the American Conservatory of Music in Chicago, she re-
ceived second place in the piano division in the finals of the Young
Artists' Auditions sponsored by the National Federation of Music Clubs.
She received her BM degree from the Conservatory in 1927, graduating
with honors. She studied piano with Olga Samaroff-Stokowski on a fellowship in the Graduate School at Juilliard (1927–29) and with Nadia
Boulanger at the American Conservatorie in Fontainebleau, France, in the
summer of 1930. She taught at the Dalton School in New York (1931–45)
until her husband became director of the School of Music at Union Theological Seminary (1945) until his death in 1960. She composed the hymn
"Christ the Lord Is Risen Again", arranged from a German folk melody
in 1958. Her hymn tune appeared in the *Presbyterian Hymnal* (1990).

POSEGATE, MAXINE WOODBRIDGE (b. 1924–)
   Tune—"Woodbridge"
A composer and organist, born in Modesto, California, on June 5, 1924,
she was educated at Modesto Junior College, Wheaton College (BS) and
California State University at Long Beach (MA). She is married to
Robert Posegate, director of admissions and records at Northwestern
College, Roseville, Minnesota. He also teaches hymnology, and she
teaches music theory and class piano at the college. She has been a
church organist, and has composed over 50 anthems that have been published. Her tune above, set to the hymn, "Gentle Mary Laid Her Child"
(words by Joseph S. Cook, 1919), was published by The Hymn Society
of America in *The Hymn* for July 1981.

POTTER, (ETHEL OLIVE) DOREEN (1925–1980)
   Tune for—"Jesus, Where Can We Find You?"
A composer, she was a citizen of Jamaica, born in Panama, and taught
music and English at St. Catharine's College, Liverpool, England. She
obtained a licentiate of music degree at Trinity College, London. She
wrote the music for Fred Kan's hymns: "Break Not the Circle," "God
Has Set Us Free," "God of Bible and Tradition," "Help Us Accept Each
Other," "Let Us Talents and Tongues Employ." Her tunes were pub-
lished in *Pilgrim Praise, Cantate Domingo, Sing a New Song, New
Songs of Asian Cities, Praise for Today, Break not the Circle,* and *Creation Sings* (1979). She died in Geneva, Switzerland. [Information from
Ann Lodge of Riley, Kansas, editor of *Creation Sings* (Philadelphia:
Geneva Press, 1979)]

POWNALL, MARY ANN (1751–1796)
"Washington"
Composer/singer/actress, she was born in February 1751 in London, England. She performed in London as Mrs. Wrighten, having made her debut at age nineteen at the Drury Lane Theatre. After coming to New York City in 1792 with her second husband, Mr. Pownall, she was the first song plugger for a publishing house in America. She plugged "Primroses" and other songs by James Hewitt. She became a member of the Old American Opera Company in Philadelphia and had the female lead in James Hewitt's *Tammany* in 1794, the first opera composed by an American. She collaborated with James Hewitt in writing *Six Songs for the Harpsichord* (1794). She sang her song "Washington", in praise of President Washington at a concert in Boston on August 1, 1794. Pownall sang "Washington and Liberty" at the City Theatre in Charleston, South Carolina, on February 22, 1796 and "Address to the Ladies". Her "Grand Concert Spiritual" in Charleston on March 24, 1796 was so successful she gave a repeat concert two days later. Unfortunately, she died in Charleston on August 11, 1796, at age forty-five.

POZZI, ESCOT, OLGA (1933–)
Lamentus
Composer of French-Moroccan background, she was born October 1st in Lima, Peru. While studying mathematics at the San Marcos University in Lima, she also studied music at the Sas-Rosay Academy of Music (1949–53), then immigrated to the United States where she attended Juilliard School in New York City (MS, 1957) and also studied at the Hamburg Hochschule fur Musik (1957–61). She taught at the New England Conservatory (1964–67) and Wheaton College, Norton, Massachusetts, since 1972. She has received a number of commissions. She married Robert Cogan and they published two books on sonic design. Her instrumental works include *Lamentus* (Trilogy no. 1), 1962; *Cristhos* (Trilogy no. 2), 1963, and *Visione* (Trilogy no. 3), 1964.

PREVIN, DORY LANGDON (1925–)
"Last Tango in Paris"
Singer/songwriter, she was born on October 22nd in Rahway, New Jersey. With her husband Andre Previn she wrote the lyrics for "Pepe", the "Theme from the Valley of Dolls", and "You're Gonna Hear from Me". With Fred Carlin, she wrote "Come Saturday Morning", with Bruce Broughton, "We're Home Here", and with Gato Barbieri, "Last Tango in Paris".

PRICE, FLORENCE BEA (1888–1953)
   "Songs to the Dark Virgin"
Composer, born Florence Beatrice Smith on April 8th in Little Rock, Arkansas, she achieved greatness as the first black American woman composer. After being taught on the piano by her mother, she attended the New England Conservatory in Boston, where she studied with Chadwick, Converse, and Cutter and graduated in 1906 with a diploma in piano and organ. From 1906–10, she taught at Shorter College in North Little Rock, then became head of the music department at Clark University in Atlanta. Later she married Thomas J. Price and move back to Little Rock. Due to racial tension in the south, they moved to Chicago in 1927, where Mrs. Price studied with Leo Sowerby and others. Her Symphony no. 1 in E minor won the Wanamaker Competition in 1932, which was performed by the Chicago Symphony Orchestra in 1933. Mrs. Price wrote symphonies, chamber and choral music, songs, piano and organ works. Marian Anderson performed her "Songs to the Dark Virgin" with a text by Langston Hughes in 1941. She died in Chicago on June 3, 1953.

PRIESING, DOROTHY (1910–)
   "Carol of the Children"
Pianist/composer/songwriter, she was born on July 31st in Nantucket, Massachusetts, and educated at Juilliard, Columbia University (BS, MA), American School of Music at Fontainebleau, France. She wrote "Carol of the Children", "Noel", "Now Is the Caroling Season." ASCAP.

PRUSSIA, ANNA AMALIA, PRINCESS OF (1723–1787)
   Passion oratorio—*Tod Jesu*
Composer, and sister of Frederick the Great, she was born in Berlin, Germany, on November 9, 1723. She studied music with her brother and with the cathedral organist, Gottlieb Hayne, and with Johann P. Kirnberger. She composed many chorals and some instrumental works, but is best known for her music for *Tod Jesu,* which was later also set to music by Karl H. Graun. She died in Berlin on March 30, 1787.

PTASZYNSKA, MARTA (1943–)
   Spectri sonori
Composer and percussionist, she was born on July 29th in Warsaw, Poland. After she earned diplomas with distinction in composition, theory, and percussion from the Warsaw Conservatory, the French government awarded her a grant to study with Nadia Boulanger in Paris (1969–70). She then studied with Duff, Erb, and Weiner at the Cleveland Institute of Music (1972–74) under a Kościuszko Foundation grant. She taught at Bennington College, Vermont (1974–77) and since then as

composer-in-residence at the University of California at Berkeley and at Santa Barbara, in between trips to Europe. Her orchestral piece *Spectri sonori* had its premiere presented by the Cleveland Orchestra in 1974. She was written an opera and numerous vocal and instrumental pieces.

PULKINGHAM, BETTY CARR (1928–)
Tune—"Alleluia No. 1"
Composer, she was born on August 25th in Burlington, North Carolina, the daughter of Bett Knott and judge Leo Carr and was educated at the University of North Carolina at Greensboro (BS in Music, Piano, Theory, magna cum laude, 1949) and the Eastman School of Music at Rochester, New York. She married the Rev. Graham Pulkingham, they had six children, and reside in Aliquippa, Pennsylvania. She made an arrangement of "Alleulia No. 1" for *The Hymnal of Worship & Celebration* (Baptist 1986) and the *Presbyterian Hymnal* (1990).

-Q-

QUEEN LATIFAH (1970–)
"Must Have Been an Angel"
Rapper/actress/songwriter, hometown Wayne, New Jersey, new resides in Los Angeles. Her father was a member of the Newark Police Department. She performed her hit "Fly Girl" from the album *Ladies First,* on the Fox TV show *Rock the Vote* in September 1992. Her albums include *All Hail the Queen,* "Latifah's Hat it Up 2 Here" Grammy winner 1993. She is currently on the Fox TV soap *Living Single* (1993–95).

While on a 1995 visit to New York City Latifah and rapper Shawn Moon were approached by someone as they sat in Lahifah's car. They were robbed, her auto was carjacked, and Shawn Moon was shot and taken to a hospital. Queen Latifah wrote a song about that night called "Must Have Been an Angel Who Saved Him."

-R-

RAINEY, MA (1886–1939)
"Moonshine Blues"
Singer/songwriter, she was born Gertrude Malissa Nix Pridgett on April 26th in Columbus, Georgia. At age twelve she appeared in a talent show in Columbus. After she married vaudeville actor Will "Pa" Rainey in 1904, the two toured in tent shows in the south in F. S. Wolcott's Rabbit Foot Minstrels. Ma Rainey became known as the "Mother of the Blues". Her piano accompanist was Lovie Austin. She was the first blues singer to record for Paramount. She composed "Bo-weavil Blues" (1923), "Moonshine Blues" (1923), made some 100 recordings and

recorded "Jelly Bean Blues" with Louis Armstrong in 1924. She toured with her Georgia Jazz Band in the 1920s, which at various times included Coleman Hawkins, Tommy Ladnier, and Joe Smith. She retired in 1935 and died on December 22nd in Columbus, Georgia. In 1994 her album *Ma Rainey's Black Bottom* was available for purchase.

RAITT, BONNIE (1949–)
"Feeling of Falling"
Guitarist/singer/songwriter, she was born on November 8th in Los Angeles, California, the daughter of baritone John Raitt. She attended Radcliffe College (1967–69) and performed with Howlin' Wolf, Sippie Wallace, and others. Her husband, Michael O'Keefe, is an actor/poet/songwriter and wrote the words for her songs in her album *Longing in Their Hearts* issued in 1994. Her other albums available now include *Bonnie Raitt, Bonnie Raitt Collection*, rated B plus by Entertainment Weekly, *Give it Up, Green Light, Home Plate, Nine Lives, Street Lights, Sweet Forgiveness, Takin' My Time, The Glow*. *Nick of Time* (1989) sold 4 million copies and was a Grammy sweeper; *Luck of the Draw* (1991) was rated A by Entertainment Weekly, sold 5 million copies, and was a Grammy sweeper.

RAMBO, DOTTIE (1934–)
Tune—"Behold the Lamb"
Guitarist/singer/songwriter she was born Joyce Reba Luttrell on March 2nd at Morganfield, Kentucky, one of 11 children. Her grandfathers, Isaiah Burton and Edward Luttrell, were both full-blooded Cherokee Indians. At age twelve she was singing country songs and playing the guitar on a weekly show on a local radio station. After converting to Christianity at age twelve, she left home to sing at church revivals in various towns and slept in the homes of the local preachers. On July 1, 1950, Dottie married Buck Rambo.

They called themselves the Gospel Echoes. When their daughter Reba was thirteen, Reba joined her parents and they called themselves the Singing Rambos. In the 1960s their album *The Soul of Me* won a Grammy, and Dottie became the first white woman to win the award singing soul music. Dottie has written the words and melody for over 2,000 gospel songs. In 1967 Buck, Dottie, and Reba sang for our troops in Vietnam. They were flown there in military aircraft and paid $8 a day, of which $3 went for lodging and $5 for food.

Disaster struck in 1986 when Dottie suffered spinal cord damage and had a long period of recovery. They had lived in Nashville, California, Atlanta, Georgia, etc., then moved back to Nashville in 1991. Dottie Rambo was inducted into the Gospel Hall of Fame on April 6, 1992. Her hymn above was included in *The Hymnal for Worship and Celebration* (Baptist, 1986).

RAMBO, REBA (1951–)

Tune—"A Perfect Heart"

Gospel singer/songwriter she was born on October 17th in Madisonville, Kentucky, the daughter of gospel singers Buck and Dottie Rambo. At age thirteen Reba was singing with her parents as The Singing Rambos. Reba married Landy Gardner, son of a Pentecostal preacher from Huntington, West Virginia. Reba quit singing with her parents and went out on her own. She was the only white woman in a group of black soul/gospel singers, Andre Crouch & the Disciples.

After Reba divorced Gardner she married Donny McGuire. They had a daughter, Destiny Rambo McGuire, and a son, Israel Anthem McGuire. She composed the music for "A Perfect Heart" and her husband wrote the words for the hymn that appeared in *The Hymnal for Worship & Celebration* (Baptist, 1986). She has written over 1,000 gospel songs, including *Lift Him Up,* "Sacrifice of Praise", "Because of Whose I Am", "With My Song", "Shadow of Your Wings," "Let Every Nation". (Information from Dusty Wells, RMR Music Group, Nashville & "The Legacy of Buck & Dottie Rambo" by Buck Rambo as told to Bob Terrell, Nashville: Star Song Publishing 1992).

RAMON, ELIZABETH T. B. (1894–Dec'd.)

"Amada Mia"

Composer/songwriter born on September 7th in New York, New York, and educated by private tutors, she wrote "Amada Mia" and "Dear Heart, Gentle Heart".

RAN, SHULAMIT (1949–)

Concert Piece

Composer/pianist, she was born on October 21st in Tel-Aviv, Israel. As a child she took lessons on the piano with Miriam Boskovich and Emma Gorochov and composition with A. U. Boskovich and Haim and at age thirteen was an accomplished composer. She studied at Mannes College of Music in New York City on a scholarship and was graduated in 1967. She then toured the US and Europe and her *Concert Piece* was performed in July 1971 by the Israel Philharmonic Orchestra under Mehta. She was appointed associate professor of composition at the University of Chicago in 1978. Ran has composed piano pieces, chamber and orchestral works, and vocal ensembles. As of 1994 her available album was *Con Da Camera II, Hyperbole.*

RANEY, SUE (1939–)

"Blue Tears"

Composer/singer/songwriter born on June 18th in McPherson, Kansas, she studied voice privately and sang on records. With Ed Yelin she wrote a number of songs, "Blue Tears", "Burnt Sugar", "Be Warm", "No Place to Go", "No Use", "Statue of Snow".

RANDALL, NAOMI W. (1908–)
"When Faith Endures"
Hymnist born in North Ogden, Utah, she married Earl A. Randall and they have one daughter. She is the author of childrens' books and has been a church worker. Her hymn above and also "I Am a Child of God" appeared in the Mormon hymnal (1985).

RAY, AMY (1964–)
"This Train"
Folk/rock guitarist/alto singer/songwriter she was raised in Decatur, Georgia, the daughter of Dr. Larry Ray, a radiologist. In 1974, Amy met Emily Saliers, and in 1980 they formed the duo Saliers and Ray. While both women were undergraduates at Emory University in Atlanta, Georgia, they formed the duo Indigo Girls in 1980 and played in clubs.

Their first album *Indigo Girls* went platinum in 1989; they also had a video *Live at the Uptown Lounge*; and the albums *Rites of Passage* (1993 Grammy winner) and *Swamp Ophelia* (1994). Their hit singles are "No-mads, Indians, Saints", "Let It Be Me" 1992, and "This Train". After a visit to the Holocaust Museum in Washington, DC, the lines in the song were changed to "Piss and blood in a railroad car/one hundred people, Gypsies, queers and David's Star". Both singers are gay. Ray lives outside Atlanta with her female companion Cooper Seay.

REDDY, HELEN (1942–)
"I Am Woman"
Singer/songwriter, she was born on October 25th in Melbourne, Australia, and came to the US. Her hit song "I Am Woman", which she wrote, became a feminist theme song. She toured the US in 1990. Her albums available in 1994 were *Greatest Hits, Helen Reddy's Greatest Hits, Lust for Life*.

REED, NANCY (1928–)
"Look At Us, We're Walking"
Composer born on May 29th in Pittsburgh, Pennsylvania, and educated at Juilliard in New York City. She was a singer and pianist with the Skitch Henderson and Benny Goodman orchestras. With Moose Charlap, Betsy Gettinger, Bob Hilliard, and John Murray, she wrote a number of songs, "The Apple, Wind and Stream", "Balboa", "Sleepy Little Space Cadet", "Toodle-EE-You-Doo", "Look At Us, We're Walking" (theme song for the National United Cerebral Palsy Telethon). ASCAP.

REICHARDT, C. LUISE (1779–1826)
Tune—"Armageddon"

A composer and daughter of the composer-teacher Johann Friedrich Reichardt, she was born in Berlin, Germany, on April 11, 1779 and studied with her father. She made her debut as a singer in 1794 and settled in Hamburg, Germany, in 1814, where she taught at a vocal academy. Shortly before her wedding, her fiancé died, and later her voice failed, so she put her full attention into composing music. She wrote numerous popular songs in addition to hymn music. Her tune appeared in Part III of Layriz's *Kern des deutschen Kirchengesangs* (1853) and appeared in *The Church Psalter and Hymn-Book* (1872). She died in Hamburg on November 17, 1826. More recently her tune was set to the hymn "Who is on the Lord's side?" and appeared in *Hymns for the Living Church* (1974). She also wrote the music Schlaf, Kindlein, Schlaf for "Sleep, baby, sleep! Thy mother watch doth keep." Her songs were popular in Germany and published as recently as 1922 by G. Reinhardt of Munich.

REISER, VIOLET (1915–Dec'd.)
'New Dawn Fantasy'

Composer/organist born on July 3rd in New York, New York, and educated at college. She studied with Clarence Adler, David Brown, Herman Schwartzman, and Gary Sheldon. She was an organist/pianist in theaters and on radio. Her instrumentals include *Waltzing Ballerina, Valse Elegante, Dancing Sunbeams, Tiny Toe Dancer, Holiday in Holland*.

REISS, FAYE LOUISE (1934–)
"Lover Boy"

Composer/singer/songwriter born on September 10th in Fresno, California, she sang in the Horace Heidt and Ralph Flanagan orchestras and sang in government shows during the Korean War. With Patricia Ann Johns, she wrote "Lover Boy".

REMSEN, ALICE (1896–Dec'd.)
"Arizona Moonlight"

Composer/singer/songwriter born on November 24th in London, England, she studied at the London School of Music. She sang in vaudeville and musical comedies in London, Paris, and in the US. She wrote "Arizona Moonlight", "The Dream I Dreamed Last Night", "Irish Rain", "Lovely Is the Lee", "One Time", "Prairie Wind", "Vagabond of the Prairie". ASCAP.

RENDLE, LILY (1875–1964)
Tune—"Vesper Hymn"

A composer, born in London, England, on May 14, 1875, she was educated in London and Paris and won a gold medal and an associateship at the Guildhall School of Music studying piano, composition, and voice. She taught at the Bechstein Hall in London for 20 years. She moved to Eastbourne in East Sussex, England in 1922 to care for her invalid mother, who died in 1944. After her mother's death, she taught a few pupils in Eastbourne and died there on July 27, 1964. Her hymn tune appeared in the *Methodist Hymnal* (1964).

RENIE, HENRIETTA (1875–1956)
Elegie
Harpist/composer, she was born on September 18th in Paris. At age eleven she was awarded first prize for harp at the Paris Conservatoire. She was so popular that the queen of the Belgians came to Paris to hear her play. Meanwhile in Lenepveu's class, she won a prize for harmony and composition. Mlle. Renie played her own compositions at Lamoureux concerts in 1901. She played the harp at Parisian symphony concerts and toured Europe. Renie composed an *Elegie* for harp and orchestra performed at the Lamoureux concerts (1907), two pieces for violin and harp, a sonata for cello and pianoforte, and pieces for harp solo—*Ballades, Contemplation, Legendie,* etc., and songs. She died on March 1st in Paris.

RENNES, CATHARINA van (1858–1940)
(Cantatas and songs)
Singer/composer, she was born on August 2nd in The Netherlands. After studying with Richard Hol and Johannes Messchaert, she taught pianoforte in Utrecht, then at Hilversum. While teaching at The Hague, one of her pupils was Princess Juliana, later Queen Juliana. Catharina composed many cantatas and songs for children in the Dutch language. She died in Amsterdam on November 23rd.

REYNOLDS, MALVINA MILDER (1900–1978)
"What Have They Done to the Rain?"
Songwriter, she was born on August 23rd in San Francisco, California. After studying piano with Rita Mooney, she was graduated from the University of California at Berkeley (BA, 1925), (MA, 1927), and (PhD, 1939); she was unable to obtain a teaching position, having been blacklisted for her political activities. Her songs were recorded by many noted performers, such as Harry Belafonte, who recorded "Turn Around" (1957), by Joan Baez, who recorded the one mentioned above in 1962, and by Peter Seeger for "Little Boxes" (1963). She played the piano and toured Europe and Japan. Reynolds wrote some 500 songs, many dealing with the environment and peace. She died on March 19th in Berkeley.

RHODES, SARAH BETTS BRADSHAW (1829–1904)
"God who made the earth,
The air, the sky, sea."

Composer, hymnist, and sculptress, she was the wife of J. Alsop Rhodes, a master silversmith in Sheffield, England. A Congregationalist, she wrote her hymn for the Sheffield Sunday School Union Whitsuntide Festival in 1870, and also wrote the tune for her hymn, which appeared in the *Methodist Sunday School Hymn Book* (1879). After her husband's death, she became head of a girl's school at Worksop, Notts, England, where she died. More recently her hymn appeared in *Episcopal* (1940); *Presbyterian* (1955) hymnals, and in the English *Baptist Hymn Book* (1962).

RICH, GLADYS (1892–Dec'd.)
'Journey of Promise'
Composer born on April 26th in Philadelphia, Pennsylvania, and she was educated at the New England Conservatory in Boston; the University of Utah (BA); New York University (MA). She studied with Edward Barnes, Harvey Gaul, and Frederick Schleider. She entertained troops at a YMCA in Paris during World War I. Her works include: cantatas — *Journey of Promise, Triumph of Faith, Messengers of Mercy;* operettas — *Aloha Sugar Mill, Garden Magic, Renting the Hive, The Toy Shop, Walk the Plank,* and *The Lady Says "Yes".* She also wrote a number of songs.

RICHARDS, MAE
Cut the Ribbons
A composer, her off-Broadway musical, *Cut the Ribbons* was produced at the New Hope Performing Arts Festival in New Hope, Pennsylvania (1994).

RICHMOND, VIRGINIA (1932–)
"Buffalo"
Composer/songwriter born on January 28th in New York, New York, she studied privately. She wrote "All My Life I Have Been Searching for You", "An Old-fashioned Wedding Song", "At the Fair", "Betcha", "Buffalo", "Doctor", "Down, Down, Down", "In My Sloppy Serape", "It Was Just a Moment", and "You Made a Boo-boo".

RICHTER, MARGA (1926–)
'Landscapes of the Mind'
Composer/pianist, she was born on October 21st in Reedsburg, Wisconsin. As a child she learned to play the piano and was composing at age eleven. While at the Juilliard School in New York City, where she studied piano with Tureck and composition with Bergsma and Persichetti, she had three of her compositions performed at the Composer's Forum in New York City. She earned her BS and her MS in 1951. She was commissioned by the Harkness Ballet to write the scores for two ballets and her series of works called *Landscapes of the Mind,* composed between

1968–79, were inspired by paintings of Georgia O'Keeffe. Many of her works have been performed by the Minnesota Orchestra, Oakland Symphony Orchestra, National Gallery Orchestra, etc. She has composed orchestral, chamber, and vocal works.

RIO, ROSA (1914–)
   "In My Caravan of Dreams"
Composer/organist born on June 2nd in San Francisco, California, she studied with John Hammond at the Eastman School of Music in Rochester, New York; also with Jesse Crawford and Joseph Schillinger. She was an organist in theaters, then with ABC and NBC. She taught music and wrote "If I Could Love You", "Just to Be Alone with You", "Memories of the Past", "The Moon Is Blue", "You'll Come Running Back to Me".

RITCHIE, JEAN (1922–)
   "Let the Sun Shine Down on Me"
Country/folk/singer/songwriter, she was born on December 8th in Viper, Kentucky, the youngest of 14 children, all musically minded. Her father, Balis, was one of 10 children, all singers, her grandfather Austin was one of 10 children, all singers, and her great grandfather Crockett was one of 11 children, all singers. After graduating from the University of Kentucky, she went to New York City in 1947, where she performed as a dulcimer player and sang with other folksingers. During the 1960s she performed at the Newport Folk Festivals. She wrote a number of songs such as the one mentioned above. "A Tree in the Valley-O", "The Cuckoo, She's a Pretty Bird", and "What'll I Do with Baby-O?". Her album *Live in Folk City* recorded with Doc Watson was available in 1994.

RITTENHOUSE, ELIZABETH MAE (b. 1915–)
   "Oh hallelujah Jesus lives within."
Composer, hymnist, and evangelist, she was born in Woodlawn, Alabama, on July 23, 1915 and was educated at a Bible Institute. She served as secretary of the Akron Ministerial Association Chartered Christian Assembly in Akron, Ohio, and conducted a radio ministry covering Akron and also Clarksburg, West Virginia. She also wrote "A Soldier for Christ," and "Search My Heart," etc.

ROBERTS, LINDA (1901–Dec'd.)
   "You Should Have Kissed Me Then"
Songwriter born on May 15th in New York City, she was educated at Cornell University, Hunter College (BA), and the New School for Social Research. With Robert Effros, Lawrence Elow, Gene Mascara, and Irving Mopper, she wrote the words for a number of songs, "Beatnick Boogie", "Charm Bracelet", "Castanets", "Love Wears a Mask", "Not

as a Stranger", "Summer Will Come Again", and "You Make Living Worthwhile". ASCAP.

ROBERTS, RUTH OLIVE (1926–)
"The Nina, the Pinta, the Santa Maria"
Pianist/songwriter, she was born on August 31st in Portchester, New York. With Gene Piller and William Katz, she wrote "Mister Touchdown U.S.A.—They always call him Mister Touchdown" and with Bill Katz "The Nina, the Pinta, the Santa Maria—There were three little ships in the harbor."

ROBINSON, JESSIE MAE (1919–Dec'd.)
"Railroad Porter Blues"
Composer born October 1st in Beaumont, Texas, she received a high school education. She wrote "Blue Light Boogie", "Clean Head Blues", "The Bachelor's Tune", "In the Middle of the Night", "The Lover Waltz", "When I See You", "Keep it Secret", "Let's Have a Party", "The Other Woman", and "You Let My Love Get Cold". ASCAP.

RODGERS, MARY (1931–)
"In a Little While"
Composer/songwriter born January 11th in New York, New York, the daughter of composer Richard Rodgers. She was educated at Wellesley College. With her sister Linda Rodgers Melnick, Marshall Barer, Martin Charnin, she wrote a number of songs: "Counter Melody", "Normandy", "Shy", "In a Little While", "Very Soft Shoes"; also stage scores for *The Mad Show, Once Upon a Mattress, Three to Make Music;* marionette score for *Davy Jones Locker;* her albums are *Ali Baba, Some of My Best Friends are Children, Children's Introduction to Jazz.*

ROE, GLORIA ANN (1935–)
Tune—"Be Calm My Soul"
Pianist/composer, she was born on January 5th in Hollywood, California. Her first hymn was published by Word Publishing Company, a subsidiary of the American Broadcasting Corporation, when she was a senior at the El Monte High School. She studied piano under Frances Zulawinski (a student of Paderewski) and as a concert pianist at age eleven made her debut in Carnegie Hall, New York City. She now lives in Diablo, California, and is an instructor at the local high school. Roe is the mother of four children. The Gloria Company consists of Gloria Roe, guitarist/composer Jannetje, vocalist/songwriter Chris, a teenager, and pianist Rebecca. They perform concerts at high school assemblies. In 1977 Gloria was elected to the Sacred Music Hall of Fame and has received the coveted Bank of America Fine Arts Award. Her hymn tune and hymn "Be calm my soul,

faint not with care" appeared in *The Hymnal for Worship and Celebration* (1986 Baptist). She has 11 albums to her credit, including those with the Stockholm, London, and Israel Symphonies.

ROGERS, CLARA KATHLEEN BARNETT (1844–1931)
'Song Cycle'
Singer/composer, she was born on January 14th at Cheltenham, England, the daughter of composer John Barnett. When she was only twelve years old, she was accepted at Leipzig University where she studied piano and singing and was the youngest student ever accepted at the university. She wanted to study composition, but at that time such study was closed to females. After she was graduated with honors in 1860 and further studies, she embarked on a singing opera career in Italy, England, and America. After her marriage to Boston attorney Henry M. Rogers, she taught singing at the New England Conservatory. She composed a piano forte, string quartet, and a number of songs including her *"Song Cycle"* based on Browning's poems between 1893 and 1903. She died at Boston on March 8th.

ROGERS, LELA EMOGEN (1890–1977)
"The Ten Commandments"
Songwriter born on December 25th in Council Bluffs, Iowa, and educated at business school. She was the mother of actress Ginger Rogers. With Bill Snyder and Victor Young, she wrote the lyrics for "Tahiti, My Island", "The Ten Commandments", "This Is Me Loving You." She died on May 25th at Palm Springs, California.

ROMA, CARO (1869–1937)
The Wandering One
Soprano/composer, she was born Carrie Northey on September 10th in East Oakland, California. After performing as a child, she directed an opera company in Canada when she was a teenager. She studied at the New England Conservatory in Boston and graduated in 1890, whereupon she sang with the Castle Square Opera Company in Boston as Caro Roma and sang at the Tivoli Opera House in San Francisco for eight seasons. While touring Europe, she sang with the Turner Grand Opera in London in 1906. After moving to Miami in 1919, she taught at the Florida Conservatory of Music and Art. She composed the song cycles *The Wandering One* and *The Swan* and numerous popular, sea, and sacred songs. Roma died on September 23rd in the town of her birth.

ROOBENIAN, AMBER (1905–Dec'd.)
"Concertino Espagnol"
Composer/organist born on May 13th in Boston, Massachusetts, and educated at the New England Conservatory with Henry Dunham she also

attended the Eastman School of Music in Rochester, New York. She married composer/songwriter W. Clark Harrington. Her works include "Reverie", "Antique Air", "Desert Solitude", "Long Gone Jublo"; choral: "In an Old English Garden", "The Willow Tree", "The Tryst", "Two Red Roses Across the Moon", "Vigil"; organ: "Samarkand"; song: "Mother Never Told Me".

ROSALES, SYLVIA (1917–)
"Prayer for Peace"
Composer/songwriter/director born on June 14th in New York City and educated at New York University (BA), she wrote college and nightclub revues, special material for Carol Channing, Imogene Coca, Jack Carter, and Milton Berle, as well as for TV shows. With her husband, Mario Rosales, she wrote a number of songs and wrote and produced TV shows in Spanish. ASCAP.

ROSNESS, JUANITA M. (1897–Dec'd.)
"Chicago Beautiful"
A composer/singer/songwriter born on May 13th in Chicago, Illinois, she was educated in high school and studied music. She sang in vaudeville, light and grand opera, and in films. She wrote "Behold. Tis Day", "Fragrance", "Little One", "Music from a Box", and "Window shopping". ASCAP.

ROSS, ANNIE (1930–)
Sings a Handful of Songs
Singer/songwriter, she was born Annabelle Short Lynch in Mitcham, Surrey, England. She was a member of the Lambert, Hendricks, Ross Trio (1958–62), then operated her own nightclub in London. She recorded with baritone saxist Gerry Mulligan, saxist/clarinetist Zoot Sims, and other jazz musicians. She performed at the Grand Finale in New York City in September and October 1980. As of 1994, her albums available were *Sings a Handful of Songs,* with Gerry Mulligan *Annie Sings a Song with Gerry Mulligan,* and with Zoot Sims *A Gasser.*

ROSS, HELEN (1912–Dec'd.)
"Hearts Were Never Meant to Be Broken"
Composer born on July 31st in New York City, she was educated in high school. With Horace Linsley and Benny Ross, she wrote: "Hold Me Forever", "'Till You Come Back to Me", "I Wanna Be 17 All of My Life", "Love, Don't be a Stranger", "What Am I to Do?", "I Wanna Gal You Can Dance Me a Cha Cha", "I Hope You Won't Hold It Against Me", "Shake Hands with a Guy in Love", and "Sightseeing". ASCAP.

ROUNSEFELL, CARRIE ESTHER PARKER (1861–1930)
    Tune—"Manchester"
Composer and singer, the daughter of Clara and James A. Parker, she
was born in Merrimack, New Hampshire, on March 1, 1861. She was
raised in Manchester, New Hampshire, where she met and married
William E. Rounsefell, a bookkeeper for a paint and wallpaper firm
there. As a singing evangelist, she toured New England and eastern New
York State with a small autoharp. Later she became a member of the
Church of God. Her hymn tune was used for "It may not be on the moun-
tain's height" by Mary Brown. She wrote her tune while attending a revival meeting of the Baptist Church in Lynn, Massachusetts. She died in
Durham, Maine, on September 18, 1930. Her hymn tune appeared in the
Baptist Hymnal (1956).

ROWEN, RUTH HALLE (1918–)
    "I Have Decided to Become an Old Maid"
Composer/songwriter born on April 5th in New York City and educated
at Barnard College (BA), Columbia University (MA and PhD), she
taught at City College of New York. With Bill Simon, she wrote "I Love
Who Loves Me", "The Needle's Eye", "Somebody Cares for Me",
"Whoa, Mule, Whoa". ASCAP.

ROWLEY, GRIETJE TERBURG (1927–)
    Tune—"Be Thou Humble"
Composer/pianist born in Florida and educated at the University of Miami, Florida (BA in music education), she now lives in Salt Lake City,
Utah, and has played the piano in various church programs for many
years. She composed the music and wrote the words for the above
hymn—"Be thou humble"—in the Mormon hymnal (1985).

ROWSON, SUSANNAH HASWELL (1762–1824)
    "Slaves in Algiers"
Actress/lyricist/librettist, she was born in Portsmouth, England, and was
brought to America at age five by her father, a lieutenant in the British
army. At age sixteen she returned to England and in 1786 she married
William Rowson, a musician. She wrote the novel *Charlotte Temple*
(1790). Susannah and her husband came to America in 1793 to work for
Thomas Wignell. She appeared on the stage in Annapolis, Baltimore,
Philadelphia, and Boston. She wrote lyrics for songs by James H.
Hewitt, Benjamin Carr, and Peter Van Hagen. With music by Alexander
Reinagle, she wrote the lyrics for *Slaves in Algiers* (1794) and the libretto
for the comic opera by Reinagle, *The Volunteers*. She died in Boston,
Massachusetts.

RUBIN, ADA ROETER (1906–)
"The Meetin's Called to Order"
Pianist/composer born on July 1st in New York, New York, and educated in public schools, she had private piano study. She recorded as a jazz pianist, made records, with Joe Davis and Andy Razaf wrote a number of songs, "Alexander's Back in Town" and "Fair and Square".

RUBIN, RUTH (1906–)
Singable English Translations (Yiddish songbook)
Composer/songwriter/folklorist born in September 1st in Montreal, Quebec, Canada, and she received a high school education. She taught at the New School for Social Research in New York City and wrote/compiled *Treasury of Jewish Folksong, Voices of the People,* and *The Story of Yiddish Folksong.*

RUNCIE, CONSTANCE FAUNT LE ROY (1836–1911)
"Silence of the Sea"
Composer, she was born in Indianapolis, Indiana. She married James Muncie, an Episcopal priest in Madison, Indiana (1861–71), later in St. Joseph, Missouri. She wrote "Hear Us, Oh Hear Us", "Round the Throne", "Silence of the Sea", "Take My Soul, O Lord", "I Never Told Him", "Dove of Peace", "I Hold My Heart So Still", and "My Spirit Rests". She died in Winnetka, Illinois.

RUPP, ANNA T. (1909–)
"You Are My Sweetheart"
Composer/songwriter born on January 25th in Quincy, Illinois, she was educated at a business school. She wrote "Dreaming", "It's Love", "Love Me", "Loving Only You", and "Janie". ASCAP.

RUSH, MARY JOE (1909–Dec'd.)
"America's Way of Life"
Composer/songwriter born on April 11th in Mannington, West Virginia, and educated at West Virginia University (BA), she appeared in Broadway shows and films. With Irving Bibo she wrote "Buenas Nochas, Maria", "Chilly Willy", "Lonely", and "Love Never Changes". ASCAP.

RUSHEN, PATRICE LOUISE (1954–)
Straight from the Heart
Flutist/pianist/singer/composer, she was born on September 30th in Los Angeles, California. She toured with Melba Liston, Abbey Lincoln, The Sylvers, Gerald Wilson, and others. Albums available in 1994 were *Anthology* and *Straight from the Heart.*

RUSSELL, ANNA (1911–)
"I'm Sitting in the Bar All Alone"
Comedienne/composer/singer/songwriter born on December 27th in London, England, she was educated at the Royal College of Music in London. She composed and sang in several musicals, wrote "Feeling Fine", "I Love the Spring", the albums *Anna Russell Sings?, Anna Russell Sings? Again, Anna Russell in Darkest Africa, A Practical Banana Promotion,* and *Square Talk on Popular Singing.* ASCAP.

RUSSELL, BRENDA
Kiss Me in the Wind
Pianist/singer/songwriter, she was born in Brooklyn, New York. Her hit song was "Piano in the Dark" (1988). Her album *Greatest Hits* (1992) included Grammy winners "Piano in the Dark" and "So Good, So Right". Other albums include *Get Here, Kiss Me in the Wind, Brenda Russell,* and *Soul Talkin* (1993).

-S-

SABIN, ZARA (1892–1980)
"With Humble Heart"
Hymnist born in Bellwood, Nebraska, she served as a Latter-day Saint in Great Britain and was a researcher for the Utah Genealogical Society for 15 years. Her poetry appeared in many publications and her hymn above in the Mormon hymnal (1985).

SADOFF, MELISSA M. (1933–)
"Honolulu Honky Tonk"
Composer/pianist/songwriter, she was born on May 1st in Belgrade, Yugoslavia and educated at the Music Academy in Belgrade. With Frankie Carle and Dorothy Wayne, she wrote the songs, "Aloha Paradise", "Melissa", etc.

SAGAL, KATEY
"Some Things are Better Left Unsaid"
Actress/singer/songwriter, she was a backup singer for Bette Midler, Bob Dylan, and Etta James before becoming an actress on the TV soap "Married . . . with Children." She co-wrote nine of the twelve songs on her debut album *Well* (1994).

SAGER, CAROL BAYER (1947–)
"They're Playing My Song"
Lyricist, she was born on March 8th in New York City. She married composer Burt Bacharach. With music by her husband, she wrote "You

Don't Know Me"; with her husband and Neil Diamond, "Heartlight" and "Turn Around"; with Bacharach, Christopher Cross, and Peter Allen, "Arthur's Theme"; with Bacharach and Bruce Roberts, "Making Love"; with Peter Allen, "Don't Cry Out Loud" and "You and Me"; with Bruce Roberts, "Starmaker" and "You're the Only One"; with Melissa Manchester, "Come In From the Rain" and "Midnight Blue"; with Albert Hammond, "When I Need You"; with David Wolfert, "Heartbreaker"; with Michael Masser, "It's My Turn" and "Some Changes Are for Good"; and with Marvin Hamlisch—"Fallin'", "Fill in the Words", "I Still Believe in You", "If You Really Knew Me", "If You Remember Me", "I'm on Your Side", "Just for Tonight", "Nobody Does It Better", "One Hello", "Theme from Ice Castles", "When You're in My Arms", and "They're Playing My Song".

SAINTE-MARIE, BEVERLY "BUFFY" (1941–)
"Now That the Buffalo's Gone"
Singer/guitarist/songwriter, she was born on February 20th on the Piapot Indian Reservation in Saskatchewan province, Canada. A Cree Indian, she was adopted by a Micmac Indian family in Wakefield, Massachusetts. After teaching herself to play the piano and to write songs as a child, she studied oriental philosophy at the University of Massachusetts at Amherst and sang in coffee shops. She sang at the Gaslight Cafe in New York City during the 1960s. She wrote "Cod'ine", "The Universal Soldier" (1963), the song mentioned above, "Incest Song", "It's My Way", and "My Country, 'Tis of Thy People You're Dying." She has written over 300 songs, and won an Oscar for the best song in the film *An Officer and a Gentleman* (1982). As of 1994 her album *Coincidence and Likely Stories* was available.

SALIERS, EMILY (1963–)
"Nomads, Indians, Saints"
Folk/rock guitarist/singer (soprano)/songwriter, she was raised in New Haven, Connecticut, the daughter of the Rev. Don Saliers, a Methodist minister. In 1974, the family moved to Decatur, Georgia, where Emily met Amy Ray. In 1980, they formed the duo Saliers and Ray. While attending Emory University in Atlanta, Georgia, in 1983, they played in clubs and called themselves the Indigo Girls. After signing with Epic records in 1988, they scored with *Indigo Girls,* a platinum album (1989). Their hit singles are "Nomads, Indians, Saints", "Let It Be Me" 1992, "This Train"; their video is *Live at the Uptown Lounge;* their albums are *Rites of Passage* (1993 Grammy winner) and *Swamp Ophelia* (1994).

After a visit to the Holocaust Museum in Washington, DC, they changed the lines of "This Train" to "Piss and blood in a railroad car/one hundred people, Gypsies, queers and David's Star". Both singers are gay.

SALPETER, SOPHIE (1916–)
"Gather up all the oranges"
Composer/songwriter born on November 19th in New York, New York, and she was educated at Brooklyn College. She worked in the editorial department of *Liberal Judaism* for three years. With Arthur Gordon, John Habash, and Rose Murphy, she wrote the songs, "Climbing Some Other Hill", "Innismore", "Look Away", and "Watcha Gotta Lose?". ASCAP.

SALTER, MARY TURNER (1856–1938)
Lyrics from Sappho
Composer/singer born on March 15th in Peoria, Illinois, she studied singing with Alfred Arthur, John O'Neil, Herman Rudersdorff, and Max Schilling. She taught singing at Wellesley College (1878–81) and appeared in concerts and choral groups. With lyrics by the ancient Greek poetess Sappho she composed the music for the song cycle *Lyrics from Sappho;* also music for other cycles: *A Night in Naishapur, From Old Japan, Love's Epitome.* She died on September 12th in Orangeburg, New York.

SANDERS, ALMA M. (1882–1956)
"That Tumble Down Shack in Athlone"
Pianist/composer, she was born on March 13th in Chicago, Illinois. She composed chamber music, songs, and was a music teacher. With Richard W. Pascoe and Monte Carlo, she wrote "That tumble down shack in Athlone—Oh' I want to go back to that tumble down shack." She died on December 15th in New York City.

SANTONI, LINDA R. (1936–)
"Another Day"
Composer/songwriter born on July 6th in Greenwich, Connecticut, and educated at Syracuse University (BA), she worked for Arthur Godfrey Productions and wrote the songs "Another Day", "Linda Rose", and "March Berg".

SARLOW, MARY K. (1912–)
"The Holiday Polka"
Songwriter born on May 28th in Brooklyn, New York, she received a high school education. She wrote songs for circuses and minstrel shows, with Caesar Giovannini, Don Large, Beatrice Lever, and Arthur Korb. She wrote the words for "The Holiday Polka", "I Keep Wishing", and "The Lord Has His Arms Around Me".

SARNOFF, JANYCE (1928–)
"I Wonder"
Songwriter born on November 25th in Dubuque, Iowa, she was educated at Clarke College and the University of Dubuque. With Ivan Lane, she wrote the words for "I Wonder", etc. ASCAP.

SAUNDERS, CARRIE LOU (1893–1976)
"Stay Close to God"
A composer, she was born in Mexia, Texas, on August 13, 1893 and was educated at Texas Technological College in Lubbock, Texas. She sang in choirs and also wrote the music for "My Savior Came" and other hymns. She died on February 3, 1976.

SAXON, GRACE (1912–)
"A Christmas to Remember"
Composer/singer born on November 23rd in New York, New York, she was educated at the New York Professional School. She was a child performer with her family act. Member of the Saxon Sisters who performed in clubs, in theaters, and on radio, she wrote "Give Me a Sign", "Lonely Christmas", "Why Do I Cry for You?", and "You Were Made for Love". ASCAP.

SCHAFF, SYLVIA (1916–)
"How Could You Forget Me?"
Composer born on March 24th in Brooklyn, New York, she was educated at Brooklyn College and Manhattan School of Music. She sang and played the piano on radio. With Gene Roberts, she wrote a number of songs, "Hey Mister", "Just One More Time", "Deny", "Lover Be Careful", "Only Yesterday", and "Tinsel and Joy". ASCAP.

SCHERCHEN-HSIAO, TONA (1938–)
L'Invitation au Voyage
Composer, she was born on March 12th in Neuchatel, Switzerland. She was taken to China at age twelve and studied Chinese music and pipa at the Peking Conservatory (1958–60) and at the Shanghai Music Academy. After her return to Switzerland, she studied under Hermann Scherchen at the Gravesano Studio (1960–61) and under Hans Werner Henze at Mozarteum in Salzburg (1961–63); composition under Olivier Messiaen at the Conservatoire National Superieur de Musique in Paris (1963–66), and private composition under Gyorgy Ligeti in Vienna, Austria (1966–67). She has been a guest lecturer at Basel and Zurich in Switzerland, in Denmark, and a research associate at Yale University, New Haven, Connecticut (1979–84). She has received several awards and now resides in Paris. She has composed choral and instrumental

works, chamber music, ballets, electro-acoustic music for cello, piano, percussion, etc. Her *L'Invitation au Voyage* for chamber orchestra (1977) was first performed in Paris in 1978.

SCHUH, MARIE (1922–)
"In the Soft Twilight"

Composer/singer/songwriter, she was born on April 17th in Milwaukee, Wisconsin, and educated at Hagen Piano Studio; Weidner International Conservatory, Boston; and the Wisconsin Conservatory. She wrote "Broken Promises", "I Hold Your Picture", and "We Can't Bid Our Love Goodbye".

SCHUMANN, CLARA JOSEPHINE WIECK (1819–1896)
"Souvenir de Vienne"

Pianist/composer, she was born on September 13th in Leipzig, Germany, the daughter of pianist Frederick Wieck. After studying the pianoforte under her father, at age nine she made her debut in public on October 20, 1828. After giving her first concert at Gewandhaus in Leipzig on November 8, 1830, she gave a series of concerts there in the 1830s. In 1837 she visited Vienna and played there. Clara had an ongoing romance with composer Robert Schumann at this time, and they were finally married on September 12, 1840. In 1844 the Schumanns visited St. Petersburg, Russia, but due to Robert's poor health, they moved from Leipzig to Dresden, then to Dusseldorf in 1850. Robert Schumann died on July 29, 1856 at Endenich, near Bonn, Germany. Clara resided with her family in Berlin, then settled in Baden-Baden in 1863 until 1874. Ms Schumann gave numerous concerts at the London Philharmonic in the 1850s, then again in the 1860s–80s. She composed some 20 pieces for the pianoforte. She died on May 20th at Frankfurt am Main, Germany.

SCHUYLER, PHILIPPA DUKE (1931–1967)
"Manhattan Nocturne"

Composer/pianist, she was born on August 2nd in New York City. As a child she studied piano and at age six was composing music and gave her first formal recital. She studied under Antonio Brico, Dean Dixon, Josef Hoffman, and others. After playing Saint-Saens's Concerto in G minor on July 13, 1946 with the New York Philharmonic at Lewisohn Stadium, she attracted attention and performed at Town Hall on May 12, 1953. She is best known for her orchestral work *Manhattan Nocturne* (1943), *Rhapsody of Youth* (1948), and *Nile Fantasy* (1965). While working for a New Hampshire newspaper, the *Manchester News-Leader* and helping evacuate children in Vietnam, on May 9, 1967, she was killed in a helicopter crash.

SCOTT, ALICIA ANNE SPOTTISWOODE (1810–1900)
"Annie Laurie"
Songwriter, she was born in Spottiswoode, Berwickshire, Scotland. She married Lord John Douglas Scott. Lady Scott wrote "Annie Laurie—Maxwellton's Braes Are Bonnie" and other songs. She died on March 12th in Spottiswoode.

SCOTT, CLARA H. JONES (1841–1897)
"Open my eyes, that I may see
Glimpses of truth thou hast for me."
Tune—"Scott"
Composer and hymnist, she was born in Elk Grove, Illinois, on December 3, 1841 and attended C. M. Cady's Musical Institute in Chicago, Illinois. At age eighteen she began teaching music in the Ladies' Seminary at Lyons, Iowa, and in 1861 she married Henry Clay Scott. She published the *Royal Anthem Book* (1882), which was the first collection of anthems published by a woman, and she contributed hymns to H. R. Palmer's *Collection*. She was accidentally thrown from a buggy by a runaway horse and killed, while on a visit to Dubuque, Iowa, on June 21, 1897. Her hymn appeared in the *Baptist* (1975); *The New Broadman Hymnal* (1977); *Hymns for the Family of God* (1976); *The Methodist Hymnal* (1966); and *Hymns for the Living Church* (1974).

SCOTT, HAZEL DOROTHY (1920–1981)
"Nightmare Blues"
Composer/pianist/singer born on June 11th in Trinidad, West Indies, she was educated at Juilliard in New York City. She made her debut at age five with her mother's all-girl band American Creolians. She was a singer/pianist in nightclubs, and married Congressman Adam Clayton Powell, Jr., in 1945. She had her own trio at the St. Regis and Sheraton Hotels in New York City. She died on October 12th of cancer of the pancreas in New York City.

SCOTT, LESBIA LOCKET (b. 1898–)
"I Sing a Song of the Saints of God"
Composer and hymnist, born in London, England, on August 11, 1898, she was educated at Ravenscroft School, Sussex, and in 1917 she married John Mortimer Scott, an officer in the Royal Navy. She wrote poems for her children, which were published in 1929 under the title *Everyday Hymns for Little Children* by the Society of SS Peter and Paul Ltd., London. The words, music, and illustrations were all done by Mrs. Scott. She was also a playwright and produced her own plays wherever her husband was stationed. Among her produced plays were *Malta Cathedral Nativity Play* (1931); *That Fell Arrest* (1937); and *Then Will She Return*

(1946). "I am her daughter and I'm happy to say that my mother is still alive and well. . . . A few years after his retirement my father took Holy Orders and was appointed Rector of Gideigh, a tiny village on the Eastern slopes of Dartmoor, some of the most beautiful scenery in Britain. They were also there for thirteen years until my father's retirement from ill-health in 1967, when they went to live near Stratford-on-Avon, near my sister, their eldest daughter. My father died three years later, and my mother has recently moved to the ancient market town of Pershore, Worcestershire, where, I am glad to say, she enjoys excellent health and is still writing and still painting at the age of eighty-three." (Letter of March 1982 from her daughter, Mary Morton, of Chagford, Devon, England) Her hymn appeared in the (American) *Episcopal Hymnal* (1940).

SCOTTOLINE, MARY R. (1923–)
   "Cara Mia"
Composer/songwriter born November 3rd in Philadelphia, Pennsylvania, she was educated at West Philadelphia Catholic Girls High School. She wrote "Beholden", "Flat Tops Special", "Roland Rock", and other songs. ASCAP.

SEAVER, BLANCHE EBERT (b. 1891–Dec'd.)
   "Just for Today"
Composer, hymnist, and songwriter, daughter of Theodore Ebert, she was born in Chicago, Illinois, on September 15, 1891 and was graduated from the Chicago Musical College (1911). On September 16, 1916 she married Frank R. Seaver. Active with the Los Angeles Symphony Association, Hollywood Bowl Patroness Committee, various hospitals and orphanages in Los Angeles, California, she was named the *Los Angeles Times* "Woman of the Year" in 1964. She received honorary degrees from the University of Southern California (LHD, 1966), Pomona College (LLD, 1970) at Claremont, California, and Oklahoma Christian College (D. Humanities, 1972) at Oklahoma City, Oklahoma. Hymnist and composer, one recording of her hymn was reported by *Phonolog Reports* of Los Angeles (1978). She also wrote "Close at Thy Feet, My Lord" and other hymns, and a *Pontifical Mass*. She won the Jane Addams Award from Rockford College in Illinois. Her hymn was sung at the Eucharistic Congress in Dublin, Ireland. (Information from the Public Library, Los Angeles, California)

SEEGER, MARGARET "PEGGY" (1935–)
   Now is the Time for Fishing
Folksinger/songwriter, the daughter of music teacher Charles L. Seeger, she was born on June 17th in New York City. As a child she received

private lessons, studied music at Radcliffe College at Cambridge, Massachusetts, and sang folk songs. She sang with her sisters Barbara and Penny on the LP record *Three Sisters,* traveled through China and Europe (1955–56), married Scotch folksinger/songwriter Ewan MacColl, and became a British citizen in 1959. With MacColl they sang their songs on *Long Harvest* and the album mentioned above. As of 1994 her albums available were *Familiar Faces* with her brother Mike—*American Folk Songs for Children,* with Mike and Penny—*American Folksongs for Christmas.*

SEELY, MARILYN JEANNE (1940–)
"Between Today and Tomorrow"
Singer/songwriter, she was born in Titusville, Pennsylvania. She started singing with radio station WSM Grand Ole Opry in Nashville, Tennessee, in 1966. She wrote "Enough to Live" and "Between Today and Tomorrow". Her albums are *I'll Love You More, Little Things, Jeannie Seely, Seely Style, Thanks Hanks,* and with Jack Greene *Jack Greene and Jeannie Seely.*

SELLE, MAUDE MARSHALL (1906–)
"Wyoming"
Composer/songwriter born on March 23rd in La Fayette, Tennessee, she was educated at Peabody College and also had private music study. She wrote "In Summertime", "Kisses", "Love and Kisses", and "Suddenly I Knew".

SELMER, KATHRYN LANDE (1930–)
The Princess and the Pea
Composer/singer/songwriter born on November 6th in Staten Island, New York, she was educated at the Eastman School of Music and at Juilliard. Singer/composer on NBC TV for *Holiday House* and *Captain Kangaroo* she collaborated with Wade Denning. Her operas are *Shoemaker and the Elf, The Princess Who Couldn't Laugh,* and the one mentioned above. She also is known for her song "Let's Go to the Toy Shop"; and the collections *For Sleepyheads Only, Let's Have a Party,* and *Songs for Little Folk.*

SEMEGEN, DARIA (1946–)
Lieder auf der Flucht
Composer, she was born on June 27th in Bamberg, Germany. After coming to the US in 1951, she became a US citizen in 1957. While at the Eastman School, she studied with Phillips and Adler (BM, 1968), then won a Fulbright scholarship to Warsaw, Poland. She studied at Yale University (MM, 1971), then taught at the Columbia-Princeton Electronic

Music Center (1971–75). She also taught at SUNY at Stony Brook after 1974 and managed the electronic music studio. She composed chamber, instrumental, vocal, and orchestral works.

SEVERSON, MARIE (1913–)
"Ingomar the Walloping Swede"
Composer/songwriter born on August 19th in Athens, Wisconsin, she received a high school education. She wrote musical commercials and songs.

SHAPIRO, SUSAN (1923–Dec'd.)
"All that Any Heart Can Hope For"
Songwriter born on November 4th in Baltimore, Maryland, she was educated at Monticello Girls College. She married composer/pianist/publisher Ted Shapiro and wrote a number of songs to his music: "Ask Anyone in Love", "The Merry Christmas Waltz", "Time", and "Your Love Has Made Me Young". ASCAP.

SHARPE, EVELYN (1884–1969)
Tunes—"Bulstrode" and "Platt's Lane"
Composer, the daughter of an architect, she was born in Battersea, England, on September 2, 1884 and educated privately. In 1919 she married Lewis John Saville. Her publications include many songs and part-song stage performances and were test pieces at several musical festivals in England and in the Daminions. Her tunes appeared in *Songs of Praise* (London, 1931). She died on August 25, 1969.

SHEARER, WINIFRED JACOBS (1883–1966)
Tune—"Filia"
Composer, daughter of the Rev. Henry E. Jacobs, a Lutheran pastor, she was born in Gettysburg, Pennsylvania, on September 3, 1883, and was educated at the Philadelphia Conservatory of Music and at the Leefson-Hills Holdander Conservatory in Philadelphia. In 1907 she married Mr. Shearer, a violinist. She was first organist at the Church of the Ascension, Mt. Airy, on the campus of the Lutheran Theological Seminary in Philadelphia. Later she was organist at St. Peter's Church in North Wales, Pennsylvania. She died at Gwynedd Valley, Pennsylvania, a Welsh settlement, on June 24, 1966. Her tune appeared in the *Lutheran Common Service Book* (1917; 1958).

SHEAROUSE, FLORINE W. (1898–1974)
"Jesus Has a Birthday"
Hymnist, she was born in Atlanta, Georgia, on December 19, 1898 and educated at Kate Baldwin Kindergarten Training School and at a Vocational

Training School. She was a charter member of the Poetry Society of Georgia, and later resided in Miami, Florida. Olive Dungam composed the music for her hymns and songs. She died on February 14, 1974.

SHEETS, DOROTHY HOWELL (1915–)
Tune—"Bingham"
Composer, she resided in Muskegon, Michigan, and was educated at the Peabody Conservatory and the School of Sacred Music of Union Theological Seminary and studied composition with Seth Bingham. She composed the tune "Bingham" as a setting for Vanstone's hymn "Morning Glory, Starlit Sky". Her composition appeared in the *Episcopal Hymnal* (1982).

SHELLEY, GLADYS
"Does It Hurt to Love?"
Dancer/actress/lyricist, she was born in Lawrence, New York. She was educated at Columbia University, New York City. Shelley wrote lyrics for Broadway musicals with music by Buddy Greco—"For a little while she's mine" (1972). It was about a man's little daughter. Frank Sinatra, Danny Thomas, and Ethel Ennis sang her hit songs "Show's On Me Tonight" and "Does It Hurt to Love?" at the National Governors' banquet (1972). With music by Morton Gould, she wrote the words for "Pavanne"—"Here's the history of a dancing dolly in a toy shop".

SHIPP, ELLIS REYNOLDS (1847–1939)
"Father, Cheer Our Souls Tonight"
Hymnist born in Davis County, Iowa, in 1852, she was taken to Salt Lake City, Utah. At age eighteen she went to live in the Beehive House on the request of Brigham Young. After she married Milford Shipp and bore him five children, he took on four more polygamous wives. In 1875 she moved to Philadelphia, where she attended medical school, bore another child, and with poor finances graduated with honors. After returning to Salt Lake City, she practiced medicine there, helped found the Deseret Hospital, bore four more children, taught nursing for 60 years, and helped deliver 6,000 babies. Her hymn above appeared in the Mormon hymnal (1985).

SIBERRY, JANE
"Calling All Angels"
A singer/songwriter from Canada, her albums are *Bound by Beauty, No Borders Here, The Speckless Sky, The Walking,* and *When I Was a Boy* (1993) on which art-rock maestro Brian Eno produced two songs and k.d. lang collaborated on the duet "Calling All Angels".

SIDEBOTHAM, MARY ANN (1833–1913)
Tune—"Europa"
Composer, organist, and hymnist, she was born in London, England, and spent most of her life with her brother, the vicar of St. Thomas-on-the-Bourne in Surrey, England, serving as his housekeeper and organist in his church. She was also a pianist and lifelong friend of Henry Smart. She contributed 12 tunes for Mrs. Carey Brock's *Children's Hymn Book* (1881), published under the auspices of the Society for Promoting Christian Knowledge, of which Sidebotham was editor. She wrote *The Bird's Nest,* a collection of 50 songs for children, and with Brock compiled *A Collection of Twelve Christmas Carols* (1894). She died on the Isle of Wight on February 20, 1913. Her hymn tune appeared in the *Supplement to Hymns Ancient and Modern.* Her hymn, "Lord, Thy mercy now entreating," appeared in the *Children's Hymn Book* (1881); the *Scottish Hymnal* (1884); and more recently in *The Pilgrim Hymnal* (1958).

SIEDHOFF, EDNA ELIZABETH (b. 1885–Dec'd.)
Tune—"Boston"
Composer, pianist, and organist, she was the daughter of Fredericka Levi and William H. Siedhoff, an upholsterer, and was born in Lockport, New York. She studied piano at the Longy School in Boston, Massachusetts, and was a pupil in composition with Frank Converse. (Information from letter dated June 10, 1982 from I. Richard Reed, County Historian, Niagara County, Lockport, New York.) She left Lockport in 1911 and studied piano in Berlin, Germany, with Breithaupt and Schnabel, composition with Leichtentritt, and organ with Walter Fischer during her three-year stay there. She was the first woman organist to play at the American Church in Berlin. She left Germany at the outbreak of World War I. Her tune to the hymn, "Thou art the way," appeared in the *Christian Science Hymnal* (1932). We have been unable to locate her place and date of death.

SILBERTS, RHEA (1900–1959)
The Nightingale and the Rose
Composer/singer born on April 19th in Pocahontas, Virginia, she was educated at Ethical Culture School, and Juilliard, and had private voice study. At age seven she made her debut as a pianist and toured the US; later she became a concert singer and was involved in opera. She wrote *The Nightingale and the Rose* for orchestra, narrator, soloists, and chorus, and *Fantasie Ballade* for piano. She died on December 9th in New York City.

SIMMS, ALICE D. (1930–Dec'd.)
"Goombay"
Composer/songwriter born on January 13th in New York, New York, she was educated at Cornell University (BA) and Damrosch Institute. At age

eleven she gave concerts and later wrote radio scripts. With J. Fred Coots, Leonard Joy, Jimmy Lunceford, and Al Trace, she wrote a number of songs: "Buzz' Buzz' and Buzz'", "Encore Cherie", All Suit' No Man'", "Basket on Head", "I Spoke Too Soon", "Reserved", "Island Woman", "Calypso Island", "Like Ma-a-ad", "Tell the Lord" (Christopher award), "Mucho Closer" (Cuban medal), "Goombay" (Princess Margaret citation). ASCAP.

SIMON, CARLY (1945–)
Heartburn
Singer/songwriter, she was born on June 25th in New York City, the youngest of three musically inclined daughters of a co-founder of the publishing house Simon & Schuster. She was educated at Sarah Lawrence College, Bronxville, New York, and then organized the Simon Sisters with her sister Lucy. She wrote and recorded "That's the Way I've Always Heard It Should Be" (1971) and "One More Time". She married singer James Taylor in 1972 and won a 1972 Grammy Award as Best New Artist. Her recording hits were "Anticipation" (1972); "Nobody Does It Better" for the 1977 James Bond film, *The Spy Who Loved Me*. In 1985 she was commissioned by director Mike Nichols to write songs for the film *Heartburn*. Simon composed an opera for children, *Romulus Hunt*, performed at Lincoln Center, New York City, in February 1993. As of 1994 her albums available were *Another Passenger, Anticipation, Best of Carly Simon, Boys in the Trees, Carly Simon, Coming Around Again, Greatest Hits Live, Have You Seen Me Lately?, Hello Big Man, Holocakes, My Romance, No Secrets, Playing Possum, Spoiled Girl, This is My Life, Torch.*

SIMONE, NINA (1933–)
"I Wish I Knew How It Would Feel to Be Free"
Jazz/pop/soul singer/songwriter, she was born Eunice Kathleen Waymon on February 21st in Tryon, North Carolina. She studied at the Juilliard School in New York City and later with Sokoloff at the Curtis Institute in Philadelphia. After singing in a nightclub in Atlantic City, New Jersey, her recording of "I Loves You Porgy" from Gershwin's *Porgy and Bess* brought her national attention in 1954. Simone sang at the Apollo Theater in Harlem, New York City, and wrote the black protest songs "Backlash Blues" (words by Langston Hughes), "Turning Point", the song mentioned above, and "Go Limp" with Alex Comfort. In the 1970s she sang at the Newport Jazz Festivals in New York City. As of 1994 her available albums were *At the Village Gate, Best of Nina Simone, I Put a Spell on You, Let It Be Me, Pastel Blues, Walkman Compact Jazz,* and *Wild is the Wind.*

SIMPSON, VALERIE (1948–)
"Ain't No Mountain High Enough"
Soul singer and songwriter, she was born on August 26th in New York City. After meeting Nikolas Ashford, the two in 1966 began a lifetime ca-

reer of writing pop-gospel songs, with Ashford writing the lyrics and Simpson the tunes. They wrote "Let's Get Stoned" (1966), recorded by Ray Charles, then became staff writers for Motown in Detroit. They wrote "You're All I Need to Get By" (1968), "Ain't Nothing Like the Real Thing" (1968) and "Ain't No Mountain High Enough" recorded by Diana Ross, which reached No. 1 in 1970. After they left Motown they produced *Exposed* (1971) and *Valerie Simpson* (1972). They were married in 1974. Later albums were *The Boss* (1979) for Diana Ross, *About Love* for Gladys Knight and the Pips (1980). More recently, *The Best of Valerie Simpson*.

SINGLETON, MARGARET LOUISE (1935–)
"Moonlight Music"
Singer/songwriter, she was born in Coushatta, Louisiana, and attended high school in Shreveport. She wrote "Not What He's Got" (1956), "My Picture of You" (1957), "Love Is a Treasure", "Take Time Out for Love", "Shattered Kingdom", "Moonlight Music" (1958), and with Leon Ashley, "Laura, Laura, hold these hands and count my fingers".

SIOUXSIE SIOUX (1957–)
British singer/songwriter Susan Dallion of Siouxsie and the Banshees. They made their debut at London's 100 Club Punk Festival in 1976 with a spooky rendition of "The Lord's Prayer." Known early as Gothic rockers, Siouxsie married Budgie, her drummer and they live in a chateau outside of Toulouse, France where they write their own music. Their albums and CDs are *Hyaena, John Hands, Juju, Kaleidoscope, Kiss in the Dream House, Nocturne . . . Live* (2Lp), *Once Upon a Time, Peepshow, Superstition, The Scream, Through the Looking Glass, Tinderbox* and *The Rapture* which includes the songs "O Baby", "Not Forgotten", "The Lonely One" and "Forever" (1995).

SKAGGS, HAZEL GHAZARIAN (1924–)
"Impressions of Snow"
Composer/pianist born on August 26th in Boston, Massachusetts, she was educated at the New England Conservatory and studied piano with Clarence Adler, Goding, Levy, Ondricek; at Northeastern University; the University of Wisconsin; and the University of Colorado. She gave piano concerts in the New England area. Her instrumentals are "Basketball", "Impressions of Snow", "Petite Ballerina", "Polka Dot Clown", and "Spring Showers".

SLEETH, NATALIE ALLYN WAKELEY (1930–1992)
Tune—"Go In Peace"
Composer/organist, she was born on October 29th in Evanston, Illinois, and was educated at Wellesley College (BA in Music Theory, 1952), awarded an honorary doctorate by West Virginia Wesleyan College

(1959) and by Nebraska Wesleyan College (1990). Her husband, Dr. Ronald E. Sleeth, died in 1985; they had two children. She composed over 180 selections for church and school, which were published by various companies. Her tune "Promise" appeared in *The Hymnal for Worship & Celebration* (Baptist 1986), and her tune "Go In Peace" was published in the *United Methodist Hymnal* (1989).

SMITH, ALICE MARY (1839–1884)
Ode to the North-East Wind
Composer, she was born on May 19th in London, England. She was a pupil of Sterndale Bennett and Sir George A. Macferren. Smith married attorney Frederick Meadows White, who later became a judge. Her cantatas *Rudesheim or Gisila* was performed in Cambridge in 1865, *Ode to the North-East Wind* in Kingsley in 1880, and *Ode to the Passions* at the Hereford Festival in 1882. Between 1862–70, she composed a number of string and pianoforte quartets, two symphonies, overtures, and the cantata *Red King* in 1884. She died on December 4th at London.

SMITH, ALICIA (1931–)
"The Fable of Chicken Little"
Songwriter born on August 13th in Miami, Florida, she was educated at the University of California at Los Angeles (Phi Beta Kappa). She married composer/conductor Gregg Smith. With her husband she wrote the above song, as well as *European Madrigals* in two volumes and *Bible Songs for Young Voices*. ASCAP.

SMITH, ANITA (1922–)
'Sao Paulo'
Composer/songwriter born on December 19th in New York, New York, and educated at Queens College, she also studied music on a scholarship with Karol Rathus. Her works are *Baroque Mood, Sao Paulo, Perambular Funiculi, Homage to Gershwin, 3 Settings to Carl Sandburg, 3 Concert Songs* (Lindsay), *Samba Nina*, and *Violin Suite*. Also she is known for her songs: "A Stranger's Always Welcome", "If You Fall in Love", "Heaven Moved Down to Earth", and "I'll Never Tire of You".

SMITH, DEBORAH DAVIS (1958–)
"Great Is the Lord"
Hymnist/songwriter, she was born on March 3rd in Nashville, Tennessee. She married pianist/composer Edward Russell Smith, who came to the states from London, Ontario, Canada, in 1950. Deborah wrote the words for "Great Is the Lord" (music by Michael W. Smith) and also wrote the words for some of her husband's hymns and songs.

SMITH, [DOROTHY JACQUELINE] KEELY (1932–)
"Bourbon Street Blues"
Composer/singer/songwriter born on May 9th in Norfolk, Virginia, she sang in local bands, then in the Louis Prima Orchestra from 1948; she appeared in shows, nightclubs, and on TV. She wrote "Just as Much", "Laugh and Be Happy", "Little Lover Boy", "Hey, Boy, Hey Girl", "Man, Dig That Crazy Chic", "Straight Down the Middle", "Yes We Did", "Nighty Night", "Sometime", "Swing You Lovers."

SMITH, ELEANOR (1858–1942)
"In another land and time,
Long ago and far away."
Composer, hymnist, singer, and songwriter, daughter of Matilda Jasperson and Willard N. Smith, she was born in Atlanta, Illinois, on June 15, 1858 and was educated in Chicago where she took lessons in voice with Fannie Root and studied composition with Frederick G. Gleason. Then she studied voice under Julius Hey and composition with Moritz Moszkowski in Berlin for three years. She taught at the Chicago Kindergarten College and Chicago Normal School for Teachers, then at the University of Chicago (1902–04). After meeting Jane Addams, she founded the Hull House School of Music and headed the school (1893–1935). She was an Episcopalian. She wrote *Songs for Little Children* (1887); *Songs of Life and Nature* (1899); *Modern Music Series* (1905); and the *Eleanor Smith Series* (1909–11). She never married, and died in Midland, Michigan, on June 30, 1942. Her hymn appeared in *Songs of Praise* (London, 1931).

SMITH, JULIA FRANCES (1911–)
The Shepherdess and the Chimneysweep
Composer/pianist, she was born on January 23rd in Denton, Texas. After graduating from North Texas State University in 1930, she studied piano and composition on a fellowship at Juilliard Graduate School (1932–39). During this time she was pianist for the Orchestrette of New York and received her MA at New York University in 1933. She gave concerts in Europe and in North America and taught at Hartt College (1941–46). She received her PhD at the University of New York in 1952. She composed the opera mentioned above in 1963, several other operas, orchestral and vocal works, and chamber music.

SMITH, KATHRYN E. "KATE" (1909–1986)
"When the moon comes over the mountain"
Singer/songwriter, she was born on March 9th in Norfolk, Virginia. She recorded over 2,000 songs and had 19 number one hits. With Howard Johnson and Harry Woods, she wrote "When the Moon Comes Over the Mountain" (1931). She is best known for her rendition of Irving Berlin's

"God Bless America" (1938). Her albums include *How Great Thou Art, Just a Little Closer Walk with Thee, May God be with You, Songs of the Now Generation, Kate Smith Anniversary Album, Kate Smith at Carnegie Hall, Kate Smith the One and Only, Kate Smith Today*. She died on June 17th in Raleigh, North Carolina. As of 1994 one album was available, *Best of Kate Smith*.

SMITH, LAURA
"Little Sir Echo"
A lyricist, with composer John S. Ferris (1867–1952), she wrote "Little Sir Echo".

SMITH, LEONA MAY (1914–)
'Scottish Fantasy'
Composer/arranger/trumpeter born on September 23rd in Bridgeport, Connecticut, she studied music with Murray Karpilovsky, George Mager, Walter Smith, and William Vacchiano. She was a trumpet soloist with the Goldman Band, Fred Waring Orchestra, Canadian Music Festivals, Radio City Music Hall (1943–47), and Metropolitan Orchestra. Her instrumentals are arrangements of *Alouette Fantasy, Au Clair de la Lune, Scottish Fantasy,* and *The Blue Danube*. She married George Scuffert.

SMITH, MARY CECELIA (1913–)
"Navarak"
Songwriter born on February 23rd in St. Louis, Missouri, she received a high school education. She studied dancing privately and danced in Broadway musicals and films. Later she had her own dance studio in Hillsdale, New Jersey. She married composer/conductor John Shaffer Smith, Jr. With her husband she wrote the words for the above song as well as "Now and Then".

SMITH, PATTI LEE (1947–)
"Because the Night"
Punk rock singer/songwriter, she was born in Chicago on December 30th. In 1956 the family moved to New Jersey, where she attended Glassboro State Teachers College. After college, she moved to New York City, formed a band, and wrote song lyrics. Her band in 1973 included guitarists Ivan Kral and Lenny Kaye, keyboardist Richard Sohl, and drummer Jay Dee Daugherty. They recorded "Horses" (1975). Her song "Because the Night" written with Bruce Springsteen was on the *Easter* album. The group disbanded in 1979. As of 1994 her albums available were *Horses, Easter, Radio Ethiopia,* and *Wave*.
Smith married guitarist Fred "Sonic" Smith (1949–1994) of the late

1960s rock band MC5. Patti collaborated on the soundtrack for the Wim
Wender film *Until the End of the World* (1992).

SMITH, RUBY MAE (1902–)
"Worth More Than Gold"
Composer/songwriter born on March 20th in Joplin, Missouri, she was
educated in public schools and had private music study. She led a local
quartet, Ruby Smith and The Rubytones. She established the Rubytone
Record & Publishing Company in Portland, Oregon. She wrote "The
Bells", "Hard Luck Blues", "That Beautiful City", "The Lord Will
Come", "When Jesus Shall Come", and "Rise or Fall".

SMITH, WILLIE MAE FORD (1904–1994)
"A sword in his right hand . . . Lord you said
you'd fight my battles, if I just keep still."
Gospel singer/songwriter, she was born at Rolling Fork, Mississippi,
taken to Memphis, then to St. Louis when she was twelve years old. She
formed the Ford Sisters Quartet, which sang at the national Baptist Convention in St. Louis, in 1922. In 1936 she became director of the Soloists
Bureau of the National Convention of Gospel Choirs and Choruses. She
married a Mr. Smith who was in the hauling business. She wrote the
gospel song mentioned above. In 1975 she was working as a parapro-
fessional in a mental hospital in St. Louis. (Information from the St.
Louis Public Library). She did appear at Newport Jazz Festivals in New
York City and at Radio City Music Hall. The gospel documentary *Say
Amen, Somebody* (1982) also featured her. As of 1994 there was one of
her recordings available, *I'm Bound for Canaanland*. She died on February 23rd in St. Louis, Missouri.

SMYTHE, DAME ETHEL MARY (1858–1944)
Mass in D Major
A composer and daughter of General J. H. Smythe of the Royal Artillery,
she was born in London, England, on April 23, 1858 and studied under
Heihrich von Herzogenberg at the Leipzig Conservatory. Her *Quintet for
Strings* (1884) and a *Sonata for Violin and Pianoforte* (1887) were performed at Leipzig, Germany. Her *Mass in D Major* was performed at Albert Hall in London under Barnby's direction on January 18, 1893. Her
three-act opera, *The Wreckers,* was performed at Leipzig on November
11, 1906. She was active in the cause of Woman's Suffrage and her
March of the Women became popular at processions of the Women's Social and Political Union. She composed many other works and was considered the greatest woman composer of her time. She died at Woking,
England, on May 9, 1944.

SNOW, ELIZA ROXEY (1804–1887)
"Awake, Ye Saints of God, Awake"
Hymnist born in Becket, Massachusetts, she was the sister of Lorenzo Snow, fifth president of the Church of Jesus Christ of Latter-day Saints. She was baptized in the church in 1835 and became the polygamous wife of Joseph Smith. After Smith was killed in Carthage, Illinois, in 1844 Brigham Young led the Mormons to Utah in 1847 and Eliza Snow became the polygamous wife of Brigham Young. He had some 19 to 27 wives and 56 children. Her hymn above, plus "Again We Meet Around the Board", "Behold the Great Redeemer Die", "Great Is the Lord", "How Great the Wisdom and the Love", "In Our Lovely Desert", "O My Father", "Through Deepening Trials", "The Time Is Far Spent", and "Truth Reflects Upon Our Senses" appeared in the Mormon hymnal (1985).

SNOW, PHOEBE (1952–)
"It Looks Like Snow'
Jazz/pop singer/guitarist/composer, she was born Phoebe Laub in Teaneck, New Jersey. As a child she studied the piano, then the guitar, and performed at an amateur show at the Bitter End in New York City (1972). She recorded "Harpo's Blues" in 1973 with Zoot Sims and Teddy Wilson, with one of her compositions on her album recorded by Shelter Records; she also recorded "Second Childhood" on Columbia Records (1976). She sang in nightclubs in New York City and performed with Dan Hill at the University of Buffalo (New York) jazz concert (October 1978). As of 1994 her albums and CDs available were *Against the Grain, Best of Phoebe Snow, It Looks Like Snow, Never Letting Go, Phoebe Snow, Second Childhood, Something Real,* and with others on *Live at the Beacon* (1992).

SOBULE, JILL
"I Kissed a Girl"
Singer/songwriter. Her albums are *Things Here Are Different* (1990), and *Jill Sobule* (1995). In her video for "I Kissed a Girl" she plays the fiancé of model Fabio who plays himself. The song, however, refers to kissing a neighbor's wife. Her songs are semi-autobiographical. The video became popular after airing on MTV's "Alternative Nation" and landed in the music network's Buzz Clip bin. Sobule tours the nation singing in clubs.

SOEHNEL, ZELMA (1909–)
"My Dolly Has a Broken Heart"
Composer/songwriter born on April 7th in Newark, New Jersey, she was educated at college. She married composer Ray Soehnel. With her hus-

band she wrote "A Heart Full of Love", "Daily Double Polka", "For Christmas", "I'm Looking Forward", "Just One More", "I'm Going to Saddle My Blues", and "Show Me the Way Back to Your Heart".

SOSENKO, ANNA (1910–)
"Comme une Boite Musique"
Composer/songwriter born on June 13th in Camden, New Jersey, she was business manager for singer Hildegarde for many years. Sosenko wrote "Darling, Je Vous Aime Beaucoup", "Ask Your Heart", "I'll Be Yours", "Let's Try Again", and the song above. ASCAP.

SOUERS, MILDRED (1894–Dec'd.)
Under the Greenwood Tree
Composer/choral director/pianist/songwriter, she was born on February 26th in Des Moines, Iowa, and educated at Drake University. She studied with F. J. Pyle and with Marion Bauer. She was with the Des Moines Symphony. Her collection of recital pieces: *Under the Greenwood Tree, Bar & Technique Melodies for the Dance Studio;* also the songs: "April Weather", "What Christmas Means to Me", and "The Immortal".

SPENCER, FLETA JAN BROWN (1883–1938)
"Love Make My Dream Come True"
Composer/singer/songwriter born on March 8th at Storm Lake, Iowa, she was educated at the Cincinnati Conservatory, and studied with Fannie Zeisler. She sang in vaudeville for 12 years. With Herbert Spencer, she wrote "East of the Moon, West of the Stars", "In the Candle Light", "Fancies", "Hearts Desire", "Prairie Flower". ASCAP.

SPEWACK, BELLA COHEN (1899–Dec'd.)
Kiss Me Kate
Librettist/playwright, she was born in Hungary. She came to the US and married playwright Samuel Spewack. With her husband, she wrote many Broadway comedies, as well as librettos for the musicals *Leave it to Me* (1938), in which Mary Martin made her Broadway debut, and *Kiss Me Kate* (1948), which won the Antoinette Perry award (Tony) and the Page One award for 1949.

SPIEGEL, LAURIE (1945–)
"Realization of Kepler's Harmony of the Planets"
Composer, she was born in Chicago, Illinois, on September 20th. After attending Shimer College in Mt. Carroll, Illinois (BA, 1967), studying composition with Druckman at Juilliard (1969–72), and studying at Brooklyn College, CUNY (MA, 1975), she also took private lessons. She taught at the Bucks County Community College in Pennsylvania

(1971–75) and at Cooper Union in New York City. Although she has written instrumental music and dance scores, she is best known as a composer of electronic and computer music.

SPRATT, ANN BAIRD (b. 1829–)
Tune—"Kedron"
A composer, she was born in England and her tune is used for Horatius Bonar's hymn "No, not despairingly, I come to Thee." It is one of two of her hymn tunes first published in the *Book of Common Praise* (1866). It also appeared in J. Ireland Tucker's *The Parish Hymnal* (New York, 1870); in Tucker's *Tunes Old and New* (1872); the *American Presbyterian Hymnal* (1874) where it is called BETHEL; *The Methodist Hymnals* (1905; 1911; 1935); and in the *Baptist Hymnal* (1956). We have been unable to locate her date of death.

STAFFORD, OTTILIE (1921–)
"Father, Grant Us Your Peace"
Hymnist, she was born on February 12th in Middletown, New York, and was educated at Atlantic Union College (BA) and Boston University (MA and PhD). She is a professor of English at Atlantic Union College and a member of the Seventh-day Adventist Church. Her hymn, a translation, appeared in *The Baptist Hymnal* (1986).

STAINER, ROSALIND F. BRIDGE (1884–1966)
Tune—"Bethsaida"
Composer, and daughter of Sir Frederick Bridge, she was born at the Cloisters, Westminster Abbey, London, England, on February 10, 1884 and studied music at home, studying the piano and viola with visiting masters, and harmony with her father. In 1907 she married Dr. Edward Stainer, F.R.C.P., second son of Sir John Stainer, who was organist at St. Paul's Cathedral in London. Her hymn appeared in the English *Methodist Hymn-Book* (1904; 1935). She died on July 1, 1966.

STAIR, PATTY (1869–1926)
'The Interrupted Serenade'
Composer/organist/conductor she was born Martha Greene on November 12th in Cleveland, Ohio. After attending the Cleveland Conservatory of Music in the 1880s, she taught there from 1889 and at the University School from 1892. Stair also served as an organist in several Cleveland churches and taught organ and piano privately. She became a member of the American Guild of Organists in 1914 and conducted choruses of the Cleveland's Women's Club. She composed songs, anthems, and orchestral works. Stair died on April 26th at Cleveland.

STAIRS, LOUISE E. (1892–Dec'd.)
"Lord Speak to Me"
Composer/organist/teacher, she wrote her music under the pseudonym Signey Forest. She composed the music for the above hymn written by Frances Ridley Havergal.

STANLEY, HELEN (1930–)
"Tear Drops"
Pianist/violist/composer, she was born on April 6th in Tampa, Florida. With Roy Calhoun, Barry Goldner, and Edwin Charles, she wrote "Tear drops—I sit in my room looking out at the rain." She composed chamber music piano pieces and songs.

STASSEN-BENJAMIN, LINDA (1951–)
Tune—"Sing Alleluia"
Composer/singer she was born on September 19th in Indiana, and was educated at Ball State University in Muncie, Indiana, at El Camino College in Via Torrence, California. She sang with the groups David (1974–75) and New Song (1975–77) and now composes songs for New Song Ministries. "Sing Alleluia to the Lord" appeared in *The Hymnal for Worship & Celebration* (Baptist 1986).

STEELE, HELEN (1904–Dec'd.)
'America, Our Heritage'
Composer/conductor/pianist/songwriter, she was born on June 21st in Enfield, Connecticut, and educated at Mt. Holyoke College (BA); she also had private music study. Piano accompanist to singers in the US and Europe, she also directed vocal groups and worked with Guido Vandt and Enrique on the compositions: "America, Our Heritage", "Duerme", "Lagrimas", "The Legend of Befana". ASCAP.

STEELE, LOIS (1910–)
"Make America Proud of You"
Composer/pianist/songwriter born on February 24th in Chilicothe, Illinois, and educated at the Cosmopolitan School of Music, Chicago, she was a concert pianist who also played the piano in nightclubs and theaters. With Jack Fulton, she wrote "Ivory Tower", "Peace", "Sweetie Pie", "Wanted", and the song above. ASCAP.

STEINBERG, CAROLYN (1956–)
Cors de chasse
Composer, she was born on May 17th in San Antonio, Texas. After studying theory at North Texas State University in Denton (BM, 1978)

and composition at the Manhattan School of Music in New York City (MM, 1980), she studied privately with Cathy Berberian (1980–81); at Accadenia Chigiana in Siena, Italy (1981–82); Staatliche Hochsschule fur Musik, Freiburg, West Germany (1983). She studied composition under British composer Brian Ferneyhough and married him in 1984. She studied conducting privately under Francis Travis (1985–86), then at the Juilliard School of Music in New York City (DMA, 1989). She divorced Ferneyhough in 1989. She has received several prizes and has lectured. She has composed choral and instrumental works, chamber music, and the opera *Cors de chasse,* which was first performed on June 8, 1990 in New York City.

STELZER, FRANCES C. (1895–Dec'd.)
"I Never Get Enough of You"
Composer/songwriter born on May 1st in Milwaukee, Wisconsin, and educated at Columbia College, New York University, and Pace Institute. She wrote the song above and "Keep Me in Love".

STEPHANIE (1965–   )
"Winds of Chance"
A singer/songwriter, Stephanie Grimaldi, Her Serene Highness Princess of Monaco, was born February 1st, daughter of Prince Rainier III and the late Princess Grace (Kelly). She wrote most of the songs on her first album *Stephanie* (1991), including "Winds of Chance" and "Born Blue" dedicated to her mother, Princess Grace. In November 1992, Stephanie gave birth out of wedlock to a son, Louis, by her former bodyguard and boyfriend, Daniel Ducruet; then on May 4, 1994, Stephanie gave birth to Pauline (6 lbs. 5 ozs.) with her boyfriend.

STEWART, DOROTHY M. (1897–1954)
"God Bless Australia"
Composer/pianist/songwriter born on March 21st in Melbourne, Australia, she was educated at St. Peter's School, Lara College in Melbourne; at Juilliard in New York City; and she studied music with Gustave de Chancet and Hortense Fyffe. She wrote "Be True", "Give Me Your Hand", "Hear These Words", "Now Is the Hour", "A Rose, a Book and a Ring", "Magic Island", and "Wedding Bells". She died on June 18th in New York.

STIRLING, ELIZABETH (1819–1895)
Psalm 130
Composer and organist, she was born in Greenwich, England, on February 26, 1819 and studied piano and organ with Edward Holmes and harmony with G. A. Macfarren and J. A. Hamilton. At the age of twenty she

was appointed organist at All Saints', Poplar, and held this position for almost 20 years, then at St. Andrew's, Undershaft. During the early 1850s, she attended Oxford University and in 1856 passed the examination for the degree of Mus. Bac., and composed the work, *Psalm 130* for five voices with orchestra, which Oxford accepted as satisfactory. But the University refused to give her the degree she had earned, stating they could not give a degree to a woman. In 1863 she married F. A. Bridge, and continued as organist at St. Andrew's until 1880. Besides organ transcriptions from classical works, she also composed organ pieces and part-songs, "All among the barley" being very popular. She died in London, England, on March 25, 1895.

STOCK, SARAH GERALDINE (1838–1898)
"Let the song go round the earth."
Also Tune—"Moel Llys"
Composer and hymnist, the elder sister of Dr. Eugene Stock, editorial secretary of the Church Missionary Society, she was born at Islington, London, England, on December 27, 1838 and became active in missionary work for the Church of England. Her hymns appeared in the *Church Missionary Hymn Book* (1899) of which she was co-editor and in the enlarged 1902 edition of *Hymns of Consecration and Faith*. Julian's *Dictionary of Hymnology* lists 29 of her hymns in common use by 1915. She died at Penmaenmawr, Wales, on August 27, 1898. More recently her hymn appeared in the *Baptist* (1975); *Broadman* (1977); and *Christian Worship* (1953) hymnals. Her hymn and tune appeared in the English *Baptist Hymn Book* (London, 1962).

STONE, ELAINE MURRAY (1922–)
Lament for the Sunken Galleons
Pianist/composer, she was born on January 22nd in New York City, the daughter of a composer with the CBS Symphony. Stone studied piano at age five and began writing music at age nine. After graduating from Ashley Hall, a private prep school for girls in Charleston, South Carolina, she studied piano and composition at the Juilliard School of Music and the New York College of Music in Manhattan; and organ at the Cathedral of St. John the Divine at Columbia University. She obtained her Licentiate in organ from Trinity College of Music in London.

Her piano piece *Colonial Suite* won first prize in a national competition sponsored by the Daughters of the American Revolution in 1986. Her *Lament for the Sunken Galleons* for cello and piano won second place in a competition sponsored by the American Pen Women. It reflects the tragic end of the fleet of Spanish treasure ships that sank off Cape Canaveral, Florida, in 1715 during a hurricane. Her piece was performed in 1993 by cellist Dana Winograd of the American Symphony Orchestra and pianist Stone in New York City. She also composed a *Christopher Columbus Suite* for piano, which was later arranged for orchestra. A band arrangement from this suite has been performed by Marion Scott and the Community Band of Brevard, Florida, on four occasions. The third movement *Discovery 1492* was performed in 1992 by conductor Maria Tunica and the Florida Space Coast Philharmonic. Stone lives in Melbourne, Florida. A widow, she has three daughters.

STREATFIELD, CHARLOTTE SAINT (1829–1901)
"How beautiful the hills of God"
Tune—"Langton"
Daughter of the Rev. J. J. Saint, rector at Speldhurst, England, she was born there on December 31, 1829. In 1862 she married Lieutenant Charles N. Streatfield, Royal Navy, eldest son of Major General Streatfield of the Royal Engineers. She published *Hymns and Verses on the Collects* (1865); *Hymns on the Love of Jesus* . . . (1877); *A Little Garland of the Saints and Other Verses* (1877); *The Story of the Good Shepherd* (1885); and prose works, *Meditations on the Seven Last Words* (1874) and *Words of Comfort* (1875). Her hymns appeared in Mrs. Brock's *Children's Hymn Book* (1881). Her tune, "Langton," was included in *The Magnificat* (New Church, 1893) and the *Book of Worship* (*Evangelical Lutheran*, 1899). She died on September 27, 1901.

STREISAND, BARBRA (1942–)
"Evergreen"
Singer/actress/songwriter, she was born on April 24th in New York, New York. In the 1950s she appeared on the "Mike Wallace PM East" television show, in the musicals *I Can Get It for You Wholesale* produced by David Merrick and starred in *Funny Girl* (book by Isobel Lennart 1964) and in *Hello Dolly*. Her album *Barbra Streisand* won a 1963 Grammy; she won an Oscar for the film *Funny Girl*. With Paul Williams she wrote "Evergreen—Love, soft as an easy chair". She sang at a Clinton/Gore fund-raiser in Los Angeles and at the Presidential Gala in Washington, DC, in January 1993. Streisand performed at the MGM Grand Garden in Las Vegas on New Year's Eve and on New Year's Day, 1994.

As of 1994 her albums and CDs available include *A Happening in Central Park, A Star is Born, Barbra Joan Streisand, The Broadway Album, Butterfly, Christmas Album, Classical Barbra, Collection: Greatest Hits, Color Me Barbra, Emotion, Greatest Hits, Greatest Hits Vol. 2, Guilty, Je M'Appelle Barbra, Just for the Record, Lazy Afternoon, Live, Live Concert at the Forum, Memories, My Name is Barbra, My Name is Barbra, Two, One Voice, People, Pins and Needles* (1962), *Simply Streisand,*

Songbird, Stoney End, Streisand & Other Instruments, Streisand Super-man, The Barbra Streisand Album, The Second Album, The Third Album, The Way We Were (soundtrack), *Till I Loved You, Wet, What about Today?, Yentl.*

STRICKLAND, LILY THERESA (1887–1958)
"Two Shawnee Indian Dances"
Composer, she was born on January 28th in Anderson, South Carolina. At age fourteen she was composing music and attended Converse College, then won a scholarship to the Institute of Musical Art in New York City, where she studied under Gregory Mason, Perry Goetchius, and others. After her marriage to J. Courtney Anderson, the couple lived in India from 1920–29. Her early songs were based on Negro spirituals, later on American Indian music, then on Hindu music. She composed operettas, piano pieces, songs, orchestral works. Her songs include "Because of You", "At Eve I Heard a Flute", "My Lover Is a Fisherman", "My Shepherd Thou", and "The Road to Home". She died on June 6th in Hendersonville, North Carolina.

STROSKY, ROSE KATHRYN (1912–)
"Doll in the Rear View Mirrow"
Composer/pianist/songwriter born on November 20th in Calgary, Alberta, Canada, she studied music privately. She was a pianist in theaters and nightclubs. She wrote the song mentioned above.

STUTSMAN, GRACE MAY (1886–1970)
"In Bethlehem 'neath starlit skies"
Tune—"Waits' Carol"
Composer and hymnist, she was born in Melrose, Massachusetts, on March 4, 1886 and was educated at Boston University and the New England Conservatory of Music in Boston. A concert pianist, she received a scholarship for graduate study at the conservatory and also won the Endicott prize in song composition. Although not a Christian Scientist, she contributed articles for the *Christian Science Monitor* for 25 years. A symphony, choruses, songs, hymns, and string quartets are among her compositions. Her hymn and tune above appeared in the *Methodist Hymnal* (1964). "Our records show that she was enrolled in the Conservatory program from 1920 to 1922. She had teachers with the following surnames: Bridge, Johns, and Mason. And she gave a piano recital in 1922 that included three of her own works. Our records indicate that she died on April 30, 1970." (April 1982 letter from Katherine Gonzales, director of Alumni Relations at the New England Conservatory of Music)

SUMMER, DONNA (1948–)
"Dim All the Lights"
Singer/songwriter, she was born LaDonna Andrea Gaines on December 31st in Boston, Massachusetts. She married Bruce Sudano. Summer wrote "Dim All the Lights, Sweet Darlin' "; with Peter Bellotte, Greg Mathieson, and Giorgio Moroder, "Heaven knows—Baby please, don't take your love from me"; with Bellotte and Moroder, "Love to You Baby"; with Moroder, "The Wanderer—Woke up this mornin' dragged myself across the bed". Her hit songs were "Hot Stuff", "Bad Girls", "Last Dance", "She Works Hard for the Money"; her albums and CDs: *Another Place Another Time, Bad Girls, Dance Collection, Four Seasons of Love, Greatest Hits, I Remember Yesterday, Live and More, Mistaken Identity, On the Radio, Once Upon a Time, She Works Hard for the Money, Summer Collection,* and *Walk Away.*

SUNSHINE, MARION (MARY TUNSTALL JAMES) (1894–1963)
"Peanut Vendor"
Composer/singer/songwriter born on May 15th in Louisville, Kentucky, she was educated at St. Joseph Academy, Mount Vernon, New York. At age five she was an actress in melodramas with her sister as Tempest and Sunshine. She toured the US and Canada in vaudeville. She wrote: "Cuban Belle", "My Cuban Sombrero", "Havana Calling", "Voodoo Moon", "Nina", "Los Timbales", "Here Comes the Conga", "The Happy Bird", "Bossa Nova Stomp", "Mary, You're a Little Bit Old-fashioned", "Baby Sister Blues", "Have You Seen My Love?", and "I've Got Everything I Want But You". She died on January 25th in New York City.

SWADOS, ELIZABETH (1951–)
Runaways
Composer/music director, she was born on February 5th in Buffalo, New York. After studying composition with Brant at Bennington College in Vermont (BA, 1972), she joined the La Mama Experimental Theater Company in New York City and also was music director of the International Theater Group. She composed the music for *Runaways,* which was performed in New York on March 9, 1978. She wrote the music for a number of musicals, theater scores, and film scores.

SWAN, DOTTIE (1916–)
"Blue Eyes"
Singer/songwriter, she was born in Hundred, West Virginia. She wrote "Blue Eyes" (1955), "Contact", "Crying" (1956), "Red, White and Blue Christmas" (1965), and "Aunt Hattie" (1967).

SWIFT, KAY (1897–Dec'd.)
'Reaching for the Brass Ring'
Pianist/composer/songwriter, she was born in New York City on April 19th, the daughter of composer critic Samuel Swift. She studied piano and composition at the Institute of Musical Art (now the Juilliard School), then piano and composition at the New England Conservatory in Boston. After touring as a piano accompanist for a trio, she married financier James P. Warburg and settled down to raise three daughters. Swift and her husband composed songs, where he used the pen name Paul James. She composed music for musicals, instrumental, vocal, and orchestral works. Her song cycle mentioned above was started in 1953 and continued for a number of years.

SYRCHER, MADELEINE B. (1896–Dec'd.)
"Come to Me, My Love"
Composer/singer/songwriter born on May 4th in Portsmouth, Ohio, she was educated at a music conservatory and had private study. She wrote "Hold Me Close", "I Believe You", and the above song. ASCAP.

-T-

TAILLEFERRE, GERMAINE (1892–1983)
'Jeux de Plein Air'
Composer, she was born on April 19th in Parc Saint-Maur near Paris, France. While studying at the Paris Conservatoire, she won first prize in harmony, counterpoint, and accompanying. She then became a pupil of Darius Milhaud. Tailleferre became known as one of "Les Six", a group of young Parisian composers. She composed a *Pastorale* (1920); a string quartet, a violin and pianoforte sonata (1922); *Jeux de Plein Air* for two pianofortes (1923); *Ballade* for pianoforte and orchestra; ballet *Le Marchand d'oiseaux,* which was produced by the Swedish Ballet in Paris in 1923. She also composed *Le Fou sense,* a comic opera and *Le Marin du Bolivar* for the Paris Exhibition of 1937. Tailleferre came to the US in 1942. She died on November 7th in Paris.

TALMA, LOUISE (1906–)
Summer Sounds
Composer/pianist/teacher, she was born on October 31st in Arcachon, France. After studying theory and composition at the Institute of Musical Art (now the Juilliard School) in New York City from 1922–30, she studied with Nadia Boulanger in Fontainebleu during the summers. She studied at New York University (BMus, 1931) and Columbia University (MA, 1933). Talma taught at Hunter College, CUNY (1928–79) and became the

first American to teach at the Fontainebleu School during the summers of 1936–39, and again in the early 1980s. She has composed opera, choral works, mixed choral and orchestral, instrumental, and chamber music. Her *Summer Sounds,* written in 1973, was for clarinet and string quartet.

TANAKA, KAREN (1961–)
Anamorphose
Composer, she was born on April 7th in Tokyo, Nippon. She studied music from age four, then under Akira Miyoshi at the Toho Gakuen School of Music (BA, 1986); then under Tristan Murail at IRCAM in Paris since 1986. She has composed instrumental and choral works and chamber music. Her *Anamorphose* for piano and orchestra was first performed in Amsterdam, The Netherlands, in 1987.

TAÑÓN, OLGA
Siente el Amor . . .
Latin artist called the Merengue Queen, with the help of Gustavo Marquez, Victor Garcia, and Raldy Vasquez, she wrote her new album *Siente el amor. . . ,* which was recorded in the Dominican Republic and Puerto Rico (1994).

TAUBER, DORIS (1908–)
"The Land Where Cotton Grows"
Composer/pianist born on September 13th in New York, New York, and educated at high school. She studied with David Kalish. She was secretary to Irving Berlin and wrote songs for Broadway musicals. With Maceo Pinkard and William Tracey she wrote "Gotta Darn Good Reason for Being Good", "Drinking Again", "Let's Begin Again", "I Was Made to Love You", "I Don't Get It", "Them There Eyes", "Fooled", "Livin' Dangerously", and "Who's Afraid". ASCAP.

TAYLOR, CATHERINE (1944–)
"Two Straws and a Soda"
Composer/guitarist/singer born on July 26th in Winnipeg, Manitoba, Canada, she was educated at high school. She sang for the Walt Disney "Mouseketeers", toured with "California Hayride", sang in nightclubs, in films, and at military bases. She wrote the songs "Falling Star" and "My Bobby Boy"; her albums are *A Little Bit of Sweetness* and *The Tree Near My House.* ASCAP.

TAYLOR, GOLDIE PEARL (1905–)
"In My Garden of Love"
Composer/songwriter born on November 13th in Hayden, Indiana, she was educated at the US School of Music. She wrote "How Far Is It to Heaven?", "Wasting My Tears", and the song above.

TAYLOR, MARY VIRGINIA (1912–)
"Sleep My Little Lord Jesus"
Songwriter born on August 7th at Muskogee, Oklahoma, she was educated at Northeastern State College (BA). She married composer/pianist Lionel "Les" Taylor. With music by her husband, she wrote the words for the anthem above as well as the songs "Deck the Hut with Coconut", "Adaptations", "Fair Weather Love", "John Henry", and "Hosanna, We Build a House". ASCAP.

TERENZI, DR. FIORELLA (1964–)
Music from the Galaxies
Italian astrophysicist and sound-synthesis computer composer. This Ph.D. uses audio telescopes to intercept radio waves from the heavens — a galaxy 180 million light years away, feeds them into a computer, applies her sound-synthesis program to convert the data into music. Her *Music from the Galaxies* is available both in an album and on a CD.

TERESA, MOTHER (1910–)
"Serving the Poor"
Hymnist, she was born Agnes Gounxha Bojaxhiu on August 27th in Skopje, Macedonia, Turkey (now Yugoslavia). She was called to be a nun at age twelve, then at age eighteen went to India with the Loretto Order. She taught at St. Mary's High School in Calcutta, became the principal and left the school in 1946 to help the poor, founding the Society of the Missionaries of Charity. She was awarded the Nobel Peace prize in 1979. Her hymn appeared in the *Hymnal for Worship & Celebration* (Baptist 1986).

THAYNE, EMMA LOU (1924–)
"Where Can I Turn for Peace?"
Hymnist born in Salt Lake City, Utah, she was educated at the University of Utah (BA, and MA). She taught English at the university for some 30 years. She married Melvin E. Thayme, and they have five daughters. She has written poetry and some 10 books. Her hymn above appeared in the Mormon hymnal (1985).

THOMAS, CARLA (1942–)
"Gee Whiz, Look at His Eyes"
Singer/songwriter, she was born in Memphis, Tennessee, the daughter of singer Rufus Thomas. She sang on radio station WDIA with the Teen Town Singers; she was graduated from Tennessee Agriculture and Industrial State University in Nashville. She wrote and recorded "Gee Whiz" (1961), recorded "The King and Queen" with Otis Redding, and became known as the "Queen of Memphis Sound". Her albums are *Best of Carla Thomas, Comfort Me, Carla, Gee Whiz, King and Queen*, and

Queen Alone. As of 1994 her albums and CDs available were *Carla, Chronicle, Comfort Me,* and *The Queen Alone.*

THOMAS, EDITH LOVELL (1878–1970)
Arranger—St. Anthony's Chorale
A composer and arranger born at Eastford, Connecticut, on September 11, 1878, she was educated at Boston University (BRE; SRE; MEd) and the School of Sacred Music at Union Theological Seminary in New York City. She also studied at Wellesley College, and later served as professor of music and worship at Boston University and for many years was director of church school music, Christ Church Methodist, in New York City. She was the compiler of *First Book in Hymns and Worship* (1922); *Singing Worship* (1925); *Sing, Children, Sing* (1939); *The Whole World Singing* (1950); and other books. She retired to live in Claremont, California. Her hymn tune appears in the *Methodist Hymnal* (1964). She died on March 16, 1970.

THOMERSON, KATHLEEN ARMSTRONG (1934–)
Tune—"Houston"
Composer/organist she was born on February 18th in Jackson, Tennessee, and was educated at the University of Texas (BMus, MMus) and studied organ with Flor Peeters in Antwerp, Belgium, and with Jean Langlais in Paris. She gave organ recitals in the US and in Europe, married Jamie Thomerson, and they have three children. She taught organ at Southern Illinois University and at the St. Louis Conservatory of Music. She composed the tune—"Houston," "I want to walk as a child of the light", which appeared in *The Hymnal for Worship & Celebration* (Baptist 1986).

THOMPSON, ALFREDA LYDIA (1911–)
'Ballads, Blues and Boleros'
Composer/songwriter born on April 24th in Offerly, Kansas, she was educated at the Golden Eagle School. With composer/saxophonist Norris Christy Henson, she wrote for the albums *Confession: Ballads, Blues and Boleros* and *Confession.*

THOMPSON, KAY (1913–)
"You Gotta Love Everybody"
Composer/pianist/singer/songwriter born on November 9th in St. Louis, Missouri, she studied privately. She made her piano solo debut with the St. Louis Symphony, later sang in nightclubs and on TV. She was music arranger for Fred Waring, CBS, and MGM. She wrote the songs, "Promise Me Love", "This Is the Time", and the song above. ASCAP.

THOMPSON, LINDA
"I Have Nothing"
Songwriter, she lived in Memphis, Tennessee. She lived with singer Elvis Presley for over four years, then married producer/singer David Foster. They wrote "Shining Through" for Miki Howard and "Grown Up Christmas List" for Amy Grant. She wrote "I Have Nothing" for Whitney Houston on the soundtrack film *The Bodyguard* (1992).

TIDDEMAN, MARIA (1837–1915)
Tune—"Ibstone"
A composer born in England, she studied music at Oxford University. Her hymn tune was used for Martin Luther's hymn, "Flung to the heedless winds." She composed anthems, hymn tunes, and songs. Her tune appeared in the *Methodist Hymnal* (1911) and in *Hymns Ancient & Modern* (1950). She died on January 8, 1915, at Croydon, England.

TILLIS, PAM (1958–)
"Don't Tell Me What to Do"
Country singer/songwriter, the daughter of country singer Mel Tillis, Pam had her no. 1 hit above in 1991. She had a son born in 1979, later divorced, and in 1991 married songwriter Bob DiPiero. Her album *Homeward Looking Angel* was released in 1992. Hit singles were "Shake the Sugar Tree" and "Maybe It Was Memphis", which won a 1993 Grammy. With others she appeared on a CBS-TV Special in January 1993.

TISHMAN, FAY (1913–)
"Spring Again"
Composer/songwriter born on October 29th in New York, New York, and educated at New York University, she wrote "Stay Here Bluebird" and other songs. ASCAP.

TOBITT, JANET E. (1898–Dec'd.)
"A Journey in Song"
Composer/songwriter born on March 24th in England, she was educated at London University; St. Andrews University LLA; New York University; and the New School for Social Research in New York City. With Alice White she wrote, composed or arranged music for a number of books, *A.B.C.'s of Camp Music, Book of Negro Songs, The Ditty Bag, Promenade All, Our World in Song,* the book above, and the compiled "Dramatized Ballads".

TODD, DOTTY (1923–)
"I'll Never Leave Hawaii"

Composer/pianist/singer/songwriter born on June 22nd in Elizabeth, New Jersey, she was educated at business college and studied music privately. She sang with the team of Art and Dotty Todd in nightclubs, on TV, and on records. She sang on CBS and ABC radio shows. With Art Todd she wrote "Ca C'est la Vie", "Joie de Vivre", "The Busy Signal Song", "The Nearer You Are to Me", "Black Velvet Eyes", "Sweet Cha Cha Chariot", and "Ring-a-ding Feeling". ASCAP.

TOOLAN, SUZANNE (1927–)
Tune—"Leave All Things"
Composer/choral director/songwriter, she was born on October 24th in Lansing, Michigan, and was educated at Immaculate Heart College, Hollywood, California, (BA) and San Francisco State University (MA). She taught in high school (1953–80), at Russell College (1960–70), and she was director of Mercy Center, a spiritual retreat center (1981–88). She composed the music for "Leave All Things", which appeared in the *Baptist Hymnal* (1986), as well as some 30 hymns and songs.

TOURJEE, LIZZIE S. (1858–1913)
Tune—"Wellesley"
A composer and the daughter of Dr. Eben Tourjee, who founded the New England Conservatory of Music in Boston in 1867, she was born in Newport, Rhode Island, in 1858. When Lizzie, at age eighteen, was asked to set a classmate's graduation hymn to music, she panicked and rushed to her father for help. So he had her sit down at the piano with the words directly in front of her to see what their meaning meant to her. So her tune evolved, and was sung at her graduation high school class in Newton, Massachusetts. She attended Wellesley College for one year (1877–78), and her father named the tune after her college. In 1883 she married Franklin Estabrook. With the hymn, "There's a wideness in God's Mercy," her tune appeared in the *Hymnal of the Methodist Episcopal Church with Tunes* (1878) and in *Tribute of Praise* (1884) for use at the New England Conservatory. More recently her tune appeared in *The Pilgrim Hymnal* (1958).

TOWER, JOAN (1938–)
Silver Ladders
Composer/pianist, she was born on September 6th in New Rochelle, New York. After studying at Bennington College in Vermont (1958–61) and at Columbia University (MA, 1967) she founded and was pianist-accompanist for the Da Capo Chamber Players. After receiving a number of fellowships, she received her DMA at Columbia University in 1978. In 1985 she was appointed composer-in-residence with the St. Louis Symphony Orchestra. She has composed orchestral, chamber, and in-

strumental works. Her *Silver Ladders* conducted by Leonard Slatkin in the early 1980s, is available on CD as of 1994.

TRAVERS, MARY ELLEN (1936–)
"The Great Mandella"
Singer/songwriter, she was born on November 9th in Louisville, Kentucky. She started singing with Noel Paul Stookey; later Peter Yarrow joined the act, and they formed the trio of Peter, Paul and Mary and became very successful. With Stookey, Yarrow, and Milton Okun, she wrote "Gone the Rainbow"; with Stookey, Yarrow, Dave Dixon, and Richard L. Kniss, "The Song Is Love"; with Stookey and Albert Grossman, "The Great Mandella—Take your place on the Great Mandella". Their hit song "Blowin' in the Wind" won a Grammy 1963. The group disbanded in 1971 and revived in 1980. The trio sang at the American Reunion on the Mall in Washington, DC, in January 1993. As of 1994, her albums and CDs available were *Best of 10 Years Together, A Song will Rise, Album 1700, In Concert, In the Wind, Peter, Paul & Mary, Peter, Paul & Mommy, Reunion,* and *See What Tomorrow Brings.*

TRIX, HELEN (1892–1951)
"Back to London Town"
Composer/pianist/singer/songwriter born on August 21st in Newmanstown, Pennsylvania, she was educated at Albright College. She toured in vaudeville shows and wrote "Parisian Peacock Girl", "You'd Love to Live in Paris", "Follow Me", "I Never Worry about the Morning", "It's Making Me Love You All the More", and "There Will Come a Time." She died on November 18th in New York, New York.

TROKER, KATHERINE BEATON (1891–Dec'd.)
"Don't Ever Break Your Baby's Heart"
Songwriter born on December 30th in Sydney, Nova Scotia, Canada, she was educated at a business college. With Al Avellini, she wrote the words for "Broken-hearted Dolly" and the song above. ASCAP.

TRYNIA, JENNIFER
"If I Had Anything to Say"
Singer/songwriter. Her album *Cockamamie* (1995) contained her song "If I Had Anything to Say" driven by trippy/fuzzy guitars.

TUCKER, EDNA MAE (1907–)
"Here Is Everything but Love"
Composer/songwriter born on May 12th in Chicago, Illinois, she was educated at high school. She wrote "A Little Bit of Heaven", "Chasing Rainbows", "Evening", "Nothing Like", "Two", and the song above.

TUCKER, TUI ST. GEORGE (1924–)
Little Pieces for Quarter Tone Piano
Composer/recorder performer, she was born on November 25th in Fullerton, California. After attending Occidental College in Los Angeles (1941–44), she moved to New York City in 1946. She has composed symphonies, instrumental and vocal works, but is best known as a recorder virtuoso where she included folk music from her summer retreats in the North Carolina mountains. Her piece above was composed in 1972, and *Indian Summer* in 1983.

TURNER, MILDRED C. (1897–Dec'd.)
"I Wish They Didn't Mean Goodbye"
Composer/songwriter born on February 23rd in Pueblo, Colorado, and educated at the University of Wisconsin, she studied with Emil Liebling, and Corneille and Francis Schwinger. She wrote the songs "Dalmatian Lullaby", "Geisha", and the song above. ASCAP.

TURNER, TINA (1938–)
"Nutbush City Limits"
Singer/songwriter, she was born Annie Mae Bullock on November 26th in Brownsville, Tennessee. In 1956 she joined Ike Turner's band the Kings of Rhythm and then married Turner. The band toured the US and Great Britain in the 1950s–60s, and with the Rolling Stones in 1969. Tina wrote the song mentioned above in 1973. The Turners were divorced in 1976, and each pursued their own careers. Tina was the Acid Queen in the rock opera *Tommy* in 1977. "What's Love Got to Do With It?" won a 1984 Grammy; "Live in Europe" won Best Pop Vocal Performance 1988 Grammy; "The Bitch is Back" track from *Two Rooms* won a 1993 Grammy. Her albums available in 1994 were *Break Every Rule, Foreign Affair, Live in Europe, Private Dancer,* and *Simply the Best.*

TWOMEY, KATHLEEN G. (1914–)
"Johnny Doughboy Found a Rose in Ireland"
Songwriter born on April 27th in Boston, Massachusetts, she was educated at the Faelten School of Music; the New England Conservatory; and she studied voice with Margaret Gugenberger. With music by Al Goodhart, Dick Manning, and Ben Weisman, she wrote the songs, "Honey in the Horn", "Hey, Jealous Lover", "In a Little Book Shop", "Let Me Go, Lover", "Serenade of the Bells", "Wooden Heart", "Never Let Her Go", "The Robe of Calvary", "Laura's Wedding", "Why Pretend?", "Heartbreak Hill", and "Pretty Little Black-eyed Susie". Her album is *Teen Street.* ASCAP.

TYLER, GOLDIE (1925–)
"Cause you're my lover"
Composer/songwriter born on October 31st in Kittrell, North Carolina, she was educated at a business college. She lived in Philadelphia and New York. She wrote the above song. ASCAP.

-U-

UNGER, STELLA (1905–Dec'd.)
"Turn Your Frown Upside Down"
Songwriter born on December 17th in New York, New York, she was educated at Benjamin School for Girls. A columnist for the New York *Daily Mirror,* she also wrote words for Broadway musicals, songs for films *Where the Boys Are, The Horizontal Lieutenant,* etc. With music by Fred Fisher, Leopold Godowsky, James P. Johnson, Alec Templeton, and Victor Young, she wrote the words for "All Dressed Up with a Broken Heart", "A Man with a Dream", "C'est la Vie", "Don't Cry, Baby", "Love Comes Only Once in a Lifetime", and "It's a Thrill All Over Again". ASCAP.

UPTON, ANNE (b. 1892–)
Cantata—*Life of Jesus*
Composer and hymnist, she was born at Marble City, Arkansas, on June 28, 1892 and was educated at the Fred Palmer Institute. She wrote for radio and composed the opera, *Book of Ruth,* a symphonic poem, *Cattle at Eventide,* etc.

URNER, CATHERINE MURPHY (1891–1942)
Rhapsody of Aimairgin of the Golden Knee
Composer/singer, she was born on March 23rd at Mitchell, Indiana. She won the first George Ladd Prix de Paris while a student at the University of California at Berkeley, where she studied composition with Charles Koechlin. She taught at Mills College in Oakland, California (1921–24). Urner sang at concerts in the US and Europe, and her compositions were performed in Paris. In 1937 she married the California composer Charles Shatto. Her choral and orchestral work mentioned above was composed in 1936. She wrote a number of songs and instrumental works. She died in San Diego, California, on April 30th.

USTVOLSKAYA, GALINA (1919–)
Symphony No. 3: Jesus Messiah, Save Us
Composer, she was born on June 17th in Petrograd, Russia. After studying at the Leningrad Arts School (1937–39) and composition under Dmitri Shostakovich and Maximilian Steinberg at the Leningrad Conservatoire

(1940–41 and 1945–47), she studied composition there under Gregory Rimsky-Korsakov (1947–50). Meanwhile she taught composition at the Music College of Leningrad Conservatoire (1948–77). On December 23, 1966, she married Konstantin Makukhin. She has composed several symphonies, sonatas, choral, and instrumental works. Her first three symphonies were performed in Leningrad—*No. 1* (1966), *No. 2: True and Eternal Bliss* (1979), *No. 3: Jesus Messiah, Save Us* (1987), *No. 4: Prayer,* which was first performed in Heidelberg, Germany (1988).

-V-

VAN de VATE, NANCY JEAN HAYS (1930–)
  Music for Viola, Percussion and Piano
Composer, she was born on December 30th in Plainfield, New Jersey. After studying piano under Rovinsky in New York City (1947–48) and under Cecile Genhart at the Eastman School of Music in Rochester, New York (1948–49), she studied piano and music theory under David Barnett at Wellesley College in Massachusetts (AB, 1952). On June 9, 1952, she married Dwight Van de Vate, Jr., and they had three children. She continued her piano studies at Yale School of Music and composition at the University of Mississippi (MM, 1958), also privately with John Boda (1963–64 and 1967–68), at Florida State University at Tallahassee (DMus, 1968). She was an instructor of music at the University of Tennessee (1967), and at Knoxville College, Tennessee (1968–69 and 1971–72). In 1976 she divorced Dwight Van de Vate, Jr., and on June 23, 1979 she married Clyde Arnold Smith. She was dean of academic affairs at Hawaii Loa College (1979), resided in Indonesia (1982–85), and has resided in Vienna, Austria, since 1985. She has composed choral and instrumental works, chamber music, operas, etc. Her *Music for Viola, Percussion and Piano* (1976) was first performed on February 27, 1977 in Honolulu, Hawaii.

VANDYKE, MARY LOUISE (1927–)
  Tune—"Chhattisgahr"
Composer/arranger/hymnist born on February 28th in Rochester, Pennsylvania, she was educated at Oberlin College Conservatory (BMus Ed); Western Reserve University, Cleveland (MA); Kent State University, Ohio (MA in Church music). She married Dr. Donald VanDyke. She taught music in public schools; piano at Jordan Conservatory, Butler University, Indianapolis; English at Kent State University; and has directed children's choirs for almost 40 years. While her husband was a medical missionary in India, she heard the bajan or folk tune mentioned above and adapted it to a hymn by William Nelson—"As ancient sunlight reaches the earth"; the tune "Tamil" (Usani) was adapted and harmonized by Mrs. VanDyke and John Ferguson; and she wrote the words

for "On God the Spirit We Rely". All three appeared in the *Hymnal of the United Church of Christ* (1974). Her hymn "Eternal Spirit, we rely on you" appeared in *Everflowing Streams,* N.Y. Pilgrim Press (1981). Her tunes also appeared in the *Lutheran Book of Worship* (1978). Since 1984 Mrs. VanDyke has served as Project Librarian, Dictionary of American Hymnology, Oberlin College Library, Oberlin, Ohio.

VAN FORST, KATHY (1904–)
"Stranger in the Chapel"
Composer/songwriter born on April 24th in Cologne, Germany, she studied music with Madelina Dietz. She wrote and produced musicals for theater groups, sang in World War II with American Theatre Wing. With Polly Arnold, Fred Patrick, and Arthur Richardson, she wrote the songs "Come Out of the Shadows", "Closed for Repairs", "The Reason is Love", "Rosella", "Tormenting Me", and the song above. ASCAP.

VAN SCIVER, ESTHER (1907–1952)
"In a Little Canning Kitchen"
Songwriter born on June 11th in New York, New York, she served as editor of *All American Bandleader* and wrote the songs "I Ain't Never Loved Before", "I Betcha My Heart I Love You", "The Fighting Son-of-a-gun", and "The Next Time You Talk to the Lord". She died on May 14th in Nyack, New York.

VAN ZANDT, MARY O'SULLIVAN (1903–)
"It's All Accordin'"
Composer/songwriter born on September 12th in Lee County, Mississippi, she was educated at Southern Female Academy and Harris Conservatory (BA). She wrote the above song.

VEGA, SUZANNE (1960–)
Suzanne Vega
Pop/folk singer/songwriter/guitarist, she was born on July 11th in Santa Monica, California. At age two she was taken to New York City, where she was raised by her mother and Puerto Rican stepfather. After graduating from Barnard College, she recorded her own songs on her album *Suzanne Vega* in 1985. With drummer Jerry Marotta and guitarist Richard Thompson, she sang on the album *99.9 degrees F* in 1992. Other albums of hers available in 1994 were *Days of Open Hand* and *Solitude Standing*.

VERST, RUTH (1930–)
"I'll Bet You He'll Kiss Me"
Composer/singer/songwriter born on July 27th in Philadelphia, Pennsylvania, she was educated at Philadelphia High School for Girls. She

sang with bands, on radio, TV, records, and wrote the above song. AS-CAP.

VESTOFF, FLORIA (1918–1963)
"Walkin' Around in Circles"
Composer/songwriter born on April 6th in New York, New York, she was educated at Children's School in New York City. She was a dancer and then a choreographer for "Old Gold" commercials and "Stop the Music". She wrote material for Jackie Gleason and Joe E. Lewis, and the songs: "Everyone Was There But Me", "If You Change Your Mind", "Bugle Woogie", "Somebody Cares", and "The Show Is On". She died on March 18th in Hollywood, California.

VIARDOT, PAULINE GARCIA (1821–1910)
Le Dernier Sorcier
Mezzo-soprano/composer, she was born on July 18th in Paris, France, the daughter of tenor/composer Manuel Garcia and actress Joaquina Sitchez. At age four she received pianoforte lessons from Marcos Vega in New York City, then studied in Mexico. She also studied with Meysenberg and with Liszt when he was in Paris, then counterpoint and composition with Reicha. She sang in Brussels at age sixteen, then at the Theatre de la Renaissance in Paris (1838) and at Her Majesty's Theatre in London (1839), etc. In 1841 she married impressario Louis Viardot, who toured with her through Europe in the 1840s–50s. She composed the music for several operettas. The libretto for her *Le Dernier Sorcier* was written by Nikolay Ivanovich Turgenev and translated into German by Richard Pohl and performed at Weimar and Carlsruhe, Germany, and at Riga, Latvia, as *Der Letzte Zauberer*. During the Franco-Prussian War (1870–71), she left Germany and returned to Paris, where she taught singing at the Paris Conservatoire (1871–75). She died during the evening of May 17–18th in Paris.

VILLINES, VIRGINIA (1917–)
"Bird in the Bamboo"
Composer/songwriter born on November 20th in Giddings, Texas, she was educated at business school and studied music privately. She wrote the above song.

VOGEL, JANET FRANCES (1941–Dec'd.)
"This I Swear"
Composer/singer/songwriter born on June 10th in Pittsburgh, Pennsylvania, she was educated at a finishing school. She sang and toured with The Skyliners throughout the US and Europe. She wrote "It Happened Today", "Since I Don't Have You", and the song above. ASCAP.

-W-

WAGNER, MELINDA J.
Ancient Music
A composer, her *Ancient Music* for mixed choir was performed by the Hamilton College Choir at Lloyd Hamilton College in Clinton, New York, on October 8, 1994.

WAINWRIGHT, MARY LEE (1913–)
"Florida the Sunshine State"
Composer/songwriter born on April 24th in Ruby, South Carolina, she was the officer of the Florida Federation of Music Clubs and the state chairman of the International Relations Department. She wrote "A Woman's Touch", "Happiness", "It's the Truth", "Our God of All", "When You Are Near", and "Wake Up, America". ASCAP.

WALDMAN, WENDY
"Save the Best for Last"
A songwriter, with Jon Lind and Phil Galdston she wrote "Save the Best for Last", popularized by Vanessa Williams. It was a Grammy winner in 1992.

WALKER, BERTHA (1908–)
"Guess I Had Too Much to Dream Last Night"
Composer born on August 18th in Indianapolis, Indiana. With Sammy Cahn, Eddie Cantor, Bob Merrill, Jack Segal, and Kay Twomey, she wrote a number of songs; "Gotta Learn How to Love You", "Hey, Jealous Lover", "Hold Me, Hold Me", "Same Old You", "Who Told You That Lie?", "Please Believe Me", and "There's a City on a Hill By the Sea".

WALKER, CINDY (ca. 1920–)
"Lone Star Trail"
Songwriter, she was born at Marr, Texas. She wrote her first song while a dancer at Billy Rose's Casa Mañana, Fort Worth, Texas. While on vacation with her father, a cotton buyer, she met Bob Wills in Hollywood, California, in 1941. Wills and his Texas Playboys recorded four of her songs. She wrote "Lone Star Trail" recorded by Bing Crosby in 1942; "Warm Red Wine" recorded by Ernest Tubb in 1949; "Take Me in Your Arms and Hold Me" recorded by Eddy Arnold in 1950; "The Gold Rush Is Over" for Hank Snow in 1952; "Trademark" with Porter Wagoner for Carl Smith (1953); "I Don't Care" for Webb Pierce (1955); "This Is It" (1965); and "Distant Drums" (1966) for Jim Reeves. She also wrote "Bubbles in My Beer" for Bob Wills, and in 1970 was elected to the Songwriters Hall of Fame of the Nashville Songwriters association.

WALSH, PAULINE (1906–)

"So Young and So in Love"

Composer/singer/songwriter born on December 19th in Kansas City, Missouri, she was educated at Wilson Green School of Music, Washington, DC; Oscar Seagle School, New York; she studied with Edward Harris, Jean de Reszke, Anita Rio and Andrei de Segurola. She sang in an opera in Cannes, France; was a soloist with the Kansas City Symphony; was on the Rudy Vallee show, on radio, WOR, New Jersey. She wrote "Christmas Story", "My Songs Are for You", and "Polka Dot". ASCAP.

WANDERMAN, DOROTHY (1907–)

The Playful Mouse

Composer/pianist born on October 20th in New York, New York, she studied music with Philipp, Saperton, and Scoville. She composed the piano pieces *The Playful Mouse, 4 Waltzes—In a French Cafe, Swiss Alpine Waltz, In a Viennese Garden, Valse Tragic.*

WARD, DIANE (1919–)

Visiting the Bancrofts

Composer/singer born on January 10th in Jackson, Michigan, she was educated at Cleary College; Jackson Jr. College; Michigan State University (BA and MA); and the University of Michigan, Interlochen. She studied with Barre Hill at the American Conservatory; and with Laura Koch, Robert Long, Robella Manong. She was a singer in musicals, opera, radio, TV. She worked with Roseann Hammill. Her works include the opera *Visiting the Bancrofts;* choral: "2 Poems"; musical play *The Little Dipper.*

WARE, HARRIET (1877–1962)

Sir Olaf

Pianist/composer, she was born on August 26th in Waupun, Wisconsin. After graduating from the Pillsbury Conservatory in Owatonna, Minnesota (1895), and studying with William Mason and others, she married Hugo M. Krumbhaar. She composed *Sir Olaf,* a cantata, performed by the New York Symphony Orchestra in 1910, *The Fay Song,* piano pieces, and numerous songs. She died on February 9th in New York City.

WARE, HELEN (1887–Dec'd.)

(Composer of Hungarian and Slavic music)

Violinist/composer, she was born on September 9th in Woodbury, New Jersey. After studying violin with Frederick Hahn in Philadelphia and composition with Hugh Clarke at the University of Pennsylvania, she studied in Vienna and in Budapest with Hubay. After 1912 she played the violin in many recitals in Europe and the US. She was a composer and arranger of Hungarian and Slavic music.

WARNER, SARAH ANN (1898–Dec'd.)
"'Neath a Blanket of White"
Composer/pianist/songwriter, she was born on October 16th in Idaho Falls, Idaho. Later she moved to Long Beach, California, where she became a publisher. She wrote "Hello, Merry Christmas", "Our Engagement Waltz", "So Speaks My Heart", and "You Stole My Heart".

WARREN, DELLA McCHAIN (1893–1976)
"There is a name to me so dear,
Like sweetest music to my ear."
Hymnist and composer, she was born in Gastonville, Pennsylvania, on February 19, 1893 and was graduated from Douglass College. On June 27, 1917, she married James B. Warren in Glassport, Pennsylvania, where Mr. Warren was a butcher in his father's butcher shop. They lived there for 30 years, then in 1947 moved to Aurora, Colorado, where she died on August 29, 1976. (Information from her son, Hugh M. Warren) Her hymn appeared in *Rodeheaver's Gospel Solos and Duets No. 3*.

WARREN, DIANE
"Rhythm of the Night"
Lyricist/songwriter. She wrote "Solitaire" for Laura Branigan (1983). During one week in 1989 seven of her songs hit Billboard's Hot 100. She wrote "Nothin's Gonna Stop Us Now", "If I Could Turn Back Time", "If You Asked Me To", "When I See You Smile", "When the Night Comes". She made ASCAP's Songwriter of the Year for 1990, 1991 and 1993 and received ASCAP's Voice of Music award in Los Angeles in 1995.

WARREN, ELINOR REMICK (1900–Dec'd.)
White Horses of the Sea
Composer/pianist, she was born on February 23rd in Los Angeles, the daughter of a choral conductor. Her mother was a pianist. She was playing the piano at age five and composing music at age fourteen. After studying at Mills College, Oakland, for a year, she studied in New York City in the early 1920s, then toured as a pianist. Her choral work mentioned above was composed in 1932. She composed a number of songs and choral works with piano or orchestral accompaniment. She has spent most of her life in Los Angeles and was named Woman of the Year in Music in 1955 by the *Los Angeles Times*. As of 1994 her *Legend of King Arthur* was available.

WARSHAUER, ROSE (1917–)
"Gee, It's Love"
Songwriter born on July 30th in New York, New York, she was educated at Ann Reno Teachers Training and New York University. She studied music with her father, Frank Warshauer. With her father she wrote songs, including the one mentioned above. ASCAP.

WARWICK, ROSE B. (1934–)
  "Sally Ann"
Songwriter born on August 7th in New York, New York, she was educated at Bard College (BA) and Columbia University. She wrote the
above song. ASCAP.

WATERS, PATRICIA (1919–)
  "VMI Ring Waltz"
Songwriter/actress born on November 16th in Bedford, England, and ed-
ucated at Sacred Heart and St. Agnes Academy, New York City, she
acted in plays, was a writer of special material, wrote words for the
songs, "Boom-Boom", "If I Can't Have the One I Love", "Glorious—
Glorious", "Nothing Else Will Do", "Pony Tail", and "Without Your
Love". ASCAP.

WATKINS, VANJA LOUISE YORGASON (1938–)
  Tune—"Norma"
  Tune—"Edgecombe"
A composer who lived in Ogden, Utah, and was educated at Brigham
Young University (BA and MA), she married Jack B. Watkins and they
have five children. She was a music coordinator for the Ogden City
Schools, taught at Brigham Young University, and has composed mu-
sic for children. Her hymns above with the words "Families can be to-
gether" and "Press forward, Saints" appeared in the Mormon hymnal
(1985).

WAYNE, MABEL (1904–Dec'd.)
  "In a Little Spanish Town"
Popular composer, she was born in Brooklyn, New York, and studied
in Europe. She entered vaudeville at age sixteen. With Albert Baer and
words by L. Wolfe Gilbert, she wrote "Don't Wake Me Up, Let Me
Dream" (1925); with words by Sam Lewis and Joe Young, "In a Little
Spanish Town" (1926); with Gilbert, "Ramona" (1927) and "Chiquita"
(1928); with Al Hoffman and Maurice Sigler, "Little Man, You've
Had a Busy Day" (1934); with Al Lewis, "Why Don't You Fall in Love
With Me?" (1937); with Billy Rose, "It Happened in Monterey" (1940);
with Kim Gannon "Dreamer's Holiday" (1949) and "I Understand".
ASCAP.

WEAVER, MARY WATSON (1903–)
  "Rise Up All Men"
Composer/pianist/songwriter born on January 16th in Kansas City, Mis-
souri, she was educated at Smith College, Ottawa University, (BA and
BM); Curtis Institute of Music in Philadelphia; and had private music

study in France. She married composer Powell Weaver, and taught at Kansas City Conservatory, Curtis Institute, Manhattan School of Music, and the Henry Street School of Music in New York City. With her husband, her choral works include "All Weary Men, Kneel Down", "Like Doves Descending", "On the Eve of the First Christmas", and "When Jesus Lay by Mary's Side".

WEBB, JUNE ELLEN (1934–)
"The Secret of Life"
Singer/songwriter, she was born in L'Anse, Michigan. She wrote "The Party Is Over" (1957) and "The Secret of Life" (1958).

WEBER, WILHELMINE FRANCES (1916–)
"East of West Berlin"
Composer/songwriter born on February 15th in Chicago, Illinois, she was educated at college (BS). With James MacDonald, she wrote "The Harbour Bell" and the song mentioned above.

WEIR, JUDITH (1954–)
'Airs from Another Planet'
Composer, she was born on May 11th in Cambridge, England. She studied composition privately under John Tavener, then under Robin Holloway at King's College, Cambridge (1973–76). She was composer in residence for the Southern Arts Association (1976–79), Cramb Fellow at the University of Glasgow (1979–82), Fellow Commoner at Trinity College, Cambridge (1983–85), and composer in residence at the Royal School of Art, Music and Drama in Glasgow, Scotland, from 1988. She has composed choral and instrumental works, chamber music, and operas. Her *Airs from Another Planet* for flute, piccolo, obo, clarinet, bassoon, horn, and piano was first performed on October 14, 1986 at St. Andrews, Fife.

WEIR, MARY BRINKLEY (1783–1840)
The Lord of the Castle
She lived in New York City from 1802 until her death in 1840. She composed *The Lord of the Castle*.

WELCH, MARILYN "MITZIE" (1933–)
"What Did You Say to Santy?"
Composer/songwriter born on July 25th in Canonsburg, Pennslyvania, she was educated at Carnegie Tech. in Pittsburgh. She was a singer with the Benny Goodman orchestra, and married composer/singer/songwriter Kenneth Welch. With her husband, she wrote "Musical Chairs", "Three Little Girls" and the song mentioned above. ASCAP.

WELL, CYNTHIA (1937–)
"You've Lost That Loving Feeling"
A songwriter, with Barry Mann she wrote "You've Lost That Loving
Feeling" and "Saturday Night at the Movies".

WELLS, KITTY (1919–)
"Dust on the Bible"
Country music singer/songwriter, she was born Muriel Ellen Deason on
August 30th in Nashville, Tennessee. Known as the "Queen of Country
Music", Kitty and her sister first sang on Radio Station WSIX in
Nashville in 1936. After she married singer Johnny Wright in 1937, they
sang on stations WCHS in Bluefield, West Virginia; WNOX in Knoxville,
Tennessee; WPIF in Raleigh, North Carolina; WEAS in Decatur, Geor-
gia; and they were on "Louisiana Hayride" on KWKH in Shreveport,
Louisiana from 1947–52. Her husband renamed her Kitty Wells after the
folksong "Sweet Kitty Wells". She became a regular cast member of
Grand Ole Opry in 1952 and was elected to the Country Music Hall of
Fame in 1976. As of 1994 her albums available were *Country Music Hall
of Fame, Greatest Hits, The Golden Years, The Kitty Wells Story*.

WERNER, KAY (1918–)
"I Got the Spring Fever Blues"
Composer/singer/songwriter born on October 9th in Birmingham, Al-
abama, she was educated at high school. With her sister Sue Werner she
wrote a number of songs, including "Love Is the Thing So They Say", "I
Want the Waiter with the Water", "Dot It Again", etc. ASCAP.

WERNER, SUE (1918–)
"Rock It for Me"
Composer/singer/songwriter born on October 9th in Birmingham, Alabama, she was educated at high school. She went to New York City in
1935 with her twin sister Kay Werner. They wrote a number of songs,
including "Requestfully Yours", "My Wubba Dolly", "Ten Little Soldiers", etc. ASCAP.

WESSON, RUTH JANELLE SMITH (1925–)
Tune—"Who's My Neighbor?"
Composer/soprano, she was born on April 25th in Greenville, Illinois,
and graduated with honors from the St. Louis High School in 1942. She
married James Robert Wesson and they have four children and ten
grandchildren. She is also a hymnist and songwriter. She composed the
tune for "They asked: 'Who's my neighbor?'" in the *Hymnal for Worship & Celebration* (Baptist 1986).

WEST, DOROTHY MARIE "DOTTIE" (1932–1991)
"Here Comes My Baby"
Singer/songwriter, she was born in McMinnville, Tennessee. She married guitarist/songwriter Bill West; both Dottie and Bill graduated from Tennessee Tech., Cookeville, Tennessee. They wrote "Here Comes My Baby" (1964), recorded both by the Wests and by Perry Como; and "Would You Hold It Against Me?" (1966), which they recorded. With Billy Davis, she wrote "Country sunshine — I was raised on country sunshine, green grass beneath my feet". As of 1994 her albums available were *Collectors' Series* and her *Greatest Hits*.

WHITE, JANE DOUGLASS (1919–)
"Trick or Treat for UNICEF"
Composer/conductor born on April 14th in Coffeyville, Kansas, she was educated at Oklahoma University (BFA); Columbia University (MA); and Colorado College of Education. She served as a captain, Women's Army Corps, Special Services. She composed film songs, musical commercials, and the TV shows "Name that Tune" and "Stop the Music". She was musical director of the Playhouse, Paramus, New Jersey, and Playhouse, Brunswick, Maine. She wrote "Love Is a Gamble", "Aime Moi", "Say Hey"; the song above was the official UNICEF song and "Song of the Women's Army," the official WAC song, won the Legion of Merit. ASCAP.

WHITE, KAY (1900–Dec'd.)
"I Long for Your Love"
Composer/singer/songwriter born on February 27th in Hackensack, New Jersey, she was educated in public schools. She was a singer on WBNS radio in Hackensack and wrote: "Come a Little Closer", "Cry Baby", "No Heartaches", "Buzzing Around", "Jonah", "Mama Said", and "Why Can't It Be?"

WHITE, MAUDE VALERIE (1855–1937)
"My Soul Is an Enchanted Boat"
Composer, she was born on June 23rd at Dieppe, New Brunswick, Canada. After studying harmony and composition with W. S. Rockstro and Oliver May in London, she entered the Royal Academy of Music in 1876 and studied composition under Sir George A. Macfarren and under F. Davenport and Macfarren again on a scholarship (1879–81). She also studied in Vienna in 1883. She composed a number of songs to words by Herrick and Shelley, and German songs to words by Heine and Schiller, and to French songs to words by Victor Hugo. The song above was written to words by Percy B. Shelley. She died on November 2nd in London.

WHITE, RUTH S. (1925–)
'Short Circuits'

Composer, she was born on September 1st in Pittsburgh, Pennsylvania. After studying composition with Lopatnikoff at Carnegie-Mellon University in Pittsburgh (BFA, 1948 and MFA, 1949), she studied privately with Antheil and at UCLA (1951–54). White composed *Settings for Lullabies from 'Round the World* (1955) and other vocal and piano compositions for children. She has composed orchestral and chamber works and since the late 1960s electronic orchestral pieces including *Short Circuits* in 1970.

WHITMAN, FAY (1926–)
"The Doodle Song"

Songwriter born on June 14th in Little Falls, New York, she was educated at high school. She was assistant editor of *Song Dex Treasury of Humorous and Nostalgic Songs*. With music by Jack Manus, she wrote the words for "Am I Asking Too Much?", "Be I Bumblebee or Not?" and the song mentioned above. ASCAP.

WHITNEY, JOAN (1914–Dec'd.)
"Comme-ci, comme-ca"

Composer/singer/songwriter born on June 26th in Pittsburgh, Pennsylvania, she was educated at Carnegie Tech and Finch College. She was a singer with dance bands, in nightclubs, hotels, and had her own radio show. She married composer/cellist Alexander Milton Kramer (1893–1955) and they founded Kramer-Whitney, Inc. publishers in 1947; with Southside Records after 1961. With her husband and Hy Zaret, she wrote a number of songs: "Candy", "Ain't Nobody Here But Us Chickens", "High on a Windy Hill", "It All Comes Back to Me", "It's Love, Love, Love", "That's the Beginning of the End", "Love Somebody", "Money Is the Root of All Evil", "Dangerous Dan McGrew", "Far Away Places", "No Man Is an Island", "You'll Never Get Away", "I Only Saw Him Once", "My Sister and I", "Summer Rain", "No Other Arms, No Other Lips", and "Story of My Life". ASCAP.

WHITNEY, YULA A. (1922–1965)
"Song of Moscow"

Composer/singer/songwriter born on October 14th in Moscow, USSR, she came to the US in 1953 and sang in nightclubs. She wrote the songs "Hush, My Honey", "Mama, My Mama", "Sorry", "Tango Exotique", "Love Is a Daydream", "There's Wind on the Window Pane", "A Few Golden Months", "Avenue of Love", "Adieu, Many Thanks", "I Fell in Love with Someone's Eyes", "Such as You Were", and "There's a Time to be Sunkist".

WHITSON, BETH SLATER (1879–1930)
"Let me call you sweetheart"
Songwriter, she was born in Goodrich, Tennessee, and was educated at George Peabody College. She wrote verses for magazines (1900–07). With music by Leo Freidman, she wrote "Let Me Call You Sweetheart" (1910), and with Friedman, "Meet Me Tonight in Dreamland." She died in Nashville, Tennessee.

WILCHINSKI, MARTHA L. (1897–Dec'd.)
"If Love Were All"
Songwriter born on March 14th in New York, New York, she was educated at New York University. She served as a World War I sergeant in the United States Marine Corps. She wrote radio scripts. With music by William Axt, she wrote the above song. ASCAP.

WILEY, LEE (1915–1975)
"Anytime, Anyday, Anywhere"
Singer/composer, she was born on October 9th in Port Gibson, Oklahoma, and was raised in Tulsa, where she studied music. She went to New York City and sang in the dance band of Leo Frank Reisman at the Central Park Casino in 1931. She sang on radio programs (1931–35) and did shows with Paul Whiteman and others. She recorded songs by Cole Porter, Harold Arlen, George Gershwin, and with the Casa Loma Band and other bands during late 1930s–40s. She married Jess Stacy in 1943, but they separated two years later. She co-wrote "Anytime, Anyday, Anywhere" with Victor Young, and the song became a smash hit. She sang at the Newport Jazz Festival in New York City (1972). Her jazz qualities are most noticeable on the W. C. Handy 16-bar blues classic "Careless Love". She died of cancer. As of 1994 her albums and CDs available were *As Time Goes By, Duologue, I've got you under my skin, Night in Manhattan, Rarities, Sings Gershwin and Porter,* and *Sings Rodgers, Hart, Arlen.*

WILLADSEN, JANE THURSTEN LYNN "GENE" (1915–)
"Just to Be Near You"
Songwriter born on July 24th at Weekawken Heights, New Jersey, she is the daughter of magician Howard Thurston. She toured with her dad until his death. With music by Isham Jones, she wrote the words for "But I Never Do", "Just Like You", "My Best to You", and the above song. ASCAP.

WILLARD, KELLY BAGLEY (1956–)
Tune—"Servant"
Composer/pianist she was born on August 18th in Winter Haven, Florida.

She was playing the piano and composing music as a teenager. After her marriage to Dan Willard in 1977, she produced several albums, *Blame It On the One I Love* (1978), *Willing Heart* (1981), *Psalms, Hymns & Spiritual Songs, Message from a King,* and *Garden* (1991). She lives with her husband and two children in Nashville, Tennessee. Her tune for "Make Me a Servant" appeared in the *Hymnal for Worship & Celebration* (Baptist 1986).

WILLIAMS, FRANCES (1904–1978)

Choral — *In Bethlehem's Lowly Manger*

Composer, conductor, and arranger, she was born in Caernarvonshire, Wales, on June 4, 1904 and was brought to America as a young girl. She was educated at the Cornish School of Music in Seattle, Washington (on a scholarship), at Juilliard in New York City on a fellowship, and studied privately. She became music editor in chief of Harold Flammer, Inc., and was also a guest conductor at various music clinics. She wrote *Christ is the Risen Lord* (cantata) and the choral works *Give Thanks, Night Psalm XXIII,* etc. She died on March 1, 1978.

WILLIAMS, JESSICA (1948–)

And Then There's This

Pianist/composer, she was born in Baltimore, Maryland. She plays both the acoustic and electric piano. In 1976, she walked into a rock and roll session at Adelphia Records, uninvited and unannounced, and during a break sat down and played the piano, and got herself a recording contract. In 1978, in San Francisco with trumpeter Eddie Henderson and altoist Vince Wallace, she formed the 11-piece band, Liberation Army, and became known as the Queen of San Francisco Jazz. Her album mentioned above was available in 1994.

WILLIAMS, KIM

"Haunted Heart"

A country singer/songwriter, with Garth Brooks and Kent Blazy, she wrote "Ain't Goin' Down (Til the Sun Comes Up)"; with Buddy Brock she wrote "Haunted Heart"; with Philip Douglas and Aaron Tippin she wrote "My Blue Angel". She won the (female) Country Music Songwriter of the Year award (1994).

WILLIAMS, LUCINDA

"Passionate Kisses"

Country-rocker/songwriter, she sang in New Orleans, Austin, and Houston, Texas, wrote "The Night's Too Long", popularized by Patty Loveless and "Passionate Kisses", sung by Mary-Chapin Carpenter. Her albums are *Sweet Old World* (1992), *Joe Ely and Lucinda Williams*

(1993), *Happy Women Blues, Ramblin.* Her "Passionate Kisses" won 1994 Grammy for Best Country Song.

WILLIAMS, MARIAN (1927–1994)
"Holy Ghost Don't Leave Me"
Black gospel singer, songwriter, and hymnist, she was born in Miami, Florida. She joined Clara and Gertrude Ward in the Ward Singers, then left them in 1957 and joined the Stars of Faith, led by Frances Steadman. She had the female lead in *Black Nativity* with Alex Bradford, the noted black gospel singer. Two recordings of her song above are listed in *Phonolog Reports* (1978), plus two for "We shall be changed." She died on July 2nd in Philadelphia, Pennsylvania.

WILLIAMS, MARY LOU (1910–1981)
"Black Christ of the Andes"
Composer/jazz pianist, she was born Mary Elfrieda Scruggs on May 8th in Atlanta, Georgia. She was raised in Pittsburgh by her stepfather and was known as Mary Lou Burley while she was a professional pianist as a teenager. In 1925 she met saxist John Williams, joined his group, then married him. In 1929 Williams joined Andy Kirk's band and Ms. Williams played the piano and composed and arranged music for the band. Later she joined Sidney Bechet's group at the Pied Piper in the Village, New York City, later known as Cafe Bohemia, with Bill Coleman on trumpet and Wilbur de Paris on trombone. After divorcing Williams, in 1942 Ms. Williams married trumpeter Harold Baker and then she formed her own trio with Baker. She also composed scores for Tommy Dorsey, Benny Goodman, and Earl Hines. She composed "Trumpet No End" in 1946 for Duke Ellington; for Andy Kirk she wrote "Walkin' and Swingin'" and "Mary's Idea". She also composed "Waltz Boogie" (1946), "Black Christ of the Andes" (jazz hymn 1963), "Anima: Christi: Praise the Lord", "Mary Lou's Mass" (1970) choreographed by Alvin Ailey. The Mary Lou Williams Trio sang at the Newport Jazz Festivals in New York City in the early 1970s. She died on May 28th in Durham, North Carolina. As of 1994 her albums available were *Live at the Cookery, The Best of Mary Lou Williams,* and *The Zodiac Suite.*

WILLIAMS, VICTORIA
"Crazy Mary"
Singer/songwriter, she wrote "Crazy Mary" sung by Pearl Jam and "Frying Pan" sung by Evando Dando of Lemonheads on the album *Sweet Relief* (1993) to help pay her medical bills. Williams has multiple sclerosis. Her album is *Sing the Statue.*

WILSON, MABEL ELIZABETH (1890–)
"The West Is the Best for Me"
Composer/author born on December 21st in Sunbury, Ohio, she was educated in public schools. She wrote "Down the Trail to Yuma", "Rio Rosita", "Take Me Back to the Everlasting Hills", "When I Said Goodbye to Mary", and the above-mentioned song.

WILSON, MARY K. (KITTY) (1927–)
"I Know"
Bassist/singer/songwriter, she was born in Rome, Georgia, and raised in Gadsden, Alabama. At age nine she sang on local radio stations; she later married singer Smiley Wilson. They joined Circle 3 Ranch in 1945 and "Louisiana Hayride" in 1949. She wrote "Sing and Shout", "We Lived It Up" (1960), recorded by Jimmy Dickens; and "I Know" recorded by Hank Snow.

WILSON, NANCY (1954–)
"Barracuda"
Guitarist/singer/songwriter, she was born on March 16th in San Francisco, California. She sang at the Apollo Theater in Harlem, New York, in 1972, married drummer Kenny Davis and has been with the band Heart since 1972. With her sister Ann Wilson, Roger Fisher, and Michael Derosier, she wrote "Barracuda—So this ain't the end"; with her sister Ann and Susan Ennis, "Dog and butterfly—There I was with the old man, stranded again", and with Ann and Susan, "Even it up—I am the one who can please you". Her album *Drumbeat Annie* (1976) sold 2.5 million copies; *Brigade* (1990) sold 2 million albums; with her sister Ann Wilson on soundtrack *Singles* (1992). (There is another Nancy Wilson, singer, born on 2/20/37 in Chillicothe, Ohio.) After her divorce from Kenny Davis, Nancy married her director, Cameron Crowe. They have no children. Ann Wilson is three years older than Nancy. Ann is unmarried and the mother of an adopted daughter. Their latest album is *Heart* (1994).

WINBUSH, ANGELA
"Treat U Rite"
Singer/songwriter and half of the R&B duo of RENE AND ANGELA in the 1980s, she was then a background vocalist for Stevie Wonder. She wrote songs for Sheena Easton, the Isley Brothers, and Janet Jackson. She collaborated on the stirring revival of Marvin Gaye's "Inner City Blues" and with her duet partner Ronald Isley on "Baby Hold On". Her albums are *The Real Thing* and *Angela Winbush* (1994), which included her single "Treat U Rite".

WINDORF, IRENE MANGHIR (1905–Dec'd.)
"Un Baiser Cette Nuit"
Composer/songwriter born on July 14th in Brooklyn, New York, she was educated at the Winn School of Music and earned a teacher's degree. She was a piano teacher and wrote the songs, "Gypsy Serenade", "How Do I Know?" "Just a Dream", "Theresa", and the song above.

WINTER, GLORIA FRANCES (b. 1938) (SISTER MIRIAM THERESE)
"Spirit of God in the clear running water."
Tune—"Medical Mission Sisters"
Composer and hymnist, born in Passaic, New Jersey, on June 14, 1938, she was educated at Bayley-Ellard Regional High School in Madison, New Jersey, at Trinity College in Washington, DC, Catholic University in Washington, DC, (BMus), and McMaster Divinity College in Hamilton, Ontario, Canada (M. Rel. Ed.). In November 1955 she entered the Society of Catholic Medical Missionaries, also known as the Medical Mission Sisters. From 1963 to 1972 she served as Director of Public Relations for the Northeast District and Coordinator of Public Relations for the US and editor of the Society's *Medical Missionary* magazine. She was both a hymnist and composer, writing over 100 songs and hymns, and also composing the music for them, together with six Mass/Service settings. Her hymn appeared in *Hymns for the Living Church* (1974). Her hymn "God gives his people strength" appeared in the *United Presbyterian Hymnal* (1972).

WOODFORDE-FINDEN, AMY (d. 1919)
"Kashmiri Song"
Composer, she was born in Valparaiso, Chile, of British parents. Her father was the British Consul in Valparaiso. She studied with Adolph Schlosser, Winter and Amy Horrocks. Her song cycle composition *Indian Love Lyrics* was based on the verses of Lawrence Hope. She wrote "Kashmiri Song—Pale hands I loved beside the Shalimar". She married Colonel Woodforde-Finden, an officer in the British army. She died on March 13th in London, England.

WOOLLETT, BARBARA ROACH (1937–)
"God's Holy Ways Are Just and True"
Hymnist, she was born on January 30th in Southampton, England, the daughter of Gertrude Lydia Jones and Harry Roach. She was educated at the Sholing Secondary School in Southampton and married David Woollett. They have three children. She is a member of the Fellowship of Christian Writers in London. Her hymn above, "How Blest Are the People" and "How long, O Lord" are paraphrases of Biblical words. Her hymns appeared in the *Baptist Hymnal* (1986).

WOOLSEY, MARY HALE (1899–Dec'd.)
"When It's Springtime in the Rockies"
Songwriter born on March 21st in Spanish Fork, Utah, she was educated at Brigham Young University; University of Utah; and Columbia University. With music by Eugene Jelesnik and Robert Sauer, she wrote the words for the operettas *Star Flower, The Enchanted Attic, The Giant Garden, The Happy Hearts,* and *Neighbors in the House.* Also she wrote the songs, "Colorado", "Lost Melody", "My Girl in My Old Home Town", "On the Trails of Timpanogas", "O Lovely Light", "Shangri-La", and "You're an Invitation to a Dream". ASCAP.

WORTH, AMY (1888–1967)
Christmas cantata—*Mary the Mother*
Composer, conductor, organist, and teacher, she was born in St. Joseph, Missouri, on January 18, 1888, was educated in public schools, and studied privately with Jessie Gaynor, Mary Lyon, and others. She taught piano and was an organist and choir director in St. Joseph, Missouri, and later the choral director of the Women's Chorus of the Women's University Club in Seattle, Washington. She also composed the choral works *Christ Rises; He Came All So Still,* etc., and the music for "Little Lamb," "Song of the Angels", "The Evening is Hushed," etc. She died on April 29, 1967.

WRIGHT, PRISCILLA (1928–)
"Fear Not, Rejoice and Be Glad"
Hymnist, she was born on October 2nd in Dallas, Texas, and was educated at Denver Metropolitan College in Colorado (1981–82), North Lake Community College in Dallas (1983–84), and Christ for the Nations Institute of Biblical Studies (1986–88). Her hymn above appeared in the *Baptist Hymnal* (1986).

WRIGHT, SYREETA
"Signed, Sealed, Delivered I'm Yours"
Singer/songwriter, born in Pittsburgh, Pennsylvania, she married Stevie Wonder, but they later divorced. With Stevie Wonder she wrote "If You Really Love Me" and with Wonder, Lee Garrett, and Lula Mae Hardaway, wrote "Signed, Sealed, Delivered I'm Yours—Like a fool I went and stayed too long." With Billy Preston she had a hit "With you I'm Born Again" (1980).

WURM, MARY J. A. (1860–1938)
(String quartet)
Pianist/composer, she was born on May 18th in Southampton, England, of German descent. She had two musical sisters Mathilde and Adela who took the surname Verne. After studying piano and composition at the Stuttgart Conservatory in Germany, she studied with Clara Schumann and

others. She played Schumann's Concerto at the Crystal Palace in London in 1882 and played at the Popular Concerts in 1884. After winning the Mendelssohn Scholarship, she gave recitals in London and in Germany. She composed many piano pieces, a string quartet, a cello sonata, an orchestral overture, etc. She died on January 21st in Munich, Germany.

WYNETTE, TAMMY (1942–)
"Stand By Your Man"
Country music singer/guitarist/songwriter, she was born Tammy Pugh on May 5th in Itawamba County, Mississippi. After singing on a radio station in Birmingham, Alabama, in 1966 she moved to Nashville where she worked as a beautician until her first record on Epic label, "Apartment No. 9", was successful. With record producer Billy Sherrill, she wrote "Stand By Your Man" in 1968, which was included on the soundtrack of the film *Five Easy Pieces*. In 1969 she married singer George Jones, her fourth husband, and joined the cast of the Grand Ole Opry. Tammy and George toured and were very successful. She was named Country Music Association Female Vocalist of the Year 1968, 1969, and 1970. After her divorce from Jones in 1975, the duo continued singing. The video *Tammy Wynette* with Randy Travis was nominated for Country Duo 1992. She wrote a number of country songs. As of 1994 her albums available were *20 Years of Hits, Biggest Hits, Greatest Hits, Greatest Hits Vol. 3, Heart Over Mind, Higher Ground, Next to You,* and with George Jones *Greatest Hits.*

-Y-

YABLOKOFF, BELLA MYSELL (1903–Dec'd.)
"Kinder-Shpiel"
Actress/singer/songwriter born on April 5th in New York, New York, she was educated at Juilliard in New York and had private tutors. She was an actress/singer in American and Yiddish theater productions. She wrote the words for the songs in musicals: *It's a Funny World, My Son and I,* and *Uncle Sam in Israel.* ASCAP.

YODER, BERTHA (1909–)
"Rejoice Ye Christians Loudly"
Composer/hymnist born on August 17th in Urbana, Champaign County, Ohio, she was educated at Goshen College, Indiana (BS in Ed.). She taught in schools in Sarasota, Florida; Lewistown and West Liberty, Ohio. In 1960 she was awarded first place in a hymn writers' contest of the Hymn Society of America. She composes the music for her hymns. In 1975 she wrote the music for the "Oak Grove Centennial Hymn" for the Oak Grove Menonite Church Centennial; she has composed 39 Christmas carols; "Sing Alleluia" (1987), "The Great 'I Am'" (1989), "The Light of the World" (1990), "O Holy Child" (1991), "O, Israel

Your King Has Come" (1993). She versified some German hymns and composed tunes and harmony for them, "Awake, Awake, O Child of Man", "'Tis My Desire to Sing", and "Rejoice Ye Christians Loudly", which appeared in the *Anabaptist Hymnal* (1987), Deutsche Buckhandling, Hagerstown, Maryland. (The foregoing information was received in a letter dated May 17, 1994, from Bertha Yoder.)

YOUNG, CHERYL LESLEY (1949–)
"Come On, Come to the Fair"
Composer/songwriter born on November 21st in New York, New York, she is the daughter of composer/songwriter Chelsey Virginia Young and the sister of composer/songwriter Charles Chesley Young. She was educated at a UN School; Sinape Academy in Massachusetts; Calhoun School in New York City; and had private music training. With her mother and brother, she wrote "The Freedom Song" and the song above.

YOUNG, CHESLEY VIRGINIA (1919–)
"Have You?"
Composer/songwriter born on September 7th in Hamburg, Arkansas, she was educated at the University of Arkansas (BA); Teachers College, Columbia University (MA); and had private music study. She served as a captain in the WACS, USAF during World War II. With her son and daughter, she wrote the above song and "Come On, Come to the Fair".

YOUNG, IDA (1891–Dec'd.)
"Why?"
Composer/songwriter born on September 20th in Kiev, Ukraine, she was educated at public schools in Boston and had private violin study. She wrote the song "Why?". ASCAP.

YOUNG, MAUDE J. FULLER (1826–1882)
"The Song of the Texas Rangers"
Poetess/lyricist, she was born in Beaufort, North Carolina. When she was eleven years old the family moved to Houston, Texas. Maude married Dr. S. O. Young in Houston (1846), but he died during their first year of marriage. Their only son, S. O. Young, served in General John B. Hood's Texas Brigade during the War Between the States. She was principal of a public school in Houston (1868–73) and state botanist (1872–73). Young is best known for her poems "The Legend of Sour Lake" and "The Song of the Texas Rangers" (1861) set to the tune "The Yellow Rose of Texas" (1858). She was known as the Confederate Lady. She died in Houston.

YOUNG, RIDA JOHNSON (1869–1926)
"Ah, Sweet Mystery of Life"
Lyricist, she was born in Baltimore, Maryland. After being educated at Wilson College, she became an actress with E. H. Southern and others. With music by Ernest Ball and Chauncey Olcott, she wrote the words for "Mother Machree" (1910); with music by Victor Herbert, "Ah, Sweet Mystery of Life, At Last I've Found Thee" (1910); with music by Sigmund Romberg, "Will You Remember" (1917); and with Victor Herbert, "My Dream Girl" (1924). With Herbert she also wrote: "I've a Very Strange Feeling I Never Felt Before, for I'm Falling in Love with Someone" and with Herbert, "Molly — Oh, Molly Dear, the Spring Is Here".

YOUNG, ROLANDE MAXWELL (1929–)
Little Acorns
Composer/pianist/songwriter born on September 13th in Washington, DC, she was educated at Catholic University; studied with Harold Bauer at the Manhattan School of Music and with Vittorio Giannini at Juilliard. She made her debut as a pianist in 1953 at Town Hall in New York City. She wrote the piano suite mentioned above and the songs, "How Can I?", "Mighty Paul Bunyan", "My Kingdom for a Kiss", "Somehow There's Magic in You", "Sunshine and Rain", "There's a Dream in My Heart", and "When the Trains Came In".

-Z-

ZAIDEL-RUDOLPH, JEANNE (1948–)
Fanfare Festival Overture
Composer, she was born on July 9th in Pretoria, South Africa. She studied under Johann Potgieter, Arthur Wegelen, and Stefans Grove at the University of Pretoria (cum laude-BMus 1969, cum laude-MMus 1972, DMus 1979). She also studied in Germany and in Boston, Massachusetts. On September 14, 1976, she married Michael Rudolph and they have four daughters. She has lectured at the University of the Witwatersrand in Johannesburg, South Africa, since 1975. She has composed symphonies, choral and instrumental works, chamber music, and operas. Her *Fanfare Festival Overture* was commissioned to celebrate the 1985 centenary of Johannesburg and was first performed there in 1986.

ZAIMONT, JUDITH LANG (1945–)
Nocturne: La Fin de Siecle
Composer, she was born on November 8th in Memphis, Tennessee. After studying piano with LeLand Thompson at the Juilliard School (1958–64), she studied with Zaven Hachadourian at the Long Island

Institute of Music (1966), composition with Weisgall at Queens College, CUNY (BA, 1966), and with Beeson and Luening at Columbia University (MA, 1968). She also took private lessons in orchestration with Andre Jolivet in France (1971–72). She has received a number of awards and commissions. She has composed instrumentals, songs, choral works, and piano pieces, including the piece mentioned above.

ZARITSKY, LIBBY (1925–)
"Bone Dry"
Songwriter/director born on December 5th in Atlanta, Georgia, she was educated at New York University (BA, MA). She wrote and directed musical shows for theater groups, and married composer/pianist/songwriter Bernard Zaritsky. With her husband and Walter Whippo, she wrote several songs including "Zoo's Who" and the song above. ASCAP.

ZIFFER, FRANCES (1917–)
"He Don't Wanna Love Me"
Composer/conductor/pianist she was born on June 5th and educated at Peabody Institute; the Walter Damrosch Institute; and studied with Carl Friedburg and David Saperton. She was music director for theater groups and wrote the stage score *Dakota*. With Hardy Wieder and Martin Kalmanoff, she wrote the songs: "Faith Alone", "One Foot to Sea", "Say When", and the song mentioned above. ASCAP.

ZIMMERMAN, AGNES MARIE JACOBINA (1847–1925)
Presto alla Tarantella (Op. 15)
Pianist/composer, she was born on July 5th in Cologne, Germany. While only eight years old, she studied under Cipriani Potter and Steggall at the Royal Academy of Music in London, then with Pauer and Sir George A. Macferren. She obtained the King's Scholarship (1860–62) and made her debut with two movements of Beethoven's E major Concerto at the Crystal Palace in London on December 5, 1863. She composed sonatas for violin and piano, for violin, cello and piano, instrumental works and songs. Zimmerman died on November 14th in London.

ZOECKLER, DOROTHY ACKERMAN (b. 1915)
"When I Kneel Down to Pray."
Composer and hymnist, she was born in Wheeling, West Virginia, on August 19, 1915, was educated at the Cincinnati Conservatory in Ohio, and studied privately with Marcian Thalberg and others. She was organist and choir director of St. Matthew's Episcopal Church in Wheeling. She also wrote "God Speaks to Me," etc.

ZWILICH, ELLEN TAAFFE (1939–)
Symphony no. 1: Three Movements for Orchestra
Composer/violinist, she was born on April 30th in Miami, Florida. After studying with John Boda at Florida State University, Tallahassee (BM, 1956; MM, 1962) and with Carter and Sessions at the Juilliard School in New York City, in 1975 she became the first woman to receive the DMA in composition. After studying violin under Burgin and Galamian, she joined the American Symphony Orchestra under Stokowski. She has received a number of prizes, awards, and commissions. For her *Symphony no. 1* mentioned above, in 1983 she became the first woman to receive the Pulitzer prize in music. She married the violinist Joseph Zwilich, who performed and recorded a number of her works prior to his death in 1979. As of 1994 her CDs available were *Celebration/Prologue/Nelson, Concerto Grosso 1985/Mehta, Symphony no. 2/Mehta, Symphony no. 2/Louisville Orchestra*. Her *American Concerto* for trumpet and orchestra had its world premiere performed by the San Diego Symphony Orchestra, featuring Doc Severinsen on September 24, 1994, at the preview gala for the California Center for the Arts in Escondido.

Sources

ASCAP List of Members 1994, New York, New York

CLAGHORN: *Biographical Dictionary of American Music* 1973, West Nyack, N.Y.: Parker Publishing Company.

CLAGHORN: *Women Composers and Hymnists* 1986, Metuchen, N.J.: The Scarecrow Press, Inc.

CLAGHORN: *Popular Bands and Performers* 1995, Lanham, Md.: The Scarecrow Press, Inc.

DAVIDSON: *Our Latter-day Hymns* 1988, Salt Lake City: Deseret Book Company.

HAVLICE: *Popular Song Index Third Supplement* 1989, Metuchen, N.J.: The Scarecrow Press, Inc.

HITCHCOCK & SADIE: *The New Grove Dictionary of American Music* 1986, London: Macmillan Press.

STANISLAW & HUSTED: *Companion to the Worshiping Church* 1993, Carol Stream, Ill.: Hope Publishing Company.

STERN: *Women Composers, A Handbook* 1978, Metuchen, N.J.: The Scarecrow Press, Inc.

About the Author

Gene Claghorn, a retired accountant, is the author of books about *The Mocking Bird* and *Battle Hymn*; five biographical dictionaries of composers, lyricists, musicians, and singers, including *Women Composers and Hymnists* and *Popular Bands & Performers* published by Scarecrow Press. Mr. Claghorn took an interest in musical research because his great-grandfather Septimus Winner wrote "Listen to the Mocking Bird," "Ten Little Indians," "Where, Oh Where Has My Little Dog Gone?," "Whispering Hope" and several other nineteenth-century songs. Mr. Claghorn is also the author of five books about the American Revolution including *Naval Officers of the American Revolution* and *Women Patriots of the American Revolution,* both published by Scarecrow Press. One of Mr. Claghorn's ancestors was a privateer captain which led him to join several hereditary orders. He served as historian for four orders in Florida—Sons of the American Revolution, Sons and Daughters of the Pilgrims, Founders and Patriots, and Sons of the Revolution.